OCCASIONAL MOMENTS OF HAPPINESS

A MEMOIR

OCCASIONAL MOMENTS OF HAPPINESS

A MEMOIR

Shana Donyaei

Scripture quotations marked KJV are taken from the King James Version. Public domain.

ISBN 978-1-948089-03-6

CONTENTS

DEDICATION

For Barbara,
We did it . . . we finally did it!
In Christ,
Shana

FOREWORD

If I try hard enough, and look back in time further than I usually do, I can remember a little girl growing up normal as normal could be, if not better than that. She went to a school she adored, had no trouble making friends, and found happiness in everything, never second-guessing any of her motivations. Seven, eight, nine, ten years old . . . all these were happy times for her. She made a lot of memories and cherished them for as long as she could, but sadly, thanks to our humanity, she had a lot less trouble remembering the bad ones and soon forgot her childhood innocence. As she was growing up, she was not completely in the dark; she knew some things. But here's the limitation: she merely knew *of* them. And for her, knowing that they existed and could hurt her was enough to keep her far away.

That worked until eighth grade, and then everything changed.

If you haven't already guessed, the little girl is—or was—me.

I was confused by my life and scared about the future, not to mention the present, which was slipping away from me as I lost touch with what was important. I developed an eating disorder that quickly took over my life. One of the things I thought about the most during the terrible years of restricting my food and living in exhaustion was how I had made a promise to myself never to engage in restrictive behavior or compare myself to others, thinking that they had set the standard of beauty that could be set only by God alone. It had been a short time ago that I'd made that promise, so how had I ended up here?

It was only by going through this time that I went from knowing *of* this disorder to knowing *about* this disorder. I realized, finally, *why* I had made that promise. I wished every day that I could go back and undo the past, but I felt trapped—in my own body, in my own world, separate from everyone else's, where food and time took away my reasons for being alive.

Shana and I have both tried the self-motivation route when we were trying to recover from depressive, restrictive behavior. I tried journaling, praying, and force-feeding my food because I thought that was recovery. These things helped in the moment but left me unsatisfied and feeling guilty, and worst of all, unrecovered. I stopped *wanting* to recover. It didn't seem worth it. I didn't want to spend the rest of my life fighting my head with no results.

Over the years my struggles with depression kept climbing higher and higher. Every time I was certain that they had reached the top, they climbed again, and I felt buried in everything I had done and what had happened to me. Trapped between a rock and a hard place, between fear and pain, I was broken and unsure of what life even was. I would wonder every day, "Is this it?"

But I, like Shana, was missing an important piece, a step in the journey that had gone overlooked for a long time. Call it what you will, for it is different for all of us, but I think of it as commitment with brotherhood. This meant getting up after relapses. This meant getting out of bed in the morning. This meant embracing the changes in my life that came as I rebuilt, no matter how it felt in the moment.

And as I and others rebuild, we're reminding ourselves that we should not be alone or feel as if we are the only ones who are never going to make it. That statement is a lie, a scam, a trap, and it will pull you down as long as you repeat it.

Recovery is out there, and it's waiting with open arms. Shana and I have struggled time and time again, but we can attest sincerely that the struggles are worth the end result. There were times for each of us when we felt as if we were better off alone and stuck forever, but we are here today. God uses each and every one of His children for good, and as He guides them to better themselves, He is using them to inspire others.

In *Occasional Moments of Happiness*, Shana is transparent and honest with the reader, and you'll feel her pain, from destructive behavior and a negative mindset, and the joy that keeps trying to break through—until one day, by the grace of God, it succeeds.

Your story isn't over, and no matter how long it takes, you can make something beautiful, just like Shana did.

Mati Petroski

> *Don't give up. Push through the droughts.*
> *Channel the inevitable disappointments*
> *into your craft. Think. Create.*
> *But most importantly, stay alive.*
>
> —Tyler Joseph

> *I can do all things through Christ*
> *which strengtheneth me.*
>
> —Philippians 4:13

ACKNOWLEDGMENTS

I have had many crazy dreams for my future over the years. In junior high I envisioned running away to LA and living happily ever after with the drummer from Motely Crüe. After graduating high school, I believed with all my being that I was destined to be a supermodel living in Paris. At the age of twenty-four, I was convinced that my soul mate was the lead singer of Pearl Jam. I know, shocker—none of those dreams came true! After truly surrendering my life and desires for my future to the Lord, God has shown me that there is a different kind of dream—a God-ordained one. If asked in the midst of all my youthful fantasies if any one of them included writing a book, I would have responded with a blank stare. Of course not. Yet here I am. That is exactly why God has to be the first I acknowledge on this page. He birthed the idea, gave me the words to write, and sent the resources needed to make his plan for my life materialize.

I absolutely have to thank my family. My mom and dad for taking me to church as a kid, trying to instill good morals in me, and putting up with all my teenage rebellion. My sister for always being there for me. My brothers for being protectors. My husband for working so hard to support our family so I could be a stay-at-home mom, affording me the time to write this book. My kids for giving me so much joy!

To my editing angel Dori Harrell at Breakout! I prayed for

you. I knew that publishing a book was way too much for me alone, and God answered that prayer, without which this book would not have been published. Also, much thanks to Lynnette Bonner for designing a book cover that fits my personality—I can't stop staring at it.

Barbara Hughes for typing the manuscript. Sara Million, Jennifer Petroski, and Caroline Timmins for your preliminary work on the manuscript. Amy Johnson, author of *Lessons from the Crawl Space,* for going before me. Michelle Robertson for being my cheerleader. Nathan French for verbalizing that I was, indeed, a published author even when the promise seemed so far out of reach. Madi Petroski for being brave and sharing your story.

To all those who have molded and shaped me. Those who were loyal friends, brave friends, there for me when I was a functional mess. To those who drove my butt around when I didn't have a car, reached out to tell me about Jesus, taught me so many things, believed in me when I didn't believe in myself. I wouldn't be me if it weren't for all of you!

Chapter 1

THE CURSE

My maiden name is Lesser, Shana Lesser, and that was exactly how I felt growing up, lesser than everyone else. In my eyes I was too tall, a bean pole, with straight dark hair that was way too thick. My eye color was a mix difficult to ascertain. Were they green or blue, with a hint of hazelnut, just to make things interesting?

Yet my eye color was the least of my worries in light of the curse indelibly stamped on me at birth—shyness. Why couldn't I make friends easily, raise my hand in class, give it my all during PE? It was because of the curse. My bad posture, an attempt to not be seen, and my quiet voice, I blamed on the curse.

I grew up on the outskirts of Seattle, near Sea-Tac Airport, in a typical middle-class neighborhood with a dozen houses spaced closely together. We had modest backyards with plenty of grass to run on and fruit trees that bloomed every spring. With only a few months of warm weather each year, none of the homes had air conditioning. The windows in our houses were left open in the heat of summer, which meant that many anticipated soap operas were edited by the departing planes.

Growing up an introvert with what some may refer to as "natural beauty" was awkward in the classroom setting. I didn't think I was ugly, but I never received verbal validation that I was pretty. I wasn't popular, so why did some boys in my class try to get my attention in all those gross boy ways? Like in the second grade when Sam wiped his boogers on my desk. Talk about disgusting!

"Mrs. Fisher," I said in a meek voice.

"Yes, Shana?" she questioned, tapping her toe.

I hesitated. "Sam wiped a booger on my desk." Surely she didn't expect me to concentrate with his booger staring back at me.

"Sam, next time use a Kleenex," she said as she handed him a tissue.

"These are the things seven-year-old boys do to show their affection. You'd better get used to it," Mrs. Fisher said to me. "Now get back to work."

"Ha-ha. Sam's got a crush on Shana." Calvin's voice echoed through the silent classroom.

"No I don't!" Sam exclaimed in defense while the rest of the class chuckled with fingers pointed in our direction.

Meanwhile, I buried my face in my palms to conceal the three shades of crimson my face had turned.

"Yeah, you like Shana," Calvin teased.

"No I don't!" Sam insisted. "I wouldn't like her. She's not even popular."

"That's enough, class," Mrs. Fisher interjected. "Now back to your lesson, or some of you will be spending recess indoors."

It was times like these, in the late seventies, that I wished homeschooling were the norm. If I could have blended in with the chipped paint on the wall, I gladly would have, yet at the same time I longed to be included with all the popular kids. If only I were like Samantha and Audrey, the two most popular girls in grade school. They almost looked like twins, with their perfect hair and petite bodies. Never left out or alone, they were always the center of attention, acting as if every school day was a new adventure.

And then there was the humiliating task of selecting teams during PE.

First, two students were elected as team captains. Then to my horror year after year, the grueling process of elimination would begin. One by one, like a game of tennis, the elect were chosen. After that, the moderate players, then the somewhat challenged players. Finally, the few left standing, with all eyes pointed their way, were reluctantly waved over. I placed in the bottom three every time.

"Hmm . . . well . . ." Nick, a team captain one year, said indecisively.

Oh, the cruelty of it all, I thought as I stood wanting to evaporate into thin air. *Why did the public school system subject children to such brutal humiliation?*

"Shoot. Well, I guess I'll take . . ." Nick resumed his internal verbal debate aloud, with an expression of one who had just sucked on a lemon as he made the excruciating decision.

"Nick!" the PE coach demanded. "This is not rocket science, for Pete's sake. Choose a teammate and let's play ball!"

"All right, I'll take Andy," Nick said.

That left Shelly and me.

"Evan, choose a teammate, and let's hurry it up," the coach instructed.

"Does it really matter?" Evan replied cynically. "I'll take Shana."

"All right, Shelly, that leaves you. You'll be on Nick's team," the coach said. "Okay, teams, let's play ball."

Knowing the process of picking teams, although thoroughly humiliating, was just icing on the cake. I trailed slowly behind my fellow classmates and onto the baseball field. I hoped I could just get through PE class today as I tried to make myself scarce by hiding in the outfield. I pleaded with the softball to please not come my way. But the ball sailed smack dab in my direction. My heart stopped. What I greatly feared had come true. I stood motionless as I watched the ball sail past and drop to the ground a few feet from my disadvantaged spot! I stood motionless, terrified of that stupid softball. My teammates complained while they scrambled to retrieve the ball.

"Geez, Shana, can't you even catch the ball when it's right in front of your face?" Evan exclaimed.

No, Evan, or should I more accurately call you Mr. Full of Yourself? I can't catch the ball because I don't know how to catch a ball or throw one. That's why I am hiding here in the outfield. So please do the world a favor—shut your mouth and leave me alone! I screamed in my head, as I didn't have the nerve to answer Evan's question, which was more like an angry statement. If only I hadn't been branded a shy girl at birth, I would have surely given Evan a piece of my mind that day.

As I'd already established in elementary school that any sort of physical coordination presented my biggest challenge of each school day and that no amount of slouching would rescue me from that most loathsome hour, there was one more grueling task to accomplish each year: the dreaded do-si-do, which solidified my awkwardness. I had no concept of my right from my left when trying to follow choreographed movement, and the other students were aware of this.

"Excuse me, Shana, may I speak with you please?" my teacher asked. "Why don't you just sit this one out, hon?" she said, pointing to a chair reserved for me. "Since you have such a hard time with square dancing."

"All right," I replied blankly, staring at the empty chair. Okay, that was not so bad. *At least I won't be making a fool of myself by throwing the rest of the class out of step. I can just sit here quietly and blend into the woodwork. Heck, maybe no one will even notice me.*

"Hey, how come Shana doesn't have to square dance?" Sam complained, pointing in my direction. Leave it to Booger Boy. The same one who wiped his snot on my desk was destined to embarrass me again.

"Sam, it's none of your concern why Shana isn't square dancing. Now, everyone take your place." The teacher clapped her hands.

"But it's not fair!" Sam griped. "She's sitting there because she can't square dance worth a bean!"

Evan, who had the unofficial title of "class babe," with an attitude to match, chuckled. "Haven't you seen her?" he questioned with wide eyes. "It's like she can't figure it out or something!"

"That's enough, Evan! Class, take formation. Places please," the teacher prompted.

Thankfully, the students complied and the focus was taken off my shamed face—until next year, that was.

I wondered if one-on-one practice would give me some much-needed confidence. But this one-on-one training never took place, so I walked around slouching and loathing PE.

Along with my lack of confidence were the many labels I adhered to myself. Shyness might have held the number one spot, but I also considered myself unpopular and even academically stupid. I never shared my internal thoughts. That would be a shameful thing, to actually confess my innermost flaws. So I suppressed everything, believing something was wrong with me and that everyone else was perfect. Instead of working side by side with someone who may have helped me work out my internal shortcomings, I began my search for self-worth externally in the form of a brave friend to cling to and hide behind.

Chapter 2

THIS EVIL THING
CALLED POPULARITY

In the sixth grade, girls started their periods, wore training bras, and discovered boys. My boy discovery launched with a crush on Rob, the tall, skinny, and beautiful James Dean of the school, destined for so much more than academics. Oh, and he was popular, which meant that regardless of his parents' occupations or net worth, Rob was out of my league.

Words could not express how much my heart ached the first time I saw him holding hands with Susan, a popular girl. She was blond and had blue eyes, but she was definitely nothing to write home about. She wasn't even Rob's type. As an A student who always did the right thing, what did Susan want with a renegade like Rob? Did it really matter though, considering that she possessed the one trait that eluded me, the dreaded *p* word? Because of this evil thing called popularity, Susan had Rob, and the only thing I had was my first broken heart, all because of a guy who didn't know I existed! An entire year of stolen glances from the corner of my eye, stalking Rob, slouched low at his desk, was all for naught as I watched in horror as he asked Susan to be his girlfriend.

Who was I kidding? Why had I thought I stood a chance with Rob? Only two boys had ever asked me to be their girlfriend in my eleven years of existence.

One of the boys waited until the last day of school to ask me, and his family planned to move ten miles away, practically another state when your only mode of transportation was a bicycle! And he was one of the popular boys too.

I told him no. He deserved to be told no, the nerve of him asking me on the way home when no one else was around, a guarantee that none of his friends would find out.

The other boy, Buddy, lived on my street. We were the same age. He sat next to me at my fifth birthday party. He had wavy strawberry-blond hair and freckles, which, at the time, was charming.

Two years had passed since that birthday party. I felt so grown up, racing up and down our street. I had recently learned to ride my bike, a banana seat with tassels. We pretended to gas up at one of the large mud puddles, using a stick for a nozzle. After gassing up, he proposed. "Would you be my girlfriend?"

I was shocked, didn't he know we were just kids? I said, "I'm a girl and I'm your friend." I sped away.

Although we resided on the same street, our friendship was interrupted by popularity, and proper etiquette forbade him to speak to me anymore. If I would have said yes that day, maybe my circumstances would have been different. Maybe I would have been popular, going out with Buddy. But where would we have gone if we had, back to the local mud puddle filling station?

Toward the tail end of grade school, I became friends with

This Evil Thing Called Popularity

Tonya. She wasn't popular or one of the smart kids or jocks, which made her a good candidate for me. I so desperately wanted to have a friend that I was willing to hang out with just about anyone, even a rebellious girl like Tonya. I didn't realize just how wild my new friend behaved until I spent the night at her house. I couldn't believe my mother had agreed to let me spend the night on a school night. But I would soon wish she hadn't let me.

In the morning, after Tonya's father had left for work, Tonya complained about attending school that day. "Have you ever skipped school?" she asked.

"No. Why would I want to do that?" It was as if she spoke a foreign language, and underneath her perplexing question, I began to fear. My curly-haired, lanky new friend with an attitude wasn't kidding!

"Let's just skip school. No one will ever know," she said.

In the best nonchalant response I could muster, still petrified, I said, "Thanks, but no thanks, Tonya. I want to go to school, and if we don't hurry up, we'll be late."

"Who cares about being late? I'm tired of people telling me what to do!" she exclaimed, as if talking to someone other than me.

"Tonya, if my mom finds out I was late for school, she might not let me stay at your house again." I defended my right to go to school.

"All right, goody two shoes, you don't have to get your panties in a bunch. We'll go to school."

"Good. Can we leave now?" Tonya didn't know I had a secret fear of being late for school. The thought of walking into class with twenty sets of eyeballs on me was beyond nightmarish. I spent my existence, at least in the classroom, trying to make myself invisible. Drawing attention to myself was a big *no*.

"All right, let's go to school. We don't want to be late!" Tonya said sarcastically.

"Great!" I rushed for Tonya's front door, thrilled! Spring was in the air, the birds were chirping, and I was walking a different route to school with my friend. Nothing could spoil this moment. Until I noticed there weren't any other kids walking down the steep hill that led to our grade school. We were late, but I consoled myself knowing that I had Tonya to walk into class with. But Tonya threw me another curve ball, and I still hated catching balls.

"Oh man, I ripped my pants!" Tonya griped as she sat motionless on the pavement within a stone's throw of our elementary school.

How on earth she managed to fall down baffled me. I hadn't even seen her fall. "Are you all right?"

She rubbed her skinned knee. "I'm okay, but now I have to go home and change my pants. I can't go to school with a big tear in my pants. That wouldn't be cool."

"But, Tonya . . ." My voice trailed as I glanced at the building, so close yet so far away. "We're already so late!"

"Who cares about being late? My dad is going to kill me. These are brand-new pants!"

"No one will even notice that your pants are ripped!" I grasped for words. "And when we get to school, you can go to the nurse's office for a Band-Aid, a perfect excuse for being late." I couldn't have cared less about Tonya's pants or her scraped knee.

"You can go to school if you want, but I am going home to change my pants," Tonya said with a sly grin. She had me cornered without a wall in sight.

"Fine." Defeated, I turned to face the hill I had just come down. I felt sick—so sick that if a slice of pepperoni pizza were in front of me, I wouldn't be tempted to take one bite.

"Don't worry. We'll be quick!" Tonya gave another mischievous grin.

No wonder I felt sick. I was too shy to lead, so I gravitated toward the courageous souls. Tonya fit that bill, a brave soldier unfazed by what others thought of her. The only problem? I was now stuck following my new friend to places I didn't want to go.

Once we arrived back at Tonya's house, she complained about school again. Miraculously, the limp she'd acquired from the fall had disappeared, replaced by malice.

"Honestly, I don't even like school. I plan on dropping out as soon as I can, and since we're already so late . . ."

In the middle of some awful nightmare, I clung to Tonya's front door. I had to convince my reckless new friend that skipping school wasn't an option. "Tonya, I don't know about you, but we are beyond late. So whether you follow me or not, I'm going to school!" Shocked by my own exclamation, I waited for Tonya's response, hoping she would say okay and this terrible situation would be over.

"You know, I'm going to have to say no. I don't want to go to school. I'm going to the mall," she declared with a radiant smile, as if finally in control of her eleven-year-old life.

"You're kidding, right?" I knew she wasn't.

"No." She stared me down at the entrance of her front door. "Are you going to come with me to the mall or show up to school an hour late?"

Had she read my diary? Was she like an animal that could

sense fear? How did she know that I would cower under the pressure she was so skillfully administering? I had never encountered someone like her. She had me just where she wanted me: squirming. Oh, how I loathed being me!

"Fine, I'll go to the mall with you, but I am warning you—if my mom finds out, I will never be able to talk to you again!" I threatened, even though I had lost the battle of the wills.

How could having a new friend be so tragic? All should have been perfect in my world, except for PE. At this point though, I would have given anything to be in PE about then. Instead, I played follow the leader along the highway, and Tonya's devious ways had no apparent end in sight.

"It's not safe to walk on the side of the road. A cop might see us and pick us up. We'll have to walk through the woods to get to the mall." She pointed to a dense section of woods that ran along side of the freeway.

"Are you joking? No one walks in those woods! It's full of thick brush, not to mention wild animals and no sunlight!" I exclaimed, aware that Tonya called all the shots.

"It's the only way." She marched on toward the tall patch of forest, knowing I would trail behind her like a lost pup.

Once inside the woods and concealed, Tonya tried to lighten things up. "Don't you like adventure?"

"If I want adventure, I'll watch TV." I hadn't even experienced this much adventure when camping.

"TV?" Tonya questioned, pushing a thick branch out of her path. "That's not living! Don't you want to experience life for yourself? There's a huge world to explore!" She stopped to look at me.

"This," I said, showing her a thorn I had pulled from my hand, "is enough exploration to last me for the rest of my life!"

This Evil Thing Called Popularity

After what seemed like several hours, Tonya and I made our way out of our up-close-and-personal experience with nature to the safe mall setting. What could possibly happen here? It's not like I hadn't been to the mall a thousand times before!

Inside the mall, Tonya led the way through department stores laden with the latest clothes, shoes, and purses. Neither of us had any money, and we were surrounded by stuff we could never buy, not that anything interested me. Nausea mixed with a sinking feeling in my stomach.

"Let's check out the perfume counter." Tonya beelined for the colorful bottles. "Wow, smell this one!" she yelled.

Before I could take a whiff, the saleslady behind the counter asked, "Why aren't you two girls in school?"

Tonya gave a lame excuse and motioned for me to follow her out of the store. "It's not safe for us to be in the mall. We better leave," she said as she ushered me out to the large parking lot. "Actually, the parking lot isn't safe either."

I was at the mercy of her adolescent mind.

She began her campaign while we sat on the ground at the back of the parking lot. "We have to watch out for the cops. The last thing I want to do is get busted!" she said like a seasoned pro.

"School will be out soon anyway, and we can head home," I suggested.

"I don't even want to go home. We should forget about going home. I mean, do you really want to get busted for skipping school? We could run away together. It'll be just like the movies."

"I don't want to run away!" I exclaimed, mad at myself for getting into such a mess.

"Just think of how much freedom you would have—no

one telling you what to do," she said with an angry smirk. Then she changed her tone and smiled sweetly. "And no one telling you to clean your room!"

"I don't even clean my room. My mom does! And she also buys me yummy food and lets me watch my favorite TV shows after school." I rose to my feet.

"Wow, lucky you," Tonya replied. "I guess not all of us have it so good. But I'm ready to run away. I don't even want to go home and get a change of clothes. Good thing I already changed my pants!" She laughed.

"I am not going to run away."

"Fine. Good luck to you," Tonya said, standing.

She had called my bluff. The girl I had been meekly following was walking away. Was I seriously going to take a stand now? If so, why on earth hadn't I taken a stand earlier and walked into class alone? Was I going to walk away from my leader now?

From several yards away, Tonya turned. "Are you coming or not?"

"Yes. I'm coming." I ran to catch up. I was on a wild roller-coaster ride with Tonya, and all I could do was hope I didn't throw up and that the ride would end soon.

After winding through the mall's parking lot and onto the busy street, we faced a predicament. Where to go next? Tonya came up with the bright idea of camping out underneath a dark, cold overpass. Then my grade school leader had the even brighter idea to cross the busy freeway.

We dashed across the first several lanes of oncoming traffic, only to get stuck in between the north and south lanes. A cop spotted us and whisked us into his patrol car. I was home-free at last! Sure I would have to face my parents. They would scratch their head in amazement, wondering what could have possibly gotten into me. But who knew what might have happened if I had continued to follow Tonya on her amusement park ride of a life. Our friendship ended that day, and for the first time, I was grateful to be friendless.

After parting ways with Tonya, I acquired Veronica as my best friend. She was the new girl in school, and more importantly, in need of a friend too. We had a blast together, listening to music, talking about cute boys, and when her mom permitted, sleepovers. Veronica might not have been the prettiest girl at school, but she had confidence, which was worth its weight in gold.

Her mother always told her how beautiful she was. I wondered if it was better to be pretty and not receive verbal affirmation, or was it better to be less than average, yet completely built up in the esteem department? I made a mental note of the physical and verbal affection Veronica received from her mother. It seemed that Veronica wasn't lacking anything in the sense of feeling loved, even when a couple of mean boys bullied her for what they saw as her imperfections.

My coming of age story happened with the most unexpected person—Buddy. Although we lived on the same street and attended the same school, we were usually on nonspeaking terms, since the popular Buddy didn't want to ruin his reputation. But since it was the weekend, nearing the end of our sixth-grade year, none of our classmates were around to remind Buddy that he wasn't supposed to associate with me.

It was a warm evening. My parents left for a church function. Church, it was just what my parents did. They were dutiful parents that took all of us kids to church each Sunday during our adolescence. But for me, Sunday morning church was enough, and this evening I was ecstatic that Veronica was staying the night! Buddy's best friend was also staying the night at his house, and his best friend just happened to be . . . Rob (the love of my life)!

The four of us had a great time running up and down the street at twilight. We darted from yard to yard, past the large weeping willow tree, and finally ended up in yet another unsuspecting neighbor's yard. It was there, in a secluded spot surrounded by a maze of hedges, that I experienced my first kiss. After choosing partners and me being too shy to admit my love for Rob, I found myself eyeball to eyeball with Buddy.

Not having been around this block before, I was petrified. I didn't know how to kiss a boy, let alone Buddy, whom I had seen too many times to count over the years. I choked under the pressure only seconds into my first kiss. I tried to address him by name, only to hear a muffled echo mid-kiss. At least I hadn't been paired up with the love of my life, only to fumble the ball worse than any PE nightmare.

The sound of my father's voice in the distance prompted a hasty exit back to the safety of my bedroom.

Regardless of how haphazard my first kiss was, it was still an exciting event.

The following Monday Buddy approached me as the recess bell rang on the playground. "Shana . . . psst. Come here for a second." Buddy motioned to me in a hushed tone.

"What is it?" I questioned with a surprised look. Buddy never talked to me at school.

"Don't tell anyone about what happened," he warned.

"You better not tell anyone either!"

In our brief clandestine conversation on the foursquare court, we swore that neither would tell a soul. I was embarrassed, and Buddy was embarrassed of me. How humiliating. My own neighbor whom I was growing up with, being embarrassed of me.

Maybe it was better that I had been too shy to admit that I wanted to kiss Rob that night. Not that it felt warm and fuzzy watching my best friend pair up with the love of my life. But what if I had kissed Rob that night, and instead of Buddy approaching me on the foursquare court, it had been Rob? Surely my yearlong crush would have crushed my heart into pieces if Rob had sworn me to secrecy the same way Buddy did. At least I had no feelings for Buddy.

But in my heart, I knew I'd settled for less, just like my last name. The label I shamefully wore steered my young life. Not only did I believe I was lesser than everyone else, I therefore settled for less. I didn't strive for what I wanted. I watched others shoot for the stars as fear gripped me. Even though my dreams were bigger, like being rich and famous. Silly as it sounds, sometimes when walking home alone from school, I pretended I was being interviewed by a famous talk show host. And at least one time a passing car screamed out, "Who are you talking to?" I kept these crazy aspirations hidden in my heart. Never did I strive for them, and never did I tell a soul.

Later at sixth-grade graduation, I stood alone in front of a crowded gymnasium to accept the most embarrassing award ever—quietest voice. Our class had voted on giving everyone a certificate. So alongside best hair and most athletic, was me, voted quietest voice. Did they not consider that someone voted quietest by their peers would not want to stand up in front of everyone?

After surviving the ceremony, my mom and dad gave me a lovely plush unicorn that was in vogue. With the blushing over with, Veronica and I, in our matching jean cowgirl skirts, new high heels, and our first pair of nylons, celebrated the joyous occasion with her mother at a local diner. Not only had we completed seven long years of grade school, we were so grown up.

Chapter 3

BESTIES

The first day of seventh grade, my heart pounded as I anticipated my first bus ride to my new middle school. With my stomach full of butterflies, I sat on my friend Kayla's bathroom counter. I had known Kayla throughout grade school, but as she was a year older, we never officially became best friends. On that day, I was thankful to have her, considering Veronica had abruptly moved at the end of summer, leaving me to face my first school bus ride alone. Not only was Kayla my new security blanket, but she also promised to show me the ropes at my new school.

"But first things first," insisted my third-generation Italian-American friend. "Makeup. It's a must if you want to snag a boyfriend this year!"

Not that Kayla or I had ever snagged such a thing, aside from in our daydreams, but we were embarking on a new era. Even if technically she had already spent a year in this new era without finding a boyfriend, there was always hope, if not for her, at least for her friend. Kayla insisted I couldn't start this new year bare faced.

I entered into a realm of curling irons, trendy clothes, periods, and boys.

"Now watch carefully so you'll know how to put makeup on when I'm not around," she said.

"Kayla, I don't even own any makeup." My feet dangled, nervously kicking her bathroom cabinets.

"You better go get some, sugar!" she said. "Because I see a gorgeous hunk of a man in your future."

"Where did you learn to talk like that?" I asked.

She paused to wet the eye shadow brush. "Soap operas!"

"Kayla, you seem well beyond your thirteen years of existence!"

"And don't you forget it!" she joked, motioning for me to close my eyes. "I'll be fourteen soon . . . early birthday." She reminded me how much older and wiser she was.

After Kayla finished my full face of makeup, I barely recognized the image staring back at me. I could have stood there for an hour, marveling, but I didn't want to miss the bus.

While we walked to the bus stop, I asked a million questions about middle school. Kayla patiently answered my questions, while I secretly dreamed of a new life. I hoped for a second chance at being one of the pretty, popular girls. Something that had evaded me year after grueling year in grade school was, maybe, finally within reach! Maybe the popular girls would ask me to sit with them at lunch. Maybe I would have a boyfriend to walk hand in hand with down the halls between classes. Who knew what the future held, but for the first time in years, I felt hopeful that maybe, just maybe, I could get rid of my shy-girl title and tear off that mental label Shana-Lesser-than-Everyone-Else.

Besties

When Kayla and I finally reached the bus stop, my bubble burst at the visual reminder. There stood the popular girls from my grade school, huddled together with scented lip-gloss smiles on their anxious faces. The popular boys from my grade school also clustered together, one of them Buddy. Unbelievably, Buddy and his friends looked curiously in our direction. I imagined their conversation by the sinister expressions on their faces. Uncomfortable, I tried to make eye contact with Kayla and forget that one of the sinister-looking boys was the same boy I had kissed just a few months earlier. Buddy hadn't uttered a word to me since our hushed conversation on the foursquare court, even though our bedroom windows were a stone's throw away, so why was he now staring my way?

I imagined his conversation with his friends.

Look, Buddy, check out the new girl, Evan said as he nudged Buddy in the ribs. *I wonder where she lives.*

I know where she lives, Buddy said numbly.

You do? Evan questioned.

Across the street from my house, Buddy replied in a sarcastic tone.

Huh? Evan said blankly. *I don't remember seeing any houses for sale on your block.*

Duh, that's Shana, the same girl who's lived across the street from me forever. Buddy shook his head in disapproval. *I guess her mom bought her some new clothes.*

Well, someone should tell her what she's wearing should have stayed at the mall. Evan tried to save face.

Why don't you go tell her? You're the one that was checking her out. Buddy laughed, nudging Evan in the ribs.

When the yellow school bus finally pulled up that morning, I stayed close to Kayla, letting her take the lead onto the bus. The popular kids made a mad dash for the back of the bus. I couldn't help but hear their laughter and chatter during the bus ride. How could they all be so relaxed? From my vantage point near the front, I envied these popular kids. Call it multitasking, but I was engaged in a conversation with Kayla, yet aware of my popular peers sitting coed on the long backseat. We had all grown up together, and the path they were headed on seemed to be such a lucky one. And no matter how much I tried not to care, all I ever dreamed of was to be one of those pretty, popular girls sitting at the back of the bus, flirting with the cute boys!

My heart pounded the entire fifteen-minute ride. I was still clinging emotionally to Kayla when we stepped off the bus. Then my heart sank all the way to the pit of my stomach. It was time to leave the security of my older friend, who didn't share any classes with me. It was time for me to go it alone with no one by my side. Maybe I'd run into Veronica, but there was no guarantee we'd share any classes. The comfort of the familiar had disappeared. I now faced the intimidating task of learning to maneuver through my new school, and even scarier, the chore of making friends with no one to hold my hand. I hoped my new friends would be popular ones! But even if they weren't, I knew one thing for sure—I would never turn down the offer of friendship, because it was better to have a friend than to stand alone.

Midyear, with no new best friend yet, I stood at my locker, grabbing the books for English. The noise of chattering kids filled the hall as a flood of students made their way to their next class. In the midst of the busyness was the familiar face of Veronica, who was about to ship out to another middle school. Her single working mom was moving once again, which meant my friendship with Veronica would be even harder to maintain. But Veronica heading out of my life led me to my new best friend.

"Shana, this is Lisa. It's her first day. She just moved here," Veronica said. Turning to Lisa, she waved a quick goodbye. "Sorry. I have to get to class. I'll leave you with Shana. You two will get along great. Bye!"

"Hi," Lisa said with a sweet little smile and gestured wave that matched her petite frame. She had shoulder-length caramel-brown hair, curled back like all the other girls in middle school, but unlike me, her hair actually held a curl! Lisa had piercing green eyes and the cutest little button nose. Within minutes we discovered we lived only two blocks from each other. It couldn't have been any more perfect, and we became instant best friends. We made a good pair, me being the tall, shy girl with a serious personality, who held people at a distance. And Lisa was everything physically and emotionally that I wasn't, a charming spitfire with a loving heart and fearless attitude who would become one of the most influential people in my life.

When around her, I felt empowered by her boldness. It rubbed off, and even though I still wore the label of shy girl when alone, I became someone else with Lisa by my side. I could face the intimidating world around me. For the first time in my life, I felt brave as Lisa led and I followed. I never let Lisa know that she was the source of my newfound empowerment. I was too shy to admit to anyone that I was shy. But my world opened up with my new best friend leading the way, even to the back of the bus! I wasn't a back-of-the-bus type. I envied the confident teenagers who thought nothing of holding their heads high with straight shoulders and attitude as they effortlessly maneuvered their way to the back of the bus.

My life took on an interesting dimension with Lisa, but sometimes the interesting turned embarrassing.

The day I embarrassed myself in front of my seventh-going-on-eighth-grade crush was the day that Shana came out of her shell . . . for a moment at least. It all started when Lisa and I discovered that both the boys we had crushes on lived in the same apartment complex. We walked the three miles from Lisa's house to the complex, hoping to run into them. Lo and behold, when we arrived at their apartment building, we spotted them shooting hoops. With Lisa at the lead, we walked up to them and started talking about what thirteen-year-old-girls talk about in the presence of cute boys. Everything was going OK. The two boys weren't impressed with us, but they at least talked to us.

Until I decided it would be a great idea to pull out my camera to snap a photo of my crush. *Mass babe* were the words I'd plastered next to his tiny picture in my school yearbook. That picture wasn't enough to quench my thirst for this babe, and I wanted something in a larger color glossy. I snapped photos, and my crush tried to pull away. If that wasn't out of character enough, I grabbed his shirt so he wouldn't get away, and the next thing I heard was a loud rip followed by a shocked look. The shirt was the much-desired concert shirt everyone was wearing. A coveted garment, a status symbol. A conversation piece.

"Hey, you ripped my shirt!" Garrett exclaimed.

I stood there dumbfounded. I could have melted into the cement we were standing on, but instead I froze.

"Whoa, dude, I can't believe that weird chick just ripped your shirt!" his basketball partner and love of Lisa's life said.

Besties

"Tell me about it! I don't know how these chicks figured out where I live." Garrett shook his head.

"Do you know them?" his friend asked.

"Dude, they go to our school. I thought you knew them. That's the only reason I was talking to them!" Garrett looked at his ripped shirt.

"Dude, go change your shirt," his friend said. "By the time you get back, they'll be gone." He shot us a glare that commanded our exit.

"And make sure they don't see what apartment I live in," Garrett warned his friend as he turned to walk away.

Lisa and I took off. My crush ended while I figured out how to hide from Garrett for the rest of the school year!

The early eighties crested with the new-wave era, and middle school kids embraced the current fad. With bands like Culture Club and Flock of Seagulls playing on MTV, teenagers were hooked. I chucked hard rock bands like AC/DC and added green food coloring to my newly spiked feathered hair.

Lisa and I hung out at her house on the weekends, enjoying the freedom of Lisa's working-mom's absence. We'd hop on the bus to the mall or walk down the busy highway to grab a bite to eat. It didn't matter what we were doing—we were never bored. All we cared about was music, cute guys, and the next fast-food burger.

Whenever parents weren't around, freedom reigned. By the time we turned fourteen, we had already kissed boys and smoked cigarettes and pot. The only thing that eluded us was in the boy department. Neither of us had had any luck snagging a boyfriend, but we still had visions of double dates dancing through our teenage minds. We wanted to be grown up, like the girls who sat in the back row at the movie theater and made out with their boyfriends. Lisa and I were just a summer away from entering high school, but as we matured, the boys did too. The innocence of middle school relationships had graduated to a new level. Cute guys didn't seem content with making out and late-night talks on the phone . . . not that I had anyone calling me late at night on the phone. Times were changing, and I felt the pressure to be like everyone else. I didn't want to get left behind. I didn't want to be the inexperienced shy girl.

The summer before high school, I took a cross-country trip with my parents to visit relatives. I was sad to leave Lisa for a whole month, but excited about the family reunion.

Certain that my summer vacation would include an encounter with a cute guy, surely I would have more luck in a different state. I planned on filling Lisa in on all the juicy details when I returned home. It was the juicy part, though, that I feared the most.

So off we drove in our eighties van, complete with convertible sleeper and retractable dining table. I began the trip with Motley Crüe playing on my boom box. In Montana, I wore a turquoise sweatshirt with a pair of matching Lawman jeans.

I loved Jackson Hole, Wyoming. I felt like I was on the set of a movie in the Old West. Mount Rushmore was okay. Maybe it'd be beautiful at night under a canopy of stars. What was really a trip and a half, though, was running into one of my classmates at the Corn Palace in South Dakota.

I stepped inside an enormous building filled with all things corn. Surrounded by an array of souvenirs, I was admiring the large cowbells. I had to have one! It looked like the exact same bell the love of my life, Tommy Lee, pounded on. *I simply must convince Mom to buy one for me!*

Suddenly, my eyes locked on to a familiar face. *No,* I told myself. *It couldn't be.* The face stared back just as intently from only a few yards away. *There's no way! What are the chances of running into one of the boys from my middle school in South Dakota, at the Corn Palace?*

The boy had been in a class that Lisa and I shared. The only time I'd talked to him was when my courageous friend Lisa was by my side. She made talking with boys easier because she initiated the conversations.

There I was without my security blanket, convincing myself that our parents couldn't possibly have planned the same summer vacation route and chose the Corn Palace as a must-see destination stop . . . on the same day!

Apparently my classmate felt likewise as we passed each other, both of us turning to look back as we continued on our way without saying a word.

When we finally arrived at my relative's big house in the country, I had a blast! We went to amusement parks, saw the Amish riding through town on their horses and buggies, and swam at the outdoor public swimming hole. And at the month's end, I still had no memorable story to come home with. What was a girl to do?

I called Lisa the minute I arrived home. It had been four whole weeks since we'd seen each other, and we had a lot of catching up to do. I invited her to stay at my house for an all-night session of music and talking.

My parents were already asleep when Lisa arrived, and we beelined for the family room, located at the far end of our one-story rambler, which meant that all three bedrooms were yards away. I cranked up Motley Crüe on my boom box and walked the length of the house, past the living room, kitchen, and down the long hallway, until I reached the end where my parents' bedroom was. All was clear, and I couldn't hear even a peep of the live version of "Too Fast for Love" that Lisa was rocking out to. I sauntered back to our headquarters for the evening. What would I tell Lisa? I hadn't been successful at losing my virginity. She would want details, but I didn't have any to give.

Entering the room, the first words to spill from her lips were, "So tell me. I'm dying to know! Who did you meet and what did you do? Did you meet someone?"

"Yes. I met the cutest mass babe I have ever seen," I lied. "He looked just like Tommy Lee, only his hair wasn't as long, but he was tall just like him. His name is Buck."

"Buck? Where did he get a name like Buck?" she asked as she lit up a cigarette.

"What are you doing, Lisa? My parents will know that we've been smoking in here!"

"Don't worry so much. The smoke from the woodstove will cover up the smell of the cigarettes," she reassured and offered me a hit off her cigarette.

I indulged in a couple of quick drags, worried my parents would walk in, and even more worried about the big fib I was about to tell my best friend.

"Let me get this straight. You got together with a mass babe that looked just like Tommy Lee, except his name happened to be Buck?" she joked.

"Yes. He comes from a small town and is named after his grandfather."

"All right, forget about his name or the cowboy boots and flannel shirt that he wears," she said.

"For your information, he has about a hundred concert shirts and wears a baseball cap, not a cowboy hat."

Besties

"All right, so tell me. Did you have sex with him?" she probed.

"I did!" I hadn't.

"That is totally cool, man. Tell me everything, and start from the beginning." She lit up another smoke.

I proceeded to tell her the whole story from beginning to end of how I met Buck.

Buck and I had our fictitious first encounter at the local pool. He had offered his apologies to me after his little brother rudely threw blueberries on my cute one-piece bathing suit. Instead of being white and purple striped, it was now highlighted with blue as well. Buck had been sweet enough to throw his little brother into the pool to teach him a lesson. We talked all day, and I was sad to leave that afternoon. But he promised to call me at my relatives'. By the time I returned, the phone was already ringing. I arranged to meet Buck that evening while our parents went to the movies.

Lisa hung on every word of my fairy tale, constantly asking, "And then what happened?" By the time I finished my fable, Buck and I were lying next to each other in his family's barn.

"He's a hick. I suppose he wears Wrangler jeans too." She laughed. "And what the heck is a firefly?"

"Oh, they're these bugs that light up the sky at night." Then I added more spice to the story by telling her that our flashlight had stopped working, and the moon, well, it was nowhere to be found. We were lost in the pitch dark, so Buck grabbed an old jar, and we caught fireflies until we had enough to use for a light.

"No way! That is so totally cool, man." She smiled, nodding her head in disbelief.

It was the perfect summer fling.

Chapter 4

PALM-TREE DREAMS

As all the kids from middle school were busy trying on their new school clothes, Lisa and I decided to run away to California, where we would find famous boyfriends, like the babes in Motley Crüe. Our lives would be full of warm weather, palm trees, and hanging out with rock bands. We didn't want an average existence of school bus rides and fluorescent lighting!

We contrived a plan while the rest of our peers spent the last days of summer in anticipation for their freshmen year of high school. Our plan wasn't the best, but it was the best last-minute scheme that two fourteen-year-old girls could come up with. We knew that once school officially started and we were not in class, we would have to get out of town quick. We intended to panhandle to scrap together enough money to take the bus to LA. When we arrived in LA, we would go hang out at the famous places on Sunset Strip and Hollywood Boulevard we'd read about.

Whether I truly wanted to ditch high school and move to LA was irrelevant. I would be tagging along on any adventure my best friend was going on because I had one motto after years as the shy, lonely girl in school: "Go where your best friend goes, regardless of the consequences!" I had a deep-seated fear of facing life alone. I couldn't attend high school by myself. The thought of walking through those huge, intimidating hallways with all the popular kids grinning from ear to ear, as if they had won the lottery, made me nauseous.

As far as I was concerned, they had won the lottery as a child when they weren't afraid to make friends with any kid on the playground or chase after the damn ball in PE. I wanted to be one of those outgoing kids so bad, but instead I was the girl who got left out. I was so desperate in grade school that I befriended teachers' assistants every year. I wrote them letters when they landed full-time teaching positions, and I even sent one of them an envelope full of rocks, as if it were buried treasure.

I made friends with adults because they were much less intimidating than my own peers. When I met Lisa, she was the answer to all the insecurity inside me, and she didn't even know it. She hadn't a clue how helpless I felt without her, and I wouldn't let her know my secret. Instead I followed along with any plan she had, and if it involved not attending high school, then I was prepared to skip my education.

Just before the first day of our freshman year, Lisa and I met a guy at the mall. He had his own apartment in downtown Seattle and also wanted to move to Los Angeles. For several days we took the long bus ride downtown to hang out at his apartment until school got out.

After two weeks of our routine, the school called my house. My brother Allen had answered the phone and was the first to confront me as I walked in the door. Terrified, I decided to make a break for it. My parents took long walks every night for an hour or so. This was my only chance to escape before they learned the news. I was alone in the house. It was time to make my move. I packed my suitcase and stole twenty dollars from my mother's wallet. I walked out the front door with a huge suitcase and ran the distance of our long dead-end street.

When I reached the main road that led to Lisa's, I stopped to catch my breath. Hopefully, my neighbors were not peering out their windows, because I must have looked ridiculous. All I had was two more blocks to go, and then I would seek refuge in an empty building near Lisa's house. I had already called Lisa to tell her to meet me once her mom was fast asleep. Hopefully, after a few days, we could get together enough money to catch a bus to LA.

I spent an hour in silence while I waited for Lisa. It would be dark soon. This small building was the perfect place to hide until we could leave for California. We had all week long to shack up there if need be, and with the building's close proximity, we could even go to Lisa's house to eat. Her mom worked all day, so our showers and phone calls could be done while her mom was gone.

While I went over the plan in my head, my mother's screaming brought me back to reality.

"Where is Shana?" she demanded in the loudest voice I had ever heard.

Lisa stated meekly, "I don't know where she is."

I could hear the entire conversation being broadcasted out loud. My mother threatened in a blood-curdling voice, "You'd better tell me where my daughter is right now, Lisa."

Lisa eventually broke under the pressure.

I sat on the little building's bare floor, frozen. The yelling had stopped, and I immediately saw the glare of headlights approaching. My mother had been successful with her scare tactics, and I had been caught. Lucky for Lisa, she didn't have to deal with my mother's wrath any longer. Now her anger would be directed my way instead. I had never been so frightened. I saw a silver lining though—the same feeling I had with Tonya, a sense of complete relief. I could go home to my own bed. I didn't have to run away. I'd been caught! Even though I was scared to death of the dreaded confrontation with my mom (that's right—my mom, not my dad!), I was now free from the nutty idea of dropping out of school and moving to LA. Sigh.

My parents and I drove back home in silence. Once inside our house, my father was calm, but my mother drilled me.

"What is going on with you, Shana? I can't believe you would do such a thing," my mom yelled. "What were you thinking? What were you planning on doing?" She asked question after question as she pulled every item out of my suitcase, screaming in the process.

"You can run away, but you are not taking a single thing that I bought with you," she seethed. "These are not your clothes! Who bought these clothes for you? If you want to leave, go ahead, but you are not leaving with a single thing!"

After what seemed like forever, my mother stopped to catch her breath and let me talk.

I told her that I had been skipping school. "I was afraid of what you would do when you found out, so I packed my bags and decided to run away." I wasn't about to tell her our crazy plan to run away to California and meet the members of Motley Crüe. "I also took twenty dollars from your purse."

The fight ended, and my mom told me to get some sleep. The next morning she enrolled me in another district. The familiar faces from grade school and middle school were but a distant memory. I would have a chance at a fresh start, but this would be a solo venture. Lisa would be attending another school. She wouldn't be by my side. I had lost my security blanket, but I was now in a much smaller, less intimidating high school. I had a new lease on life. Still shy Shana, but maybe I could live a different life at this new school . . . no familiar faces to remind me of who I was and where I'd come from.

A popular rocker chick was the first person to talk to me at the quaint school I now called home. I sat in the back of the fifth-period English classroom, with all the other kids who had no desire to learn. My mother must have been highly disturbed by her once sweet little girl turned rocker rebel, possessing no interest in an education unless it was the Motley Crüe High School for troubled teens. Yes, we students in the back row were often red eyed, just passing the time.

"What school did you come from?" The girl interrupted my daydream of Tommy Lee.

"Foster."

"That's where I want to transfer," she cooed. "I love Foster. It is such an awesome school. Why would you transfer here?"

"I got in trouble for skipping school with my best friend, so they transferred us to separate high schools," I answered.

"Wow. I heard all the guys at Foster are total babes," she said with envy, turning back to face the teacher before she could be reprimanded.

I quickly found the anesthetized group at my new high school and embraced any friends I could make. The smokers would walk across the street to indulge in a quick puff between classes. There were usually about twenty people hot-boxing their cigarettes, trying to suck one down between classes. I didn't really need cigarettes, but I just kind of went along with the crowd.

Others would walk farther down the hill and get stoned between classes. I marveled at the laid-back stoner crowd that actually seemed to enjoy getting stoned. I never liked getting stoned, but sometimes I indulged when offered. Luckily this wasn't a daily occurrence, because every time I got stoned at school, I ended up paranoid for the next couple of hours.

There was a guy in my history class who loved to make me sweat. Though I didn't make it a habit of getting stoned, when I did, he tried to rat on me. I didn't know if this fellow rocker wanted to get me in trouble or if he just loved to play the game called "Let's watch Shana freak out."

"Why are your eyes so red?" Zack questioned me from halfway across the room.

"Shut up," I replied in a hushed tone. Boy, did this guy know how to make me squirm!

"Are you stoned, Shana?" he persisted with a mischievous grin. He of course knew the answer to that question and didn't let up until he got the teacher's attention.

Lucky for me, Zack must not have been the teacher's pet. Instead of walking up to me with suspicious eyes, she yelled at Zack and told him to get back to work.

What kept me from becoming a serious pothead, aside from my paranoid state while stoned, was my mother. The one time I had come home stoned, my mom noticed. I didn't know how my friends' mothers seemed so clueless, but not my mom. She took one look at me and instantly asked what I had taken. After that day I stuck to the rule of never inhaling anything stronger than cigarettes unless I was staying the night at a friend's house.

Palm-Tree Dreams

Aside from smoking pot occasionally, smoking cigarettes more often, and failing most of my classes, school was going really well for me. The thing most important to me, having friends, had worked out. I hung out with a bunch of fellow male and female rockers.

One minor detail that occurred on my first day of school ended up plaguing me each day. I had missed my fourth-period class on the first day. All the other freshmen were already acclimated to their class schedule and high school life. Since I'd started school two weeks late, the attendant had to handwrite my schedule. In the process, she made an error. It wasn't until after lunch that I realized my math class was already half over. That was where my trouble began. I was too embarrassed to walk into class late, so I skipped it. Why didn't I get it right the next day and attend the class? I would have had to give the reason why I didn't walk into class when I found out I was late on day one. I would have to explain why I was a big fat chicken!

It was a miracle I was even attending high school without Lisa. She was so full of confidence. With her by my side, I surely would have walked into class late without a care in the world. But all alone was a different story. I didn't like being late. The whole Tonya fiasco already proved that. It seemed to me that late people received the attention of everyone in the room. I avoided being publicly singled out at all costs. The tragic thing was that I would have been early to math class if there hadn't been an error on my class schedule.

That was how I got myself in a pickle. I saw no way out, so I didn't attend math class. Instead, I took an hour and a half lunch each day. I was bored during my daily siesta and would walk a long distance to get lunch. It was a good day when I could afford a taco salad, but usually I had to scrape for change to get a hamburger. How much easier it would have been to be in my math class than wandering the street. I'd often walk along the airport highway to a nice hotel that seemed to always have a convention going on. If Lisa was home sick, I would call her, or I would hang out in the ladies' lounge fixing my overly made-up face.

After several weeks of this crazy extended lunch hour, the school finally found out what was going on. With a sinking feeling, I watched my teacher walk directly toward me with a pink slip in hand. Talk about scary! The slip instructed me to go see the principal. I had been caught. Maybe it was for the best because each time I got caught, it ended up being a blessing with a little screaming attached. At least now I wouldn't be wandering the streets aimlessly for an hour and a half every day.

The mistake my principal made was underestimating my fear of confrontation. I wasn't a fighter. I was a runner. He should have sent someone to escort me to his office, because no sooner had I left my class to "go see the principal" than I made a beeline for the main road, and I didn't look back.

That day I walked along the busy highway for several miles until I reached Lisa's school. She was on the road smoking cigarettes with her peers from her alternative high school. I would never have made it hanging around this school's crowd, and I stayed close to Lisa as her classmates stared on.

"Hi. I finally got busted. They found out I was skipping school and called me to the office. I took off as soon as I could," I told Lisa.

"Oh man! What are you gonna do?" she asked.

"I don't want to go home tonight. I am definitely in trouble."

"I don't understand why you skipped your math class for

two months, Shana," she said.

I wasn't about to confess my insecurity to Lisa.

"I have to go home and face my mother now. She is going to be so mad. I am just going to go get it over with, I guess," I muttered.

"Bye, Shana. Be brave, and call me when your mom gets done yelling at you." She chuckled.

It wasn't funny, and I held my breath as I entered the door. I knew the school had already called my mom at work and must have filled her in on my speedy departure.

After a lot of yelling and screaming, she ended with, "As far as I'm concerned, you can go jump off a bridge!"

Of course my mother didn't really want me to jump off a bridge. She most likely wished that her sweet little girl who never got into trouble would return.

My mother did get a little revenge the following day when, delayed as it was, I realized I would be attending that infamous math class for the remainder of the year.

My saving grace was a girl named Kristi. We never became close friends, but we definitely huddled together in that class for the rest of the year.

Chapter 5

I'M NOT GONNA TAKE IT ANYMORE!

The heavy-metal rock scene captivated me. Cute rocker dudes showed off their male prowess by wearing their long hair spiked up with too much hairspray. Colors like jet black and platinum blond were in high demand, and the rocker guys looked similar to the girls.

The girls had one thing on the guys though, aside from their femininity, and that was their hair. The blessed girls had the most beautiful long, spiral curls that cascaded down to the middle of their backs. I dreamed of having hair like these girls, but my hair was too thick, which meant my perm ended up resembling a frizzy poodle, not spiral, cascading curls.

The cool-looking rocker chicks also owned several pairs of tight spandex pants to be worn at the most important events ever—rock concerts! These awesome-looking pants fit like a second skin and were in solid black or leopard/zebra print. I envied these girls with their perfectly petite figures. They were not too skinny and not too curvy, but most of all, they were not too tall, like me. To top off the ensemble, they often dressed in cropped muscle shirts with pictures of favorite rock bands. Sometimes these shirts were signed by the actual band members, which made for an even cooler look and more envy on my part. These concert shirts were a must-have in any avid rocker's wardrobe.

My first concert shirt was a black muscle shirt with the face of Twisted Sister's lead singer, Dee Snider, plastered on the front. He aroused teenagers everywhere to drive their parents crazy while blasting the anthem "We're not gonna take it!" on millions of boom boxes throughout America.

I should have been content listening to my boom box and purchasing a Twisted Sister shirt at the mall, but instead I was about to make my mom mad once again.

My trouble began when Twisted Sister came to town. Seattle was only a bus ride away from our airport town. Lisa was skipping school for the day to attend the event. I was heartbroken because my mother refused to let me go to rock concerts until I was sixteen. At fourteen, it seemed like a lifetime before I could see a band play live at the coliseum.

Discontentment set in, and I usually sailed past discontentment until I reached the shores of "this is fun, but I'm definitely going to pay for it big time."

"Come on, *Shana*. Just come with me to the concert," Lisa begged from her doorstep that morning.

Her mom had already left for work, and I had stopped by Lisa's house on the way to the school bus. Probably not the smartest thing to do.

"Look at all the awesome shows you have already missed," she complained.

"I'm missing out on Twisted Sister, live. This totally sucks, man. I should just go. I mean, what's the worst my mom can do to me?" I knew the answer to that question. She could yell like no other five-foot-four-inch woman and send my heart pounding. On the other side of the concert coin was the fact that all my peers would be going to this concert and I didn't want to miss out yet again.

My mom didn't understand how excruciating it was to witness my classmates return to school after a late night out with their favorite rock band. Their ears still ringing from the night before, they walked around with an attitude, bragging about the previous night's show. "Wow, what a cool shirt," I would overhear a fellow classmate comment, practically drooling with envy. "Did you get it from the show last night?"

"Yeah, man, I was right in the front. Nikki Sixx was only three feet away, and he threw a guitar pick at me, man," the popular kid would boast. "It was so awesome, dude! I can barely hear. I have bruises all over my body, dude, from being pushed up against the stage."

Witnessing yet another bragging concertgoer the morning after was something I could no longer endure. Seriously, I wasn't in middle school anymore. I was in high school. To top things off, I had already missed my favorite band of all time, Motley Crüe, not to mention the love of my life, Tommy Lee.

What was a girl to do? "Man, I'm just gonna go. My mom can't keep me from seeing Dee Snider in person."

"All right, now you're talkin', Shana! There's that brave girl I know and love! We are gonna have a totally awesome time, man!" Lisa exclaimed. "Let's hurry up so we can stand in line and get a spot up front!"

We scattered around Lisa's house that morning with Twisted Sister blasting on the stereo while we got ready. Getting ready included spending too much time in front of the mirror, equipped with hairspray, brush, and makeup. Cheap aerosol hairspray was a must in every serious rocker's arsenal. Our hairbrushes were corroded beyond recognition as we curled, sprayed, and ratted our hair for a spiked look. Then we spent another half hour caking on too much concealer, powder, red blush, eyeliner, purple eye shadow, mascara, and lipstick. The essential eyelash curler was used many times as we curled lashes and reapplied mascara until we resembled raccoons.

Now all we needed was something to wear. Luckily, Lisa had the perfect outfits. She had just bought two new pairs of spandex, one leopard print and the other black. We topped the pants off with cropped muscle shirts.

On a sunny afternoon, Lisa and I walked to the highway to catch the public bus to Seattle. The forty-five minute ride was especially long on a standing-room-only bus filled with several other concertgoers. Lisa and I, as usual, passed the time talking while we tried to keep our noses plugged. On any given day, at least one person, ten days short of a shower, sat on the bus, often engaged in a solo quarreling match. Is that what would have happened to Lisa and me if we had run away to California? I shuddered.

"Shana, are you spacing out? Did you get a whiff of that guy on the bus, man?" Lisa asked.

"Yeah, thank goodness the ride is over, man," I replied as I stepped off the bus to join her on the busy downtown sidewalk.

"Finally, I can breathe." Lisa waved her hand in front of her nose.

Twelve city blocks flew by as we approached the concert venue. It was only 2:00 p.m., and hordes of people stood in line outside the coliseum so they could get up close and personal with the rock stars on the stage. We engaged in conversation with a couple of guys who offered to share a joint with us.

High, I began to reach my usual paranoid state when I noticed a girl in the crowd.

"Oh, man, isn't that Trisha?" I asked in horror, nudging Lisa in the side.

Lisa kept chatting with a dude instead of paying any attention to me.

I'd been terrified of Trisha ever since she threatened to kick my butt one day after school. Even though it had been two years ago and Trisha had long since moved away, I was frightened. "Lisa! Is that Trisha over there?" I asked again.

"What? Where?" she asked.

"Right in front of us by the news cameras," I said. "Oh, no! The news is here! What if my mom sees me on TV?" In my panic, I forgot about Trisha, more concerned about getting caught smoking pot on television.

"Shana, you are so paranoid. Geez!" Lisa laughed, directing her attention to the line ahead. "I think they're opening the doors soon." She squinted into the distance.

"Good!" Paranoid or not, I couldn't wait to get inside.

When the doors finally opened, I couldn't wait to attend my first concert. Our first stop was the T-shirt booth. We both picked out shirts with the lead singer of Twisted Sister's face plastered on the front. After we pulled on our new shirts, we dashed to the front of the stage. I followed behind Lisa, along with many others. We were so close to the stage that I was sure we would be able to reach up and touch Dee Snider. Before any touching would take place though we had to wait. We stood there, packed in like sardines.

The house lights dimmed, cuing the standing audience to

rush to the front of the stage. Lisa was slammed up against the wooden barricade center stage. Aside from a backstage pass, she had the best spot in the house. Frightened, I envisioned myself being trampled by the fanatical mob. Lisa kept a sturdy hold on her spot, still pinned up against the barricade with hundreds of concertgoers; she had no intention of leaving. She had waited all day for this.

I enjoyed the remainder of the show several yards back from the aggressive crowd. *No wonder my mom doesn't want me to go to these events. The people are entirely nuts!* Guys lit off M-80s in the crowd. Girls made torches with their lighters and cans of hairspray. It was unreal, and I had never experienced anything like it. Of course, I would never admit my fear to my fearless leader, Lisa. I told her it was the best night of my life.

By the time we departed Bus 174 on Pac Highway and began our ascension up the large hill to our homes, I'd already concluded that my first rock concert was not worth the wrath to come. Lisa's mom wouldn't be mad at her, but mine would be a different story. My days of being the sweet, obedient daughter had ceased with the influx of teenage friends and my fear of being left out. I had done the evil deed. I had disobeyed my parents by sneaking off to a concert that promised excitement yet left me feeling empty and sick to my stomach.

"Cheer up." Lisa smiled as we said our goodbyes.

"That's easy for you to say. Your mom isn't mad at you," I said.

"Oh, your parents won't be mad for long. They love you."

"I'll call you tomorrow," I replied with a meek smile as I turned toward my street.

"Good night," Lisa replied from several yards away.

We continued our goodbyes as we walked in opposite directions until our voices trailed off in the inaudible distance. Now to face my parents.

"Where have you been, Shana?" Mom demanded the minute I opened the door. "That's it. I've had it with you. I'm not going to go through this rebellion with you!"

Dad, calm as usual, stood there in agreement with my mother. *Boy, Twister Sister is so not worth the wrath of Mom,* I thought as I sat speechless on the living room sofa. What could I say in my defense? Everything my mother said was true. I had no excuse. All I could do was wait it out. Eventually the yelling would cease and my mother would calm down.

In my sophomore year, Lisa enrolled in my school, but I no longer clung to her like a favorite blanket. I had reached the status of acquiring my own set of rocker friends and felt comfortable at school. My grades were still dismal, but socially I thrived. The home front was even better. My parents had great-paying jobs, and I was the only one left in the family nest. All of us kids were spaced three years apart. First my sister Debbie, then my eldest brother, Michael, my stuck-in-the-middle brother, Allen, and myself, the baby of the family. It seemed every few years another sibling was flying solo. Finally I ruled the house!

To top it off, my mother spoiled me rotten on a middle-class level. Every morning I hopped in her car and she took me to my favorite drive-thru. I ordered the same thing each day—sausage and cheese on an English muffin, with orange juice. While the other students stood at the bus stop freezing their booties off, I sat in my mom's warm car listening to music.

On Thursdays my mom took me to my favorite clothing store at the mall, where I picked out a new outfit. Awesome! This was after a pit stop at my mother's shrink. She'd had an ongoing appointment with her shrink ever since I could remember. She'd had a rather miserable childhood and had some sorting out to do. With the hour already reserved each week, my mom decided it would be a good idea for me to tag along for a couple sessions to work on what she referred to as "my rebellion."

"This is my daughter, Shana," my mother said as she introduced me to her shrink.

"Hello, Shana, it is very nice to finally meet you. I have heard so much about you," he said.

While he and Mom settled into their assigned sofas, I opened up the book I brought along. I wasn't trying to be rebellious. I saw the whole thing as a bore and brought along a little company. I hoped they viewed it as a positive trait—at least I liked to read . . . just not schoolbooks.

My mother's shrink saw it in a different light.

"I see that you brought a book with you today. This is a clear display that you lack respect for authority," he said, resting his hand on his chin, studying me.

"You're not my authority." I didn't know this man from Adam, and he was talking like he had me all figured out. He got under my skin, but would I have been so outspoken four years earlier? The answer was a definite no. But things had changed since I had entered my teenage years. Maybe I was rebellious—or maybe I felt completely outnumbered.

"Can you shed some light on the issues that are causing conflict in your home?" he asked, directing his attention to my mother.

"Shana is completely rebellious and refuses to obey her curfew," my mother said.

"She wants me to come home at 10:30 p.m. on weekends.

I'm Not Gonna Take It Anymore!

All of my friends stay out until two a.m.," I complained. "For goodness' sake, I'm fifteen years old, and in a few months I'll be sixteen. That's old enough to get a license and work! They suffocate me and are so protective," I concluded, compelled to plead my case.

"All right, maybe there is a reasonable hour that everyone can agree on?" the shrink suggested. "What about twelve a.m.?"

My ears perked up. I better not refer to this man as a "shrink" anymore because if my ears didn't deceive me, he was siding with me. At least in the curfew department, which was the only thing I cared about. I drank on the weekends when I stayed the night at my friends' houses. Their moms let them stay out until midnight! We also got stoned sometimes and smoked too many cigarettes while intoxicated. I didn't see any of this secret life as a problem. I just saw my mother standing in the way of my social life. That was what I'd thought her psychiatrist would do too. But to my amazement, it seemed he was on my team for the moment! Maybe his parents had tried to make him come home early when he was a teenager too?

"If we decide on twelve a.m., then she will eventually come home at two a.m.," Mom said.

I knew a new curfew was too good to be true! While I observed my new teammate battle it out in a verbal debate, I didn't place much confidence in him. He wasn't my age, and since my parents paid him, surely he would cave. My mother would reign once again. This meant I would continue to be the only fifteen-year-old within the city limits humiliated in the sight of all my peers with a 10:30 curfew.

"Shana, can we agree on twelve a.m. for your curfew and no later?" he asked.

"Yes, I can definitely agree on twelve a.m.," I pledged. For the first time since I had entered his office, I made direct eye contact with my teammate. As if swearing an oath, I agreed to a midnight curfew.

We reigned victorious. My shame was taken away, but as far as the oath, I knew I would let down my teammate.

After a few sessions with my mother's psychiatrist, everything settled down at my house, and I reveled in my new curfew. On the school front, I wasn't skipping any classes or receiving any infamous pink slips from the principal. But my grades continued to plummet. My faltering grades paralleled my utter lack of interest in graduating high school. My report cards simply reflected my attitude, a medley of Ds, Fs, and an occasional C, thanks to art class.

Though my history teacher saw me as a lost cause, that didn't hinder him from calling on me from time to time, his expression flabbergasted when I actually answered.

"Shana, please answer the question," he prodded.

It never failed that when I tried to hide from a teacher's glaring eye by sliding down in my seat, I was called upon. There I sat halfway under my desk, staring intently at my textbook.

"Shana, do you know the answer to the question?" he repeated.

"Ah . . . Czechoslovakia," I mumbled.

"Yes. You are correct!"

I didn't know who was more amazed that day by my correct response—my fellow classmates, my teacher, or myself. I hadn't studied or finished my homework assignment and had simply chosen a country that rhymed with the previous correct answer, Yugoslavia. It was a shot in the dark, but low and behold I was right!

Chapter 6

HE ONLY WALKED ME HALFWAY HOME

My descension down the spiral staircase of life accelerated at top speed with the loss of my virginity. At the tail end of my sophomore year, just before I turned sixteen, I finally snagged what I had dreamed of for years. Ever since witnessing Susan holding hands with the love of my sixth-grade life, I had wished for a boyfriend to call my own. Someone to walk with hand in hand and spend hours talking to on the phone after everyone in the house had gone to bed. My dreams were always PG rated, and at the most I daydreamed of the first wonderful kiss. I dreamed that kiss would be so enchanting that it would be enough.

Then reality smacked me in the face. A kiss wasn't enough to hold my wish together. I relented because deep down I wanted to feel loved. I wanted someone to love me and hold me in their masculine arms. Even if he used more hairspray than me.

My first boyfriend, Vince, wasn't the most gorgeous guy on the planet, but he did have two major things going for him.

First, he somewhat resembled the bass player for Motley Crüe, or at least had the same hair. Second, he was in a band, and what could be more romantic than going out with a guy in a band? To be the girl up front—or even better than that, to be the girl backstage that he winked at while playing his guitar! In my rocker group of friends, it was the epitome of cool, and I had finally snagged this dream. I had a babe to call me on the phone, to spend hours talking about him with my girlfriends. My wish came true . . . sort of.

That night, the night my fantasy bubble burst and I caved under the pressure to perform, maybe things would have been different if I had placed any value on my virginity, but I didn't. I saw it as some ugly, embarrassing thing that I needed to get rid of, yet I was scared to death of the act of shedding it. What if the guy knew that I was a virgin? How embarrassing would that be?

Just a couple of weeks into my new relationship with Vince, after having done all the first-few-date things like going out to a restaurant and seeing a movie, Vince invited me to his friend's house to hang out. It was the weekend, and his friend lived near my home. I agreed but was scared this would be "the night."

"I'll pick you up at eight tonight. My friend Charlie's parents are out of town. We can finally be alone. I've been going crazy. I can't wait to be with you." My boyfriend sighed.

"Me too," I lied and hung up the phone.

After I had changed clothes a million times, I waited for him to pick me up. I was nervous, but what could I do? Whom could I talk to? Not my mom. Her little girl had grown up to lead a secret life of partying. Many of my friends were doing the same. This was my lot in life, and I was prepared to accept it. I wanted a boyfriend, and this was part of the territory. This was what it took to be loved.

With my stomach in knots, I hopped into the car with Vince. The sun hadn't set as we drove down my tiny dead-end street. The street that had looked so large the day I had sped off on my bicycle with Buddy's words still echoing in my head: *Will you be my girlfriend?* What a silly question, and what an even more silly response, *I'm a girl and I'm your friend!* A lot had changed since that day. *No more banana-seat bicycles, that's for certain,* I thought as Vince and I drove past the weeping willow tree. Waiting for the oncoming traffic to pass, Vince cautiously turned the corner. That is when any innocence left inside me said its last goodbye.

It took only minutes to drive to Charlie's house. I secretly wished the car ride lasted forever. It felt so good to be stuck to Vince's side with my head resting on his shoulder, and the best part of my night was already over by the time we entered the house. For Vince though, it was the moment he'd been waiting for.

"Hey, dude, howz it going?" Vince asked Charlie.

"Cool, man. I see you brought your girlfriend." Charlie smiled knowingly.

They snickered like schoolboys.

"Yeah, this is Shana," Vince confirmed.

"Hi," I said meekly.

We sat on the couch holding hands, making the necessary small talk for all of twenty minutes. The entire time my heart raced. I tried to concentrate on Vince and Charlie's conversation, but I couldn't. All I could focus on was what would happen next. Interrupting my train of thought, my aspiring rock-star boyfriend stood up and escorted me to a dark bedroom just around the corner from where we were just sitting. If only I could be back in the living room, just sitting. Vince slowly closed the door. He didn't waste a minute getting down to business. I knew it was why we were there, in the small, unfamiliar room, his friend only a short distance away.

He laid me on the bare carpet and proceeded to take from me what I was willing to give him. It was the most unfulfilling, unemotional time in my short fifteen-year life span.

"Has it been a while since you were with anyone?" he asked.

Vince obviously had no clue I was a virgin. He, on the other hand, by the ripe age of seventeen had already familiarized himself with many females. I was grateful I could barely see his face as I answered through the dark, "Yeah, it's been a while." Thankfully, it didn't take long for what I considered an ordeal to be over with.

The first thing I did was reach for my clothing. I now knew what it felt like to give my body away, even though he was my boyfriend. I couldn't articulate how I felt afterward. I had mastered the art of shoving my feelings down so deep that it was almost as if I didn't feel anything. *Dirty, used, cheap*—these words offered an accurate depiction of what had just happened to me, but what I really felt? Numb.

After returning to the living room, we spent a few more moments on the couch with his friend, and then he walked me halfway home. Vince had borrowed Charlie's car that night when he'd picked me up. At almost sixteen years of age, my self-worth was so low that I settled for losing my virginity to a boy who didn't even walk me all the way home.

After saying our goodbyes, I climbed the remainder of the hill that led to my street, in the dark and alone. I'd climbed the same hill hundreds of times over the years, almost always with someone by my side. Whether coming back from the minimart with my licorice whip in hand or during a snow day when we kids panted our way up what we had just sledded down. How could I forget the night my heart pounded out of my chest after the Twisted Sister concert, knowing my mother was waiting for me the minute I walked in the door? I had climbed this familiar childhood hill many times, but never had I ascended with soreness between my legs and numbness in my mind.

My parents, of course, had no idea, even when my mother inquired about the mark on my back a few nights later. I was getting ready for a school dance, my first school dance with my new boyfriend. I intended to wear a white silky dress embedded with rhinestones.

"What is that mark on your back?" my mom asked when I had called her to the bathroom to help me zip up the delicate dress.

"Where?" Puzzled, I tried to catch a glance in the mirror of the mark.

"It's right here." Mom rubbed the area in question with a perplexed look.

I quickly changed the subject. "Mom, I don't know what it is. I must have scraped myself. I have to hurry. He'll be here any minute."

While Mom left the bathroom, I finished zipping my dress to cover up the infamous rug burn on my lower back. It was the only thing I had to show for my lost virginity.

My relationship with Vince ended a couple weeks after attending my first school dance. I was devastated, but time has a way of mending a broken heart, and for a while I enjoyed my PG-rated love life again.

After ringing in my sweet sixteen and finishing my sophomore year of high school, I should have been on cloud nine. It was summer, the season I lived for. Not only did I love it for the weather, a time when our rainy city finally warmed up, but also because school was out and there would be no early morning wake-ups for a couple of months. Just late-night parties and lazy days spent hanging out with friends while the folks were at work.

My only problem, and the reason my favorite time of year was turning out to be just like the Bananarama song "Cruel Summer"? Lisa had decided to ditch me for an entire month. Talk about lack of dedication. It was just something that you didn't do to a longtime friend. Maybe it was payback for my previous cross-country summer vacation. Regardless of whether I was happy for Lisa or not, it didn't change the fact that while she was having a blast visiting relatives, I was left sulking on my couch watching MTV and munching on too many peanuts M&Ms. It was what I did when bored or uncomfortable. I munched away, not paying attention to what was going in my mouth.

After a day or so of complete boredom and before I needed to move up a pant size, I put down my bag of candy and picked up the telephone. I had a brainstorm. Why not call a friend from school? Even though I was bused in and didn't own a car, I had a friend from school who'd just acquired her license. Maybe she'd like to hang out while Lisa was away.

I'd met Melinda in art class during my freshman year. She was the epitome of the beautiful eighties rocker chick. She was also all the things I was not. A petite blond with natural spiral curls that cascaded down her small frame to the middle of her back. She had blue eyes and a figure to die for. Many girls envied her natural beauty—girls who spent hours at the salon bleaching and perming their hair could still not achieve what Melinda was born with.

Even though I hadn't spent much time outside of school with Melinda, I figured it was worth a shot to give her a call. Maybe she didn't already have a best friend to hang out with for the summer. With MTV still blaring in the background, I picked up the phone and dialed Melinda's number.

"Hi, Melinda, this is Shana. Howz it goin'?"

"Oh, hi! Good, I'm just sittin' around watchin' TV."

"I'm pretty bored. I was wondering if you want to go do something."

"Yeah, I'm totally bored. What do you want to do?" she asked.

"Whatever. Anything is better than what I'm currently doing, which is basically nothing. Can you come pick me up?"

"Yeah. I'll leave in a couple minutes."

I had, by one little phone call, acquired a fun best friend, one that I had a blast with day after day. Not only that, now there were no more bus rides, as the two of us rode around in style in her huge blue gas guzzler of a first car. It could fit a ton of friends, side by side, in the front and back seats. But usually, at least during daylight hours, it was just the two of us cruising around town. Even stopping at the convenience store for a hotdog was fun with my new best friend.

But something else was happening under the surface, something I barely noticed. It was an ugly thing that was no fault of my perfectly proportioned friend. At the same time, it had everything to do with her.

She ate like a bird and had not one inch of cellulite on her tiny body. She could wear anything and always look skinny. It was my turn for the first time to not be the skinniest one in a friendship. I'd always eaten whatever I wanted and probably drove my friends nuts, but I never reflected how it felt to my shorter and curvier friends. This way of life, eating whatever I wanted even if I didn't need it or might not have been hungry, was normal to me. I'd sometimes binge on food out of boredom or frustration, but the weight never caught up with me.

Until, that was, I stopped growing in height, and even then at almost six feet tall, a little extra weight didn't show much on my frame. I enjoyed this food bliss for years without ever considering how it affected the friends I hung out with.

Until that friend with more curves was me.

Everything changed when I met Melinda. My nonstop carnival ride of eating bliss had come to an end. My tall beanpole frame filled out a bit. I had a friend who'd taken my reigning crown. I wasn't the skinniest girl in the group anymore, and for the first time, I cared about what the scale said.

I embarked on my first diet while Lisa was still having a blast on vacation. I purchased my diet program at the health food store, and I walked away from the cash register with a delicious, or maybe not-so-delicious, replace-a-meal-with-a-nutritious shake.

I denied myself scrumptious donuts and marveled at my willpower. Instead of delectable fried burritos from a fast-food restaurant, I mixed my chalky shake with nonfat milk. After about two weeks, I saw results, and compliments came with my new shapely figure. The school clothes I'd purchased for my junior year fit nicely.

On the first day back to school, a popular girl commented on my new look. "Wow, you lost some weight, didn't you?"

"Yeah, I lost a few pounds this summer," I confirmed with confidence.

He Only Walked Me Halfway Home

"You look great," she exclaimed.

Here I was, a shy girl with little attention ever paid to me. The joy I felt when my peers noticed and complimented me was just the fuel I needed to set ablaze the smoldering fire inside, the part of me that craved the affirmation I didn't receive growing up. There was a little girl inside of a blossoming teenage body who so desperately wanted to hear the words, "You're beautiful," "I love you so much," "You can do anything!" Simplistic phrases I dreamed of hearing but hadn't known I'd wanted to hear. I didn't realize the driving force behind my actions. I had no idea that inside I was like a small child, unsure of herself and desperately wanting to feel loved.

At an early age I learned I could get attention through weight loss. I also discovered that guys could fill the empty part inside me . . . temporarily, that was. Even after my bad experience with a guy, I kept seeking them out, motivated by the desire to feel loved. Whatever that was, love. I just knew I wanted that feeling of being wanted by someone, even if that someone walked away and left me feeling emptier than before.

Chapter 7

SEARCHING FOR SOMEONE TO MAKE ME WHOLE

By my junior year of high school, I had officially immersed myself in the party-girl lifestyle, which meant that I spent most weekends drinking with friends and smoking too many cigarettes. When inebriated, I had one focus, and that was snagging a gorgeous guy to call my own. Most of the guys I chose to set my drunken eyes on, however, were not in the market for a permanent girlfriend—including twenty-year-old Drake, a total babe many a girl drooled over.

I first encountered this much talked-about babe at a rocker party at a rundown house a block away from the local supermarket we frequented. He approached me as I leaned up against the living room wall and contemplated my boredom. I was sober, which made me uncomfortable. My dear friend Melinda, who had driven me to the party, was outside talking to a guy she'd just met. I was left by myself, feeling lonely and bored—when in walks Mr. Beautiful to rescue me.

"Hey, what are you doing standing here by yourself? Why is such a beautiful girl like you standing up against the wall like a wallflower?" Drake asked.

I smiled shyly, giving him the signal that I was an easy target, and his plea began.

"Come home with me tonight," he begged.

I was a goner from the second he approached batting his thick black lashes that accentuated his icy-blue eyes. Drake's shoulder-length, unkempt jet-black hair went along swimmingly with his fair complexion and tall, lanky body. He was a vision from the pages of a magazine. I knew Drake was destined for something much bigger than our city had to offer.

Still, I hesitated, though unsure if I did so because I was sober or because I was afraid an older guy like Drake would pressure me into sleeping with him. I answered with a firm "No thanks." Maybe it was his brazen approach. Assumedly, no girl ever turned down Drake. Maybe that was why he didn't bother with formalities and just cut to the chase. What did he think—that I would just go to his house and sleep with him?

Within seconds of my response, he waltzed off to the bathroom, leaving me standing there like a lovesick puppy. Even though I had turned down Drake's request, any girl would love to be kissed by his perfect lips. My train of thought was interrupted when I spotted Melinda, who'd disappeared earlier and left me there to stand alone up against the wall, the very wall that I still clung to, hoping that Drake would come out of the bathroom and still want to talk to me.

"Hi. Sorry I left," Melinda said with a huge grin.

"That's okay," I replied. "You won't believe who I just met. I'll fill you in later. Now please leave. He's going to come out of the bathroom any minute!" I pushed her away.

"Geez, you don't have to push me!"

"I'm sorry, but this guy is so cute, and I don't want to lose my chance with him. I will fill you in on all the details in a sec, okay?"

"All right. I'll be waiting outside, but hurry. I have to get home soon."

"Cross my heart, I'll be right out." I nodded.

No sooner had Melinda walked away, I saw the bathroom door open, and out strutted the most gorgeous specimen on planet earth! I had neatly placed myself right next to the bathroom door, as if waiting in line.

Drake's eyes met mine the moment he stepped into the hallway. I stood there motionless, hoping he would turn his attention my way again.

"Come home with me. I won't even touch you. I promise!" he pleaded in a sultry voice as he leaned in close, locking his eyes on mine. How could any girl resist his masculine whisper, the kind that sent goose bumps up your spine? I was playing with fire, thinking I wouldn't get burned.

After much coercion on his part, and staring into his icy eyes, I agreed to go home with him. Then trying to stand my ground, I affirmed, "But no funny stuff!"

I located Melinda and let her know that I wouldn't need a ride home. "I'm going to stay at Drake's place tonight. And don't give me that look. Nothing is going to happen. He just doesn't like sleeping alone," I assured Melinda.

She clearly wasn't buying my story.

"Oh my goodness! Don't lie to me, Shana. You think you are just going over there to sleep?" Melinda, with all her sixteen years of wisdom, assured me that more than sleep was on the menu if I went home with Drake. She knew who he was—all the girls in our airport suburb knew who Drake was. He practically had celebrity status, being a popular hairstylist at a trendy salon, with fame and fortune surely in his future.

"I'll be fine. Can I tell my mom that I'm staying over at your house?" I asked.

"Okay, just call me tomorrow as soon as you get up."

After Melinda left the party, Drake and I caught a cab back to the condo he lived at. It was pitch black when we arrived, and he wasted no time taking me up to his bedroom. We kissed on his bed, but I was about to discover a sad reality. One, Drake did want more than just a make-out session, and two, guys were quite good at telling girls what they wanted to hear. Drake had experience in this department, and after much pleading, he finally chipped away at my resolve.

For the second time I gave in to a male's demands, and the experience was almost identical. Awkward and uncomfortable. I just wanted it to be over with, but unlike my experience with Vince, this time I didn't have the safety of my own bed to crawl into.

In the morning I woke up next to Drake and immediately slid out of bed to try to make myself presentable while he slept. Then I heard his mother enter the front door and call his name. I was terrified she would walk in and see me in his room. Drake slept like a baby as I frantically tried to get his attention, envisioning his mom opening his bedroom door. Surely I had guilt written all over my face. Any chance of escaping now was zero.

"Your mom is here! Wake up!"

But Drake didn't wake up, and luckily his mother didn't open the door. I sat there motionless in silence for an hour, waiting for him to rise. When he did finally get up, my problems weren't over. To exacerbate my dilemma, he couldn't give me a ride home. Why hadn't I realized the night before that I could be stuck walking home? We had taken a cab from the party, and I guessed my crush had clouded my thinking.

"Sorry. My motorcycle is at the repair shop. If you walk straight up the hill, you can catch the bus," he informed me.

He kissed me goodbye. I felt about ten inches tall as I headed toward Drake's front door, hoping to avoid his mother, although Drake didn't seem worried that she might find me there.

Talk about feeling like a fool! It was reminiscent of my first sexual encounter, having to walk myself home. Here I was supposedly all grown up and participating in grownup "things," yet something was very wrong. I felt cheap, unlike any fairy tale ending. Nonetheless, I still searched for my prince. The question was, how many frogs would it take until I finally found someone who would at least walk me to the bus stop or even splurge for a cab?

Once I reached the parking lot, still feeling Drake's eyes on me, I noticed a guy standing beside his car. He seemed older than me, at least out of high school, but his age was irrelevant. The usual shy girl that I was had left the building. At this point, with Drake still watching me from his living room window, it was now all about saving face.

The brave girl inside me who was often suppressed by fear, the girl who so desperately wanted to come out fighting, was screaming inside me that morning. "Injustice! Are you going to let that sorry excuse of a male treat you like this?" Rarely did I give heed to that brave girl. I was shy Shana and just didn't do things like give someone a piece of my mind. That was Lisa's department. She was a brave soul who always stood up for herself, or anyone who was experiencing injustice. As for me, I thought the thoughts but never dared say a word. And some-times that brave, suppressed girl in me managed to sneak past undetected, and I forgot all about being shy.

Was I seriously going to let gorgeous Drake watch me, lei-surely from his window, walking away with my tail between my legs? The answer was *no!* I had already caved under his intense persuasion, and that brave girl in me screamed, "You're not going out like that!"

I walked up to the guy standing next to his car. "Can you give me a ride to the bus stop on the highway?"

The guy quickly said yes, but his curiosity was evident.

I climbed into his car, and he asked, "Did you just come from that condo?" He pointed at Drake's window.

"Yeah, I was just visiting," I lied, glancing at Drake.

"You stayed the night?" the guy asked, turning the ignition.

"No. I just stopped by," I lied again.

It was apparent the guy knew whose condo I'd come from and wasn't buying my story. It didn't matter. I had accom-plished my goal of not only snagging a ride to the bus but also saving face in the sight of Drake's witnessing eyes.

We spent the rest of the ride in silence, and after he dropped me off on the highway, I caught the bus to meet Melinda at her dad's business. She often helped him. In return he provided her with wheels, gas, and spending money. Melinda couldn't wait to hear the details, which I disclosed in full as soon as we escaped her father's presence, in the comfort of her big blue car. When we arrived at Melinda's, I took a long, hot shower. It was the weirdest thing, how physically dirty I felt that afternoon when we arrived at her house. Then as I dried myself off, I felt so clean, like I had washed the evening off me. Like the whole unwanted sexual act disappeared down the drain, suds and all.

Searching for Someone to Make Me Whole

I later wished I could forget about Drake and move along with my sixteen-year-old life, but in my desperation to feel loved, I made a very un-Shana-like move. I made an appointment at the trendy hair salon Drake worked at. The appointment would guarantee a face-to-face encounter with him, even if I did have to pay for his time.

I imagined that Drake would take one look at me and tell me how much he'd been thinking about me over the last few weeks. Why, after my less-than-perfect sleepover at his house, would I want to see him again? I wondered. The answer was simple: I was walking around feeling like half a person, searching for someone to make me feel whole. This was my mantra, the very thing I searched for in life. Every weekend, with every drink I took, I was searching for my prince, the guy who would complete me and transform me into a complete person.

Did it make sense to allow myself to be treated like a doormat? Of course not, but there was a much deeper driving force behind the madness . . . a desperate one. And in this state, I entered the salon Drake worked at. I was his last haircut of the night, not by coincidence.

He recognized me and greeted me with a warm smile. After the usual "How have you been and what style of haircut would you like," the talking ceased. Blame it on concentration or even the blow dryer, but regardless the result was the same—dead silence. My plan hadn't worked, and I had no plan B up my sleeve. All I could do was force a smile and pay the receptionist at the front desk. The only thing I received from Drake was a friend-zone kind of grin as he bid me a good night, the exact opposite of what I had hoped for.

When I left the salon, it was already dark and pouring down rain. I felt like an actress in the middle of the scene where the leading lady gets her heart broken and, in her despair, must still run across a crowded street full of cars to hail a cab. Instead of a cab, though, I made a mad dash through evening traffic to find warm shelter while I waited for Mom to pick me up. My feet squeaked as I entered the restaurant. I tried to put on a happy face as I walked past the line of waiting customers. Heading straight for the restroom, I locked myself in a stall to sob in peace. I didn't cry often, but that night, like a little girl who had just skinned her knee with her mama nowhere in sight, I cried real tears.

Chapter 8

WHIPLASH WASN'T SUPPOSED TO BE A PREREQUISITE

*E*ven though things hadn't worked out with Drake, I was still looking for love in all the wrong places. My dream was simple—to finally meet a cute guy and have the long-term relationship. Then and only then would I be able to stop drinking every weekend. The whole point of going out every weekend was to hook up with a babe, and being so shy, I couldn't possibly meet someone when I was sober. I clung to my goal to obtain a boyfriend who would be my security blanket. With a strong, gorgeous guy by my side, I could do anything and go anywhere without any fear.

My academic education was on an upswing for the first time since middle school, much to my parents' glee. After two years of flunking classes, my school counselor enrolled me in a "special program" for people who needed extra help. I spent half the school day with one teacher in a small classroom with a handful of students. I thrived in this intimate setting, more so than I ever had since entering grade school. My grades reflected my new surroundings, and my D average quickly transformed into a B average. I had hope for the first time, educationally, even though I wasn't out of the woods yet. I would still have to take every night school and summer school class imaginable to make up for my dismal freshman and sophomore years of high school, but at least I would graduate.

By the tail end of my junior year, I was on yet another quest, to obtain my driver's license—every teenager's dream and every parent's nightmare. It also turned out to be my science teacher/driver's ed instructor's worst nightmare too. Miraculously I ended up not only in the same driver's ed class as Lisa, but we were also assigned to the same car. It was a simple class to pass, but as we embarked on our final driving exam, mischief was the only thing on our minds. I just couldn't help but slam on the brakes, waiting for Lisa's snorting laughter to come from the backseat. Whiplash was not supposed to be a prerequisite, but we couldn't contain ourselves. I played up the stupid act to arouse hysterical reactions from my instructor as he braced himself for another bumpy ride. Our instructor had the last laugh, though, when we discovered we were not passing *go*.

"I regret to inform you girls that you have received a failing grade on your driving test," our instructor stated.

"What?" Lisa griped.

"No way! My mom is gonna kill me," I whined.

"Maybe you should have thought of that before you took the course. Driver's education is not a game, and you two spent most of the time joking around."

"Please give us a second chance," we begged in unison.

"All right. I normally don't do this, but I will allow one more driving test—"

Whiplash Wasn't Supposed to Be a Prerequisite

"Oh, thank you so much!" Lisa exclaimed, giving him a high five.

"You're so awesome," I declared.

"Let me finish. The condition is that you must receive a hundred percent."

"No problem," Lisa and I said.

Days later, Lisa and I beamed from ear to ear when our instructor confirmed in amazement that we had both received 100 percent on our driving test. We didn't know why he was so surprised. When push came to shove, we knew we would nail it. Grades weren't a problem when I was motivated to achieve something, like graduating high school and obtaining independence in the form of a car. It didn't matter what make or model the car was either. I was a middle-class teenager. Having a car that ran and could fit a bunch of my friends into was all I needed to be happy.

The summer before my senior year of high school, I had my own car, an old Pinto the exact color of the cheese sauce at one of my favorite convenience stores. Melinda and I frequented the store and loved to sit on the hood of my car eating hotdogs. Being the ever delicious, messy dogs, the cheese would inevitably drip all over my little Pinto.

"Wow, your car is the exact color of this cheese!" Melinda said.

"Good to know. Now I can cover up the gray primer patches with the cheese sauce," I noted.

"Except for the whole rain factor," Melinda added.

"Darn, I thought I was on to something."

Whether the cheese sauce would cover up the gray patches on my yellowish-orange car for two days or two weeks didn't really matter. Life was great. The extent of my responsibilities was graduating high school and vacuuming the floor at home. I didn't have to hold down a job to pay for gas or have spending money like some of my peers. I didn't even clean my own room! My mom cleaned it, much to my father's dismay. I had a cushy life that was full of fun and hanging out with my friends. I knew how to cook a box of macaroni and cheese. What else did a seventeen-year-old girl need to know or worry about, for that matter? I was on autopilot, loving my easy life.

Chapter 9

A TWANG IN HER TALK
AND A SWING IN HER STEP

And to make my life even better, I received the greatest gift, a new friend. My favorite relative, Emily, moved cross country to our rainy city. I always had a blast with Emily, but our visits had never lasted more than a couple of weeks.

A blond-haired blue-eyed girl with a twang in her talk and a swing in her step, Emily had an outgoing personality and fit perfectly into my handful of close friends. Where I required alcohol for liquid bravery around the opposite sex, Emily simply waltzed on in wearing a confident smile that showed off her perfectly white teeth.

At the first party Emily attended with our group of friends, I watched her work the room. By the end of the night, she had met everyone. After that we never attended another party in our airport neighborhood. Emily changed that forever . . . in one night.

We were now in with the urban party crowd, and we would drive as far as needed, including to downtown Seattle or to the

University District, where all the college kids lived. The guys were cuter, older, and the parties lasted all night. Surely in this setting I would finally meet a cute guy and have the long-term relationship I dreamed of.

But it wasn't just the weekends that were fun. After school we would go to the mall, and I would drool over the cute guy who worked at a trendy clothing store. I never had the nerve to approach him, but I did spend many mall hours obsessing over him while Emily and I tried on yet another outfit in the store's dressing room.

"Look at this dress! It's awful," I complained to Emily in the dressing room next to me, who was complaining about the same thing.

"Well, check out this little number!" she said.

"I can see every single dimple on my butt," I moaned.

"Yeah, well, my thighs look like tree trunks in these pants."

"I have got to lose a few pounds."

"Me too."

After the saddening state of affairs in the women's dressing room, we would walk toward the mall exit with that dirty four-letter word, *diet*, on our minds. Until the aroma from the food court stopped us dead in our tracks. Only inches from the exit doors, we were goners.

"Do you smell my favorite bakery calling my name?" Emily gingerly inhaled.

"Those ham and cheese croissants are to die for!" I inched closer to the deliciously fattening bakery.

"I love their snickerdoodles," she said. "Who starts a diet in the middle of the day anyway?"

"Yes. Tomorrow." I purchased a pastry. The cute skirt would have to wait another week on the rack.

A Twang in Her Talk and a Swing in Her Step

Life was never perfect, and no matter how much fun I had hanging out with Emily, something crept in. A familiar feeling. For some reason, I felt protective of my friendship. I didn't mind group activities with several friends at the same time, but I couldn't bear being excluded. With a possessiveness driven by insecurity, I was desperate to never be left standing alone. This fear often drove me to places I didn't want to go. But that was what fear did . . . paralyzed me.

Chapter 10

CRAWLING BACK INTO MY MOTHER'S WOMB

I definitely would not be the homecoming queen my senior year. I had a large handful of friends at my high school, but I wasn't popular as far as high school popularity was defined.

That fall the entire student body elected peers they felt they could trust to share troubles with. This group consisted of a select amount of high school students from all grade levels who were at the disposal of their peers in time of need. The program was geared as an outreach to the students who might not otherwise talk to their parents or school counselors.

I was shocked to find out I'd been chosen to be a part of this group. Someone had accidentally filled in my name. Or at least, in my insecure heart that was what I believed, that I had been picked by mistake. Aside from my circle of rocker friends, who else knew I even existed?

Even though being selected seemed to be a golden opportunity, a chance to finally find purpose and meaning in my life, I chickened out. From the moment school officials sent a notice for us to take a group picture for the yearbook, my fight or flight kicked in. I was the flight girl, ready to run when things seemed intimidating. I wasn't an athlete or brainy. I'd never been challenged. I didn't like being under the scrutiny of watchful eyes. And I always, always preferred the passenger seat. I was downright petrified of learning something new, unless I was by myself or following the lead of someone else.

So from the start, I ran. While the team I was supposed to be a part of was getting the group picture taken in the gymnasium, I was hiding out in the bathroom. I didn't fit in with the group, and I didn't have a friend by my side to hold my hand. Just when I could have turned my life around, fear rose up, and I gave up an opportunity that may have changed the path I was on. Instead I decided to play it safe, for the millionth time, and continue with the mediocre life I had settled for, a life of boozing and chasing guys, even though I didn't want to disappoint my counselor. She had been so elated the day she brought me the good news. Not wanting to reveal my true feelings, all the fear and insecurity, I pretended to be happy.

"What an honor, you were selected to be a student counselor, Shana," she marveled.

"I got what?" What was she talking about?

After she explained the selection process, I stared at her in awe. "Who would choose me? I'm not popular at all?"

"It isn't popularity that counts in life. Your peers have chosen you as someone they would trust to confide in," she replied.

"You've got to be kidding. It must be a mistake."

"No, I'm not kidding, and it wasn't a mistake. You get to go on a weekend retreat," she explained. "You'll get to know the other student counselors, and they will have workshops to train you. You will make new friends. Oh, you are going to have so much fun!"

After she had finished congratulating me, I purposed in my heart that I did not want to be a part of it. I would have to spend the weekend with a bunch of preppy, popular people that I didn't know and who had never spoken to me before. On top of that, I would have to miss a weekend of parties. That meant that Emily and Melinda would be spending the weekend together. Surely by the time I got back from the retreat, they would be best friends and I would be left in the dust! I simply couldn't do it. The risk was too great. To spend the weekend with a bunch of people who would be huddled together in their cliques while I stood alone feeling like that wallflower again, then to return home and see that Emily had so much fun with Melinda and that I wasn't needed anymore. The answer was a definite no!

Despite all my internal resistance, I went home that day and told my parents the news. This probably was not the best idea in the world, considering I had already made a vow with myself not to attend the retreat and backed it up by skipping out on the yearbook picture. I didn't know what drove me to tell my parents the news. It was probably that girl inside me, the one I always suppressed. The one who waited to be unleashed from the chains of fear that bound her, to smell the fresh-cut grass and run uninhibited with the wind blowing through her hair. She was the one who wanted to share the news with my parents. She was also the one who still dared to dream.

"So how was your day, honey?" my mother asked, as she usually did.

"Okay, I guess. I was chosen to be a peer counselor," I replied.

"What is that?"

"It's someone who talks to students about their problems, when they need someone their own age to talk to."

"So how did you get picked to be a peer helper?"

"The whole school voted for the people they would most likely be able to confide in if they needed someone to talk to. I guess someone must have chosen me," I explained.

"My lands, what an honor," Mom replied with a smile.

My mother, of course, was impressed by the news, along with all my teachers at school. News traveled fast in high school, and it didn't take long for everyone to find out. Now I was faced with an even greater dilemma: How the heck would I get out of going on the retreat?

I packed my suitcase begrudgingly and found a seat on the school bus for the long ride. I hadn't been to camp since the sixth grade, and not much had changed since then. I still felt equally awkward when out of my comfort zone, which was the security of a best friend. Even though I was present on the bus ride, I was absent at heart, and I spent the entire ride penciling the directions down on a sheet of paper. They might come in handy at some point.

Once we arrived, everyone eagerly grabbed their backpacks and were off to their assigned cabins. I felt lonely and out of place among all the preppy girls I was bunking with. It seemed that everyone had his or her best friend with them, and I was the odd man out. Oh, how I loathed being the odd man out. I felt as if there were a neon sign plastered to my head that read, *I have no friends and everyone knows it.*

So I did what I normally did at times of intense insecurity, when I felt awkward and alone. I ate. Food was my unseen friend—we went way back. It was a love/hate relationship. I loved to seek this friend out when I was bored or lonely or scared, and the list went on. But at the same time I hated this friend. I hated that I wasn't outgoing and even needed her in the first place. Most of all, I hated the sick feeling I felt after my friend was long gone and I was left with the guilt of seeking her out in the first place, not to mention the unsightly pounds she left on my hips! I turned to eating subconsciously, and spent most of the first night gobbling up bite-sized donuts.

The next day we were all assigned to small groups—I'd always thrived in a more intimate setting, so I considered this a highlight. One guy in my group was popular at school, and I had never talked to him before. Even though these sessions were full of laughter, associating with people outside my circle of friends, I still didn't see myself fitting in. I automatically assumed that the popular preppy kids at my school wanted nothing to do with me. What could we possibly have in common? My friends and I shopped at thrift stores because it was the only place we could find cool vintage clothes, like men's wool cardigans that we matched with brightly colored sixties Hawaiian dresses. I just didn't belong with the whole peer-counselor crowd.

Then there was the gnawing fact that Melinda and Emily were having a great time together. Surely I would lose both my friends by the end of the weekend. With all this in mind, I pulled myself away from the refreshment table and sneaked off to the kitchen where I spotted a phone. I called Emily.

"Hi, howz it going?" I asked.

"Good, how's camp?"

"I'm totally bored. Did you go out last night?"

"Yeah, Melinda picked me up. We went to a party in the U-District. It was so fun," she replied.

"Really, did you meet any guys?"

"We met some people. There was a band playing."

"Well, I don't want to miss another night of parties. Can you come get me?" I asked.

"Sure, give me the directions," she said.

"All right. It will take at least an hour to get here. Is that okay?"

"Sure, I can leave as soon as we hang up."

"Thanks." I gave her directions before someone spotted me. The easy part was over. Now I faced the hard part of sneaking my suitcase out of my cabin and into Emily's waiting vehicle. I was too much of a coward to confront my counselor and admit I was throwing in the towel. She would ask me why, and I would have no excuse to give her. The true reason wasn't even something that I was willing to share with my best friend, let alone my teacher. Instead, I'd just run away without saying a word. It was my way of handling awkward situations. I didn't talk about my problems—I ran from them. My decision solidified my initial impression that someone had made a mistake choosing me to be a peer counselor. So since I didn't truly belong anyhow, what was the harm in leaving?

"Shana, what are you doing?" my counselor asked, catching me in the very act of throwing my suitcase into the back of Emily's idling car.

"I called for a ride. I really don't feel well. I'm going home," I stated nervously.

"Were you planning on telling anyone?" she questioned, dumbfounded.

My counselor had also been my teacher for an entire year. We had a good student/teacher relationship even though I wasn't in her class any longer. She seemed stunned by my behavior, but she had no clue of my struggle to fit in.

"I'm sorry. I'm just not feeling well. I called for a ride." Barely making eye contact with her, I held my breath, waiting for her to release me and accept my lame excuse.

"Shana, I would really like you to reconsider this." She replied, practically begged me with her eyes.

The guilt of leaving camp and the teacher who was so proud of my achievement overwhelmed me. But in my eyes the deed was already done. Emily had driven an hour to come pick me up. I had gotten myself into a huge mess this time.

Saying the words she didn't want to spill from my lips, I responded, "I'm sorry. I really have to go." Without waiting for a rebuttal, I jumped into the car and quickly closed the door. I tried to reassure myself that I had made the right choice. I tried to think about all the cute guys that would be at the party that night and how much of a bore camp was. It worked. I had mastered suppressing my true feelings.

But in the end I didn't snag a cute guy to call my own. What I did gain was a disappointed teacher. My counselor tried to reach out to me the following week by sending me a note to stop by her class for a talk. Like the chicken I believed myself to be, I never showed up. In fact, I avoided her for the rest of the school year.

And what I feared most came to pass in the second half of my senior year. My nightmare had manifested itself. Both Melinda and Emily received enough credits to attend school half days. The thing that I had strived so hard to keep from happening, was now completely out of my control. While I waited for the bell to ring, Melinda and Emily would be free. My nightmare had come true. I was left with no choice but to finally unleash my emotional death grip. It was a sobering moment to surrender and let go.

Even though it bothered me terribly, I eventually relinquished my possessiveness and started spending more time with Lisa after school. My bestie from middle school, the one I'd ditched many times to hang out with other friends, was once again by my side. She was a true friend, brave and loyal. Not flaky and insecure like me.

While Emily and Melinda enjoyed their early dismissal each day, Lisa and I drove together to our shared class at the occupational center near our high school. Our favorite part was lunch, just before the three-hour class started. We frequented the many fast-food restaurants on the busy airport strip along the way, even though our full bellies made it difficult to stay awake during class. I quickly forgot about being jealous of Melinda's and Emily's friendship. Instead, I enjoyed my carefree life and last semester of high school.

That was, until that inevitable day arrived, the one I was fully unprepared for: graduation.

After walking down the aisle to receive my diploma, my mother snapped a photo. It was a picture that said a million words, one of an utterly petrified teenage girl. This was truly what I viewed myself as, a scared little girl living inside an adult body. During the graduation festivities, I finally reached adulthood and turned eighteen. I suppressed the fear inside me, in the face of my onlooking parents, who were so proud to see their youngest child graduate.

At least someone was excited. In fact, it seemed all my friends were excited. I, on the other hand, was not prepared to embark on this new adventure called "real life." I had never had a job and possessed little skills. I clearly wasn't going to be attending college in the fall like many of my classmates, and I

Crawling Back into My Mother's Womb

wished I could crawl back into my mother's womb. Scared to death, I spent my days pounding the pavement in search of just about any job available and spent my nights on the familiar party scene.

The first job I landed lasted only four days. I worked in the airport cafeteria with Emily, who had already acquired work experience. She had held down after-school jobs and was familiar with proper work ethics. I, on the other hand, quit after four days without notice. All I knew was I couldn't possibly spend another day, let alone another hour, in a windowless white-walled cafeteria whose only source of color was the food. Surely I was destined for so much more. How could I settle for such a mundane job?

Nine months passed, and I was clueless what to do with my life. I needed a job. I couldn't sponge off my parents forever. I suffered a tremendous amount of guilt for doing nothing with my life. Many of my high school friends were working part time while earning college credits. I felt alone and desperate. I had to find a job.

My brother Michael had recently started his own mechanic business, so I took the easy route and landed on his payroll. All I had to do was answer the phone and schedule jobs. In this setting I had plenty of time to contemplate life, sitting around the office waiting for the phone to ring.

It took all of two days to realize that I loathed my job. I didn't know anything about cars, and frankly I didn't want to know anything other than how to put the key in the ignition and drive. I lived in fear of the phone and realized early on that there were now two skills I could cross off my list: dispatcher and cafeteria worker.

Chapter 11

ALL TANGLED UP LIKE OCTOPI

Have you ever known a guy named Dillon? Growing up, there was always a guy named Dillon each year in one of my classes, and he was usually one of the most popular, good-looking guys in school. Along with his gorgeous face and physique also came the attitude that he was well aware of his effect on the girls. I met a guy named Dillon just after my eighteenth birthday, and oh, what a babe he was! And just like the Dillons in school, he had the attitude and looks to go with it.

The first time I laid my drunken eyes on Dillon, it was across a crowded room full of equally drunken partiers. I fell head over heels for this green-eyed, sandy blond with shoulder-length hair, loose curls and all. He was so manly too, just like the Dillon in my PE class, and both looked great in a pair of shorts!

From the moment our eyes locked at the crowded house party just blocks from Seattle's trendy Broadway district, I had to have him.

Dillon was well beyond my eighteen years, and he didn't

waste any time taking me to his tiny sports car, where we spent an hour steaming up his windows. From that first night, our relationship was established on sex alone, but to me sex was simply a hoop I had to jump through in order to achieve what I truly desired—a cute guy to hold me tight and never leave me. In the following weeks, I had sporadic encounters with Dillon, at house parties in the city or all ages, hole-in-the-wall clubs where up and coming Seattle bands would play. Dillon never wined and certainly never dined me. I'd say that I was a cheap date but he never even took me out on an official date. I didn't care because it was the overnight encounters that kept me coming back for more. Dillon knew how to hold a girl tight, and I loved being held. I had never been held like that before. Maybe to a guy there was nothing like sex, but to me there was nothing like kissing a babe all night, entwined together like octopi.

I should have known that Dillon would have little respect for a girl who surrendered her body to him within the first twenty minutes of acquaintance. All I knew was that I wanted to feel loved. It didn't take many "sleepovers" with Dillon to get my heart stomped on. The word *doormat* comes to mind on what would become the infamous classical-music night that I spent at Dillon's apartment on his living room floor—an unfamiliar floor.

Once again, all entangled like octopi, I lay with him until the morning light with the soothing sound of classical music playing on the radio, like a melodic lullaby. These were the moments I lived for in life. Until Dillon jolted out of my arms. From my vantage point on the floor, I heard the shower turn on, and for the first time, took in my surroundings. Yes, I'd had sleepovers with Dillon but never at his place. Usually someone's parents were out of town and the two of us ended up on a sofa. The apartment was now brightly lit by the sun shining in through the blinds, and my buzz had long since passed. It was in this unfortunate setting that I was not only stark naked, aside from a blanket, but also discovered Dillon had two female roommates. After covertly grabbing my clothes and dressing under the cover of Dillon's blanket, permeated by his cologne, I sat up from my position on the floor. Folding up the blanket in awkward silence, I took a seat on the couch and tried to make small talk with his two roommates. I was anxious for Dillon to return from the shower and whisk me away. Yet to my horror, Dillon walked right past me without a word and headed straight for the front door. Was this some kind of sick joke?

One of his female roommates called out in the most embarrassing tone, as if she wanted to make sure she didn't get stuck with me, "Dillon! What about your friend?"

Halfway out the door, Dillon turned around and actually acknowledged my presence. "I'm sorry. I'm late for work." He hastily closed the door behind him.

Dillon's two roommates just stared at one another in disbelief. I figured I'd provide them with much conversation for the remainder of their day, but I had no intention of sticking around. Even though one of his roommates kindly asked if I needed a ride somewhere, I declined and quickly scampered away. Many people in the heart of Seattle didn't own a car, so she probably assumed I lived nearby. I would have rather died than admit I lived many miles away. Instead, I headed up the street to the crowded boulevard and dialed Melinda's house. It seemed like forever as I waited for her to pick me up. Melinda was my rock, the more sensible one, always less intoxicated than me. Most of all, Melinda came to my rescue each and every time. But I wondered when or if I would ever learn my lesson.

As if getting my heart stomped on in full view of strangers and my best friend wasn't bad enough, I was still stuck with an unfulfilling job. My weekdays dragged by at a sluggish pace. I passed the time at my brother's office by watching television and nervously consuming too much food from his refrigerator. The whole time, I mentally pleaded with the phone not to ring. Occasionally, Michael would let me go home early if he didn't have any jobs. That was my only ray of hope. At least I could enjoy a quick trip to the mall and spend a little money on a new pair of earrings to help me forget my plight in life.

Just over a month into my new career as a dispatcher, my sister, Debbie, saved the day by one phone call. "Hey, Shana, do you want to go to California with me?"

"Of course I do!" I exclaimed.

"We'll be gone for two weeks. We can take the 101 near the coast and spend some time in LA and San Diego."

"LA? You can count me in! I'm already packed and waiting out front for you to pick me up!"

"I'm glad you're so excited, but we won't be leaving for another week," she said. "I know you don't have much money. Do you think Mom would pay for you to go?"

"Oh, yeah, she'll pay all right," I affirmed.

"And how about getting time off from work? Can you get two weeks off?"

"Don't worry your pretty little head over it!" I assured her. Nothing was coming between me and this trip to LA. It was my dream. Ever since falling in love with Motley Crüe in junior high, I dreamed of what LA seemed to have in store for all who moved there. The land of palm trees and opportunity. A place where an unknown person living on pocket change could become rich and famous seemingly over night!

First, I needed to ask my mother to fund my vacation and my brother to allow me time off on short notice. As my mom pulled into the driveway that evening, I was there to greet her. When they are greeted at the car door, parents instinctively know their child wants something.

"Hi, Mom, how was work?" I asked.

"Fine, and how was your day?" she responded.

"Great. My favorite sister in the world called!"

"You mean your only sister?" She clearly sensed something was up.

"That too. Did you know she's driving down to California for two weeks?" I asked.

My mother had made her way through the front door and into the kitchen. She began her usual routine of preparing our evening meal. I was ready to make my move.

"Yes. She mentioned taking a trip this spring," Mom said.

"So anyway, she's leaving in a week and really doesn't want to be the only driver. Imagine after all these years—this will be the first trip that I can actually help with some of the driving."

"That would be a big help." She grabbed a sack of potatoes and started peeling. Yum. It didn't get much better than Mom's mashed potatoes.

"If it's okay with you, I'm going to ask for the time off."

"Well, sure. Why wouldn't it be all right with me if you go to California?" she asked.

"Well, there's this little issue of financing the trip . . ." The pot of water on the stove boiled. I simultaneously bit my lip.

"Oh, so you need money? Now I see what the issue is here."

"Why don't I call her, and you two can go over all the specifics?" I grabbed the milk and butter from the fridge. If my mother was going to finance my trip, I could at least help with dinner.

"All right," my mother agreed. After a brief conversation, she hung up the phone and announced she would fund my part of the vacation.

I was halfway to California. All I needed was to beg my brother for two weeks off. I could hardly sleep that night as visions of sunny beaches and palm trees danced through my head. It was one of those rare mornings where I couldn't wait to jump out of bed, no alarm required.

As I pulled up in Michael's driveway, he was just heading out for the day.

"Hey, I need to talk to you real quick," I said.

"Okay, make it snappy. I'm in a hurry." He glanced at his watch.

"Yeah, ah, I just wanted to ask if I could take a couple weeks off . . ."

"You just started this job a month ago and you want to take time off?" he retorted.

"I knew you would say that, but actually it would be doing a favor for my favorite sister," I continued.

"You mean your only sister. What does she have to do with this?"

"Well, Debbie's going to California for two weeks and she doesn't want to be the only driver," I explained.

"Okay, I have to go." He opened the truck door and slid in.

"So, is that okay a yes? I can take two weeks off?"

"Yeah, you can take two weeks off, but that's your vacation for the entire year!" He slammed his pickup door.

"That's fine!" I agreed enthusiastically. A much-needed reprieve from my dull weekday existence. No wonder I had been so scared on the day of graduation. All my other classmates seemed giddy. While they were all expectant about the future, I was wishing for a retake of life, starting back at birth!

I was elevated far past cloud nine as I endured the five-day workweek. Once I completed this arduous task, I shifted my thoughts into party mode. Not that every weekend wasn't party mode, but this one was extra special. I had run into Dillon at a party in the University District. He had promised to call me so we could go do something. Yes, the same Dillon who'd left me with his roommates, barely saying goodbye. The same jerk who'd treated me like a doormat and then went to work, leaving me to bum a ride home from Melinda. Yes, that Dillon. I supposed most girls would have nothing to do with a guy who'd treated them so shabbily. Nonetheless, no matter how lame and pathetic it looked, I couldn't wait to rekindle our romance.

I sat in my room that evening and hoped for the phone to ring. Unfortunately, Friday and Saturday night passed and Dillon still hadn't delivered his promised call. Another jerk had disappointed me. I consoled myself with the fact that in one more day I would be on my way to LA. Hopefully, Dillon would call me while away and get a taste of his own medicine. Regardless of whether he called or not, one thing was sure—I was determined to leave my sleepy airport town and Dillon far behind . . . at least for two weeks.

I waited in the driveway with my tiny seventies flowered suitcase in hand. It was stuffed to capacity with all my needed essentials. Makeup, check. Toothbrush. Affirmative. Camera, a must! Oh, and I couldn't forget my new book for hours of titillating reading pleasure. It was about a groupie's account of her wild hippy days growing up in LA and hanging out with famous bands. Being that it was currently the tail end of the eighties, with sixties fashion and music in vogue, I couldn't think of a more fitting read, embarking on my own California adventure.

My sister arrived in the driveway undetected while I was thoroughly engrossed in my book.

"Hi. Sorry I'm a little late," she said.

"No problem. I brought this great book to read along the way."

"Good. Is this all you're taking with you?" Debbie asked as she gestured toward my flower-power suitcase waiting patiently on the cement.

"Yep, that's it!" I replied.

"Okay, let's get going then."

Debbie was well prepared and had every hotel reserved from Seattle to San Diego. This was a trait I didn't possess. She must have acquired her organizational skills from our mother. She had every mile accounted for, not to mention an approximate time of arrival.

I hopped into the front seat of her car and couldn't wait to resume my reading. There wasn't a lot of scenic stimulation the first day of our trip anyway, just miles of pavement. By day two, we arrived in San Francisco and spent the afternoon taking in the sights at Fisherman's Wharf. It was a drizzly day at the Wharf, which seemed similar to Seattle, with the added bonus of lush palm trees. After getting lost in Chinatown, we continued on down the highway.

On day three, we finally arrived in Southern California. I couldn't wait for my guided bus tour that was scheduled for the following day.

All Tangled Up like Octopi

It was already warm as I dressed that next morning and stubbornly chose to ignore the well-seasoned forecaster's ninety-degree estimated high. My refusal to heed wise council was driven by an unquenchable thirst to figure things out for myself. Ninety degrees in April? Preposterous.

I was overdressed and sweating bullets as I toured the Chinese Theatre on Hollywood Boulevard and when we finally hit the infamous Sunset Strip. This is what I had traveled so many miles for and waited a lifetime to see.

There was the Whiskey A-Go-Go, the same club that had hosted Motley Crüe and the Doors. At that moment all I wanted to do was scream, "Let me out here, Mr. Bus Driver! This is definitely my stop!" It just wasn't fair. How come I didn't grow up in sunny California? How come my landscape was evergreens, not palm trees?

"Hi, how was your bus tour?" my sister asked when I arrived back at the hotel.

"Great! I saw Sunset Strip, where all the cool clubs are, and Tower Records, where all the famous bands sign autographs!" The day had gone by much too fast, and I enjoyed reliving the experience. "We also drove through Beverly Hills. Did you know the street signs are white?"

"Ah, no, I sure didn't," she responded.

"And we drove down Melrose, which is full of funky clothing stores," I continued. "By the way, I really want to spend a day there before we leave."

"I'm glad you had fun," she replied. "Did you see all the stars on Hollywood Boulevard?"

"Let's just say I saw enough of them to last a lifetime! Considering we were there for an hour because the bus driver hit a pole." Stripping off my sweaty jeans, I grabbed a pair of shorts from my suitcase.

"He hit a pole?" she questioned.

"Yeah, backed into one as we were leaving."

"Oh, what a bummer," she said.

"Man, I want to move here!" I exclaimed. "Just leave me here. I'll be just fine." I plopped onto a bed, enjoying the air conditioned room.

"Are you joking? Mom would kill me if I left you here!"

"Yep. I'll just live off the land and soak up the sunshine."

"Live off the land? Don't you have a job to go back to?" Debbie questioned.

"Job shmob. I love it here! I don't need any money. I can sleep on the beach . . ." I said dreamily.

"You're crazy, and no, I'm not going to leave you here." She threw a pillow at me.

I had adopted the idea of living off the land from a friend's older sister who had already lived the life I dreamed of. She had toured the country with a famous rock band. I loved to flip through her photos that recaptured it all. Imagine having a picture taken while hugging the members of Motley Crüe. Or what about the much-fantasized backstage pass? For some girls, it was actually a reality. And being brave enough to up and leave for an indefinite vacation in LA without a dime. If only I had an adventurous friend, I would have stayed in LA.

Chapter 12

BACK TO MY SOGGY CITY

Instead, Debbie dragged me back to Seattle kicking and screaming (at least in my mind, I was). The two weeks in California had flown by, and I was distraught, to be forced to abandon my Hollywood dream and return to my rainy city and the job I loathed. At least if I had to go back to Seattle, I was bound and determined to find another source of income. Something that didn't involve answering phones.

It was late when we arrived, and I didn't feel like talking much. I was sorry to leave California and depressed to face another day as a dispatcher.

"How was your trip?" my mother asked.

"I loved it so much, I didn't want to leave," I confessed.

"Didn't want to leave? She was begging me to leave her there!" Debbie said. My sister had a gift. She could make any event sound entertaining, even a mundane trip to the grocery store. "Mom, we were driving down the highway, and she told me to just leave her on the side of the road!"

"It wasn't the side of the road! You make it sound like I

asked you to just toss me and my suitcase out the car window," I said in my defense.

My mother didn't get a chance to respond as my sister continued to fascinate and I repeatedly interrupted with my version of the event.

"Mom, it was dark outside, we were in the middle of nowhere, and here's Shana telling me to drop her off." She threw her hands in the air. "I told her she was nuts, that you would have my head if I left her there."

"It sounds like you enjoyed yourself. I know it is hard to transition back to real life after a vacation," Mom said.

"California is so different from here. I love the weather and palm trees. It's not like rainy Seattle." I paced around the living room.

"Palm trees? You wanted me to leave you on the side of the highway in the middle of nowhere." Debbie laughed. "Mom, there were no palm trees. Just some brown grass," she added.

"Don't listen to her! She has no idea what she's talking about," I retorted. "We passed the most beautiful places. One was in Red Bluff. It was dusk, and there were these grassy hills with trees just like the ones on African safaris. You should have seen it, Mom."

"That sounds very nice," Mom said.

"And she says I don't know what I'm talking about," my sister said sarcastically. "When was the last time you were on an African safari? And let's not forget about your third-degree sunburn!"

"Sunburn?" my mother questioned.

"I kinda stayed at the pool too long in San Diego. I really thought I was dying, it hurt so bad," I explained.

"How long did you stay at the pool?" Mom asked.

"All day!" Debbie exclaimed.

"Not all day. About five hours," I said. "I couldn't come back from sunny California as white as a ghost!"

"Yeah, instead she was as red as a lobster!" my sister exclaimed. "Mom, her face was so puffed up I didn't know what to do. I thought she was going to burst!"

"What did you do?" Mom asked.

"She took me to the emergency room. We didn't want to worry you," I added.

"They took one look at her and admitted her before all the other people waiting," Debbie said.

"Yeah, I looked pretty bad."

"Pretty bad?" Debbie said with a look of disbelief. "Mom, her face looked like a marshmallow, a red marshmallow. Let's just say that she was beyond recognition."

"Gee, thanks, sis." I pinched her arm.

"I hope you are more careful from now on," Mom said.

"Believe me—I never want to lie in the sun again!"

"That's a little drastic," Mom said. "It just takes time for someone with a fair complexion to develop a suntan."

"Yeah, I know that now. I just didn't want to come back whiter than when I left." I frowned at my peeled arms.

"Our family is beyond white, more like translucent," my sister joked, then turned to look at the ticking clock. "I guess I better be getting home now. I have to work tomorrow." She sighed, turning toward me.

"Don't remind me." I pouted. "But thanks for the awesome vacation. I wish it could have lasted forever."

"Thanks for keeping me company. I'm glad your face is back to normal," she said with a smile.

After saying our goodbyes, my stomach was all in knots

over the fact that in just eight short hours, I would have to return to my job as dispatcher.

"Shana, someone named Dillon called for you while you were gone," Mom said.

"Really, what did he say?" I asked, playing it cool.

"That he would try again when you get back from California."

This was just the thing I needed to hear. Dillon had called while I was away! There was something so sweet, thinking about a guy who could be thinking about me that very second. As I lay my head on my pillow that evening, I dreamed about Dillon. He hadn't forgotten me. He still cared. Now I could sleep with a smile on my face and have the courage to face another day at work.

Chapter 13

POUNDING THE
TEMPORARY PAVEMENT

After a couple of weeks back dispatching, I mustered up enough nerve to quit my job, though I had no prospects up my short sleeves. My unfortunate plight felt like a catch twenty-two. I couldn't possibly bear another day at my current job, but I was scared to not have one.

The word "perplexed" would accurately depict the look on my brother's face when I told him I was leaving with no new job lined up.

"I think I'm going to start working for a temporary agency," I stated.

"It's up to you" was his only response.

Aside from being newly jobless, not much had changed in my life. I was still spending my Friday and Saturday nights at various parties in Seattle. I still had my same friends, although most of them were well on their way to lucrative careers in an office or busy juggling college and part-time jobs.

As for my love life, it had fizzled dramatically. Dillon still hadn't called me since I had returned from LA, and worse than that, I had even run into him. Well, I had run into the same room as him at a crowded house party in the University District. I'd been way too sober to approach him while he stood in the middle of the room conversing with a few guys from a popular Seattle band. I wished that he would have whisked me away, but that wasn't my relationship with Dillon. I was the drunken girl who'd pursued him the night we first met. Sober and a chicken, I watched him saunter away with the band. He didn't say a word to me, and I was devastated.

However, I never showed my feelings to my friends. That would be way too humiliating. I was used to it, getting my heart stomped on and hiding my feelings, feeling about an inch tall. It had become my normal routine, and I had no idea there was a reason I felt so bad. How was I supposed to know that an eighteen-year-old girl wasn't supposed to be giving her body to any cute guy who showed interest, in hopes that he would love her forever?

I didn't know why I let guys treat me like dirt. All I knew was that my heart hurt each time the phone stopped ringing and I kissed one more what-could-have-been relationship goodbye.

After another day of puttering around the house jobless, I took my mother's advice and signed on with a temporary agency. What better thing to motivate me than the fact that I was on the verge of my nineteenth birthday. Almost a year had passed since graduation, and I needed to take action. I was so busy that day running to and fro that I actually forgot to eat. By the time I returned from the agency, it was already suppertime, and I was famished.

"How did it go at the agency?" Mom asked the moment I stepped in the front door.

"Great. I took a bunch of written tests and evaluations," I replied. "They seemed to think I will get work."

"That's great," Mom said.

"I just have to call in every morning and afternoon to see if there's any work." I dished myself up a plate of food and sat at the kitchen table.

My mother knew the drill. She had acquired jobs through temporary agencies. "That's wonderful, and there's a good chance you'll get hired on permanently," she said. "Many companies like to hire people through agencies."

"Hopefully, I'll get something tomorrow," I said.

"Yes, I hope so. I know it's boring sitting at home."

After just a few days, I landed my first job assignment. I woke up bright and early to report for duty at the Auto Auction.

The first day flew by while I collected signatures from buyers on the auction floor.

The following day I was escorted to my prestigious post as a coat-check girl. This assignment brought occasional tips as I waited for the auto dealers' coats to check.

It was hustle and bustle, hanging soggy jackets up to dry. *This isn't half-bad*, I thought. *What a cool gig for a girl with little marketable skills.* Plus, all the dealers who frequented the auction were always in a good mood.

By the time I pulled my little Pinto out of the parking lot that afternoon, I was already celebrating my new position. "Shana Lesser, the Auto Auction's new coat-check girl!"

It was a breeze waking up the following day. I couldn't wait to perch myself inside the coat-check room and wait for my first raincoat.

Waiting would be the key word. Where are all the handsomely dressed dealers? In my boredom, I composed a poem.

While Walking thru Paris

While walking thru Paris, rummaging thru the fog
I slipped on a pretzel; ouch, no, I stepped on a frog.
The frog went "ribbit"; ope, nope, it must have been a rat
Cuz right there behind me, came chasing a cat.
But eww was I lucky, that cat's glasses got stuck
Stuck in the cement . . . Watch out cat, here comes a truck!
So the rat has escaped and now I am free
Because everyone knows that cat can't chase after me!

My new "career" ended up lasting less than a week. I guessed that was why they called it a temporary job. Once again, I found myself pounding the pavement. In desperation to be out of the house each day and making some money, I accepted the first job that came my way. This new stint was scheduled for two weeks and was as cold as the warehouse floor I stood on.

The job was boring and monotonous, but it was a job. Since I was a dreamer, I had plenty of time to fantasize about sunny beaches and palm trees. I also had plenty of time to mentally abuse myself, mostly about my inadequacies.

"Why wasn't I at least proficient at typing?" I asked myself. I already knew the answer. It was the same reason I sat out square dancing in grade school and the same reason I had the highest grade point in my high school occupational class but was the slowest at ten key. It was why my friends had jobs in plush offices and I stood on a warehouse floor performing manual labor.

To top things off, I had been given the prestigious title of industrial worker at the temporary agency. The office attendant's words still echoed in my ears as I stood on the warehouses uninviting floor taking inventory and recalling the first day I arrived at the temp agency.

Pounding the Temporary Pavement

"How many words a minute do you type?" the office attendant had asked.

"I can't type very well," I replied, squirming in my seat.

"How about ten-key?"

"I took a ten-key class in high school," I replied.

"Great, let's take an evaluation on the computer."

Take an evaluation on the computer? I managed to skate my way through high school without taking a computer class. The courses I took in high school wouldn't get me diddly-squat in the career world.

"All right, just take a seat at the computer and we'll begin testing," the attendant instructed.

This was the point where I'd started to question why I had come to the agency in the first place. Yes, I recalled, because my mother suggested trying the temporary job market. My mother, who types a bazillion words a minute and is highly proficient in the administrative field. But not me. I had no marketable job skills. I was thrown into the pot of unschooled workers at the temporary agency and given the title of general laborer.

"I'm sorry, but your ten-key is not up to par for the office field," the attendant replied. "And considering that you have no computer background . . . but I do have a lot of work in the industrial job market."

"That's fine," I muttered. "I just really need a job."

"Yes, and there's great potential for permanent employment through a temporary job assignment," she said.

Back to reality on the cold warehouse floor, I was thankful that my current assignment was not permanent. Standing there wearing shoes with no arch support, I wished I could jump into one of the small boxes I was in charge of taping up.

I grabbed a box from the conveyor belt and adhered another label addressed to Los Angeles, California, when the warehouse manager interrupted me.

"You do such a wonderful job," he marveled. "All your boxes look exactly the same."

Big deal. I excelled at precision. "Thanks." So what if I aligned the labels dead center on every box. That didn't change my situation. The damn box was shipping off to California, and I was stuck in a low-paying job. My life had become one huge settlement, and not the monetary kind. This was a settlement of compromise. My life had become one never-ending compromise. Why couldn't I go to college, dressing up each day? Why did I have to dress down to go to work?

My reality sucked. I was so ill prepared for this thing called life. I was a scared little girl in grownup shoes, fantasizing my days away while I stuck yet another label on a box bound for LA.

Chapter 14

TRIPPING OVER DILLON'S EGO

Life swung to an upward turn at last. Seattle's infamous rainy days had diminished, and my favorite season had arrived, summer. These few short months motivated me to make it through another year in my soggy city. It was the season I lived for, what kept me chugging along. Even though there wasn't a palm tree in sight, summer was a time of celebration each year. And what better way to celebrate this wonderful season than hanging out with my friends barefoot and full of booze!

Us group of girls often cruised down Alki Beach with the Beach Boys blaring on the car stereo. We ran around in our little tank tops and miniskirts in search of the next cute guy to collide with, which wasn't the norm for me—the whole colliding-with-a-cute-guy thing. But a girl could always hope, right? And as circumstances would soon prove, I would need much reason to hope, because Dillon was about to rear his ugly head.

It was business as usual on another tiki torch–laden evening as my friends and I entered a crowded house party in downtown Seattle. We didn't know who was renting the house, but that was nothing new. We heard about parties through word of mouth and often didn't know whose house we were at. It was never awkward to simply waltz on into a stranger's home, considering that the door was usually wide open while a sea of partiers revolved in and out. We entered this two-story house in a busy urban neighborhood. My happy demeanor soon faded though as my eyes surveyed the room and recognized a familiar face. Except instead of Dillon's usual sultry smile, his piercing green eyes locked on mine, full of vengeance. *Why is he glaring at me like that?*

From the top of the packed staircase he stood on, his voice echoed through the background music and drunken chatter. "Get that bitch out of my house!"

I stood there shell shocked, wondering why Dillon would be shouting profanities in my direction when all I ever did was dream about the guy?

"What is that bitch doing in my house?" Dillon screamed with an evil glare from the same spot.

Speechless, I searched my friends' faces for clarity. Was this actually happening to me?

"Get out of my house now!" Dillon shouted.

At this point I was more than happy to oblige Dillon's request and flee from his ugly presence and the dozens of partiers witnessing the awful scene.

I turned to my friend. "I'm going to go wait in the car. I can't believe he is calling me a bitch in front of all these people. Can I have your car keys?" I asked, trying to avoid any eye contact with Dillon. Then, with my head down while turning toward the door, a girl tapped me on the shoulder.

"Hi, I'm Monica, one of Dillon's roommates," she said.

"Hi, I'm Shana," I mumbled, trying to conjure up a smile.

Tripping over Dillon's Ego

"Don't worry about Dillon. He's just drunk. I told him to go sleep it off. What's the point of drinking if he's just going to make an ass of himself?" She laughed, apparently trying to cheer me up.

"I feel like a fool. I should leave. I'm definitely not welcome here."

"No, this is just as much my house too," Monica said with a radiant smile. "And as my guest, I would like you to stay." Grabbing me by the arm, she walked me up to the top of the stairs where Dillon had been standing. "Have a seat." She gestured toward the top step. "And don't worry—I already chased Dillon away for you. Now you can tell me all about how you know Dillon."

Sitting on the staircase next to her, I began, "I met Dillon several months ago at a party. We've gotten together a few times. I've even been to his apartment . . . well, his old apartment . . ." I lost my train of thought.

"So the two of you were going out?" She nodded.

"More like hooking up at parties, and the last time I saw him was at a party in the U-District. He was with a group of guys, and I was sober. So instead of going up to talk to him like I usually would, I just hung out with my friends, talking. I had also taken a trip to California a while ago, and when I returned home, my mom said that he called. I didn't call him back, but I never call guys . . . I wait for them to call me," I said, catching my breath.

"Okay." Monica nodded again, as if everything now made sense. "This is an ego issue. You didn't talk to him at the party, and you didn't return his call. Simple. His ego got hurt!"

"I guess, but as far as I'm concerned, all I ever did was like him." I said, nervously turning around to see if Dillon was anywhere near.

"Well, you're my guest now. Enough talk about Dillon."

"But what if he comes out and starts yelling again?"

"I'm not afraid of him. If he comes out of that room up there," she said, pointing to the door just feet away, "I'll personally pounce on him for you!" She laughed.

Monica was my angel that evening. And as for Dillon? He did rear his ugly head in an attempt to scare me away, but it didn't work.

Monica was on my side, and even though she was a petite little thing, she barked back, "Oh, shut up, Dillon, and leave this nice girl alone!" Although I would have rewound the embarrassing night if I could have, at the same time, I felt victorious knowing that Dillon didn't stand a chance against Monica. But I couldn't hide my defeat from my diary:

Dillon

It's all your fault—I blame you
You left me, made me a fool.
I get drunk, do stupid things;
Pick up on every guy, I need release.
But it's not my fault—I still blame you.
You gave up on me, but I wasn't through.
So hey, what's the deal?
Why not just give me a call?
Oh, did your ego get hurt?
Did you think I didn't like you at all?
All I can say is, you're totally wrong
If I didn't want you, would I be writing this song?

Chapter 15

FAMISHED

*E*ven though Dillon had stomped on my heart once again and left me writing many a sad poem in my diary that summer, things were finally looking up for me in the nine-to-five world. I had landed a permanent job at a print shop and opened my first bank account. It was exactly one year after graduation, and my metamorphosis had finally occurred. I was now a full-time employed adult who still resided in my childhood bedroom. Living at home wasn't the end of the world. Many of my friends still lived at home. It was the smart thing to do. Who could argue with free rent?

Now I could save money for a newer car, long overdue considering my rear window had been busted out in an attempted robbery while parked downtown one evening. What person would seriously break into a cheese-colored seventies Pinto was beyond me. They were surely disappointed when they realized the only thing in my car was a dated tape player and some spare change.

The busted window did provide entertainment for my new coworker, Sue. She was twenty years my senior, full of personality, and even better than that, had grown up in my favorite era—the sixties! I loved Sue. She made me laugh, knew all the office gossip, and was always kind enough to inform me of adverse weather conditions—my cue to drop my current task and promptly run to my parked car with umbrella in hand. With my Pinto's busted-out window, I was at the mercy of the wind whenever it rained. It was still summer, but sometimes the wind sent my trusted umbrella halfway down the parking lot, which provided much entertainment for my new coworkers. They got to laugh at the new nineteen-year-old print shop assistant chasing an umbrella as it sailed down the parking lot.

Living at home was the quickest way to obtain a new set of wheels with all its windows intact.

Shortly after I started at the print shop, my yo-yo dieting took a dastardly turn. Lisa and I were still hanging out periodically on the weekends in her neck of the woods, the all-night dance-club scene. We'd just come from a club in the University District and had burned off all the alcohol we'd consumed. We were famished.

"Hey, let's stop and get some munchies," Lisa suggested, pulling her car into the parking lot.

"Good idea. I'm starving!" I exclaimed.

"You know what sounds good . . ." Lisa hinted, with a beaming smile, as we climbed out of the car.

"A chili cheese dog!" I said, reading her mind.

"I'm not even going to worry about the calories or how much fat that sucker's going to add to my ass!" Lisa stated adamantly, heading straight for the counter.

Famished

"Yep, we'll diet tomorrow," I agreed, helping myself to the chili and cheese dispensers.

"Oh please, Shana, like you need to diet. You're so tall and thin. You make me sick," Lisa said as we made our way to the register.

"Gee, thanks!" I replied, handing the cashier some money.

"You know I love you. I'm just jealous." Lisa turned to give me a warm smile as I trailed behind her.

We continued our conversation all the way to her parked car.

"Well, you needn't be. Seriously, now that I've stopped growing vertically, I'm spreading horizontally!" I joked.

"Oh, please! You're just like my mom, tall and thin. You could gain twenty pounds and still look great," Lisa replied, hopping up onto the trunk of her car. She let out a huge sigh, as if all that dancing had taken its toll.

"Well, hopefully, this chili cheese dog won't put twenty pounds on me," I said, joining her. I raised my hotdog to my mouth. I couldn't wait to devour the sloppy, delicious mess. But before I could take my first bite, I asked, "Speaking of your mom, how is she?"

"Good. She's in the process of remodeling our house right now," Lisa replied.

"Well, she's got great style, and she's just so cute with that little button nose and adorable accent," I said with a full mouth.

"I zink you two girls are pulling zee vool over mine eyes!" Lisa said as she impersonated her mother's accent.

"Oh! Was that from the night we had her drive us down to the grocery store?" I asked.

"Yeah, don't you remember?"

"How could I forget? We told her there was a big blowout sale and it only lasted for fifteen minutes." I laughed.

"A midnight ice cream sale, to be precise," Lisa said.

"Yes! It's all coming back to me now. And we told her your favorite flavor, butter pecan, was going to sell out if we didn't hurry, and we'd have to pay full price."

"I can't believe she bought our story," Lisa said, taking a bite of her hotdog. Lisa always savored each bite of her food, a trait I didn't possess but admired.

"I can't believe she didn't notice what we were wearing until after we got back from the grocery store," I said, shaking my head.

"She about died when we got out of the car. 'You vore zat to zee store?'" Lisa mimicked.

"Those were the days, huh? Before graduation, without a care in the world. No more midnight trips to the grocery store wearing only an oversized T-shirt and pair of undies!" I reminisced, taking a sip of pop.

"Don't forget the bunny slippers!" she added. "Yes, now we actually have to hold down jobs, and the only thing to look forward to is the weekend." Lisa sighed.

"Well, and chili cheese dogs," I replied, staring down at my empty wrapper.

"And this colossal-sized pop!" Lisa raised her cup in the air.

After polishing off our early morning meal, Lisa dropped me off at my house. "I had fun. I'm glad we're hanging out more often," I said from outside the car door.

"Me too. I'll call you tomorrow," she replied.

"What are you gonna do now?" I asked, already knowing the answer.

"Probably listen to music for the next three hours!" She laughed.

"Of course, you night owl." I waved as she drove away.

Famished

Once inside my house, I tiptoed down the dark hallway to let my parents know I'd made it home. Then I was off for a quick bathroom break, a routine stop I'd made countless times before. It was the same bathroom where I'd played with my dolls during grade school. The same bathroom I'd primped in for my first school dance just days after I'd lost my virginity. It was the same bathroom where I'd bandaged scrapes and cuts and wiped away tears as a little girl.

It would also be the bathroom I would purposely throw up in for the first time.

Somewhere between shutting the door and removing my makeup, in the wee hours of the morning, I felt full. Disgustingly full. All the chili, cheese, and soda culminated in my stomach, and it felt like Thanksgiving Day all over again. The first solution that came to my nineteen-year-old mind was to throw up. I didn't know where the thought came from. It just popped into my head. So I did it. I placed my index finger down my throat and gagged. Then I watched the hotdog I'd just eaten come back up and proceed down the sink drain. I don't even recall whether or not I brushed my teeth afterward—it was that subtle. In the naivety of my teenage mind, I didn't give the act a single thought. Instead I walked straight to my bedroom and quickly fell asleep.

I had no idea the severity of what I'd just done. Not a single clue.

Chapter 16

PLAYGROUND KISSES AND GRADE-SCHOOL BEHAVIOR

It was a hot August evening when Melinda and I sat in my spanking new car, new to me that is, waiting for her boyfriend, Preston, outside his house in West Seattle. Melinda's boyfriend was tall and lanky, with shoulder-length dark-brown hair that matched his dark eyes. Preston, or Presto, as I called him, didn't need alcohol to have a good time. He was one of those people with a natural "high on life" going for him, not to mention a magnetic personality. I always believed that Presto had missed his calling as a comedian/radio disk jockey. He had the whole package, voice and all. He also had a ton of friends in the up-and-coming neighborhood he grew up in, just across the water from downtown Seattle. One of those cute friends tagged behind Preston on what was measuring up to be a very promising evening. And to top it off, my parents had just taxied down the runway to enjoy a much-needed two-week vacation, leaving yours truly to house sit.

"Ladies, you both know Steve, right?" Preston asked, motioning toward his friend.

"Yeah, we've met," Melinda and I replied in unison.

"Great. If you don't mind, he's going to hang out with us tonight," Preston said.

"Of course not. The more the merrier," Melinda responded.

"Hi, Steve," I greeted, making eye contact with Preston's good-looking friend.

Hi," he replied sheepishly as he slid into the backseat of my car with Preston. Finally, a shy guy! It was such a breath of fresh air in comparison to the arrogant jerks I'd gone out with. He wasn't shy in general. He just seemed to be with the ladies, which made him all the more appealing. Now I just had to catch a good buzz and hopefully cozy up to Steve once we reached our destination.

It didn't take long after we arrived at the crowded party that Preston's darling friend had conjured up enough nerve to make his first move. We were engaged in a casual conversation on a comfy sofa when the most unexpected words spilled from his sweet lips.

"You're so beautiful," Steve said, with an innocent smile that would melt any girl's heart.

That was all I needed for him to reel me in. I was the type who craved affection like a sweet tooth craves candy. I had unexpectedly collided with just the fix I needed.

"I can't believe that you don't have a boyfriend," he said with his darling grin. Then faster than a schoolboy on the playground, he kissed my lips. And that was it. So I waited . . . but nothing. I felt perplexed. Was he toying with my emotions, or was Steve seriously this shy? Didn't he understand that we should be cuddled up on the couch like two lovebirds by now?

Playground Kisses and Grade-School Behavior

Interrupting the silence, Preston appeared. Translation: my cue to make a break for it.

"Hey, you two, what's happening?" Preston asked.

Well, I can tell you what's not happening! I thought, but answered, "Not much."

"Man, there are a lot of people at this party," Steve commented. "What is this place? Is it a recording studio, a house, or what?"

"You know, I was trying to figure that out myself," Preston replied with a chuckle.

While those two marveled over a seemingly mundane conversation, I subtly slipped away. What a jerk Steve was, toying with my emotions. I wasn't in sixth grade looking for a quick playground kiss that would take me through the rest of the school year. And my parents were away for two whole weeks. There was no time to waste. With determination I mingled through the crowd. I would show Steve that he couldn't toy with my emotions, and I would find a cute guy to hook up with for the evening, no matter what.

I almost surprised myself with my liquid determination as I rounded the corner and collided with Curtis.

"Hi, Curtis," I greeted enthusiastically. He was a friend of a friend's recent ex-boyfriend, and by the look on his face, he was ripe for the picking.

"Hi, howz it goin?" He conjured up a smile.

"Great. Who are you here with?"

"Just a couple friends," he replied somberly. It was evident Curtis was attempting to mend his broken heart with a case of cheap beer. Although statuesque and resembling one of those men on the cover of a romance novel, his sullen face now looked like a lost puppy.

I had already heard all the gossip. Curtis's girlfriend had stomped on his heart after a six-month relationship. She was one of those girls who always had a boyfriend. Personally, I just didn't get it. Why some girls were like a magnet to guys, yet I was more like the plague? Then looking at Curtis's somber face, suddenly it all made sense. A nice guy like Curtis didn't want to date a nice girl. He needed someone the complete opposite of his personality. He needed a girl with a little attitude, even if she ended up treating him like a doormat! Hmm . . . reminded me of all the times I'd let Dillon treat me the same way. Pushing my bitter feelings aside, I reminded myself of why I was even standing there striking up a conversation with Curtis in the first place. That was right . . . I was on a mission!

"You look sad," I said. "What's wrong?"

Shameless in my buzzed state, I knew exactly what was wrong with Curtis, and did I care about his feelings? The answer was a big fat no. I had a huge ulterior motive up my short-sleeved top regardless that Curtis was vulnerable in his current lovesick state. In my defense, I was a lonely person. I believed with all my heart that if I could just find the right guy, he would alleviate my own pain, the pain of loneliness, of feeling lesser. So, fair or not, my target was Curtis.

"I'm kind of bummed out because Susanna broke up with me," he confessed. "I was shocked, you know. We'd just celebrated our six-month anniversary, and I thought everything was cool between us."

By this time I had glued myself opposite to him on a secluded spot of carpeting and was confident that I could make him forget about being dumped. "She's crazy, Curtis. Don't even worry about it," I assured him. "She obviously doesn't know a good thing when she's got it."

"Yeah, I guess you're right," he mumbled, staring at the floor.

"I'm serious." I touched him on the hand to gain his attention. "She doesn't realize what she gave up. I mean, you're so nice . . . and cute," I cooed.

"Yeah?" Curtis asked as he leaned his face closer.

"Yeah," I whispered, feeling his soft lips against mine.

Curtis's kiss was so fragile and sweet. I was in an intoxicated state of bliss. My mission was a success. I had shown Steve that I wasn't going to wither away over his sudden withdrawal of affection. Unfortunately, I hadn't calculated Preston's uncanny ability to interrupt at the worst possible time.

"Hey, Shana, everyone's ready to leave," Preston said. "Melinda and I are pretty tired, and Steve would like a ride home."

"Okay," I replied reluctantly. I pulled myself away from Curtis, who lived miles away from my neck of the woods, and said goodbye. It was time for plan B. I couldn't go home alone. "Preston, would you please ask Steve if he'll come back to my parents' place with us?" I begged, trailing behind him in search of Steve's darling face among the partiers.

"Yeah, sure, give me a second, and I'll go ask him."

Preston and I had a great relationship. He was like a really cool brother who would do anything for me, and I hoped beyond hope that Preston could convince Steve to join us for the remainder of the evening.

After a couple minutes of viewing their conversation just out of earshot, Preston returned with the verdict. "I guess Steve is going to go to his place tonight."

"Why?" I didn't want to return home with Melinda and Preston by myself. That was the story of my life, being the dreaded third wheel.

"Listen, this is nuts! I'll go get Steve, and you two can discuss this between yourselves." Preston headed off to retrieve his friend.

While Preston was in the process of capturing Steve, I was in the middle of nail-biting contemplation. It was true I didn't want to return to my empty house without a guy, yet the situation had become grade school embarrassing! Here I was practically begging Steve to spend the night with me. I was almost ready to escape to my car in shame, when Preston reappeared with Steve.

"All right, now that we're all together," Preston began, addressing Steve first. "Shana would like you to join us this evening at her parents' house. They're on vacation, she has the place to herself for a couple of weeks," he explained. "Now I'm going to find Melinda and head out to your car, Shana."

The whole thing reeked of a grade school crush.

"Okay, we'll meet you at the car," I replied, turning to face Steve. "Uh, hi," I uttered, not knowing what to say.

"Hi," he replied.

"Steve, I'd really like you to come back to my parents' house with me tonight," I admitted.

"I just saw you kissing another guy," he said. "Why don't you ask him?"

Boy, this was going to be tougher than I'd thought. "I don't even like him. I like you," I said in my sweetest voice.

"Then why were you kissing him?"

"That was just really dumb of me. I don't even like the guy. I guess I just got the feeling that you weren't interested in me." I locked eyes with him.

"Are you crazy?" he asked. "A guy would have to be blind not to be interested in you!"

"You're not blind, right?"

"No. Just stupid," he answered with an innocent smile.

"You're not stupid." I nudged him playfully.

"You're so beautiful, you could have any guy."

"If I could have any guy, then why don't you want to come over to my house tonight?" I asked with a flirtatious smile.

"Because I'm a total idiot," he confirmed, looking at me through his long, dark-brown bangs that obstructed one eye.

"So, total idiot, is that a yes?" I moved his bangs to the side to reveal his sweet face.

Steve answered my inquiry with a darling grin that was quickly becoming his trademark. His face looked like the most charming boy-next-door a girl had ever seen, and he oozed masculinity from every square inch of his lanky frame.

"We'd better get back to my car. They're waiting for us," I replied.

"All right, let's go."

Hand in hand, the two of us zigzagged through the throng of people and back to my car. I was victorious! I had snagged a total babe. Now, if I could only keep him for more than one night . . .

I faced one last hurdle.

"Melinda, I was wondering if you wouldn't mind too terribly—"

"You want me to drive."

Poor Melinda! It seemed she had the title of chauffeur tattooed on her forehead. Regardless of whose car it was, she more often than not ended up behind the wheel.

"Yeah, I kind of had too much beer, so if you wouldn't mind driving us home?" I petitioned in a feel-sorry-for-me kind of voice. I justified my actions by the fact that Melinda had a boyfriend. She spent every weekend with Preston, with me tagging along in my quest to find a mate. It was a rare occasion that I actually hooked up with someone for the evening, and I wasn't about to miss a single second of bliss. Why should I drive when I could be snuggled up to Steve in the backseat?

"Yes, I'll drive."

Chapter 17

SPOOKED BY THE DEVIL'S WEED

After arriving home, I gave Steve a tour of the house, hoping to say goodnight to Melinda and Preston. Unfortunately, Steve seemed more interested in conversing with Preston over my music collection.

"Hey, Shana, what is this stuff?" Preston asked with a chuckle.

"'Super Lover'?" Steve questioned.

"Yeah, I love that song!" It was evident I was under deep scrutiny for my musical taste, while Preston and Steve rummaged through my case of CDs.

"You call this music?" Preston laughed. "Did you actually spend money on this stuff?"

"Well, excuse me, Preston, if I don't have a vast assortment of whatever it is that you listen to."

"Lords of the New Church . . . U2 . . ." he rambled.

"Okay, excuse me if I don't have those in my collection."

"You call this a collection?" Steve said with a sweet little smirk.

"All right, I've had enough of you two music aficionados!" I scooped up my CD case.

"You know, you might want to get your ears checked next time you pay a visit to the old doc," Preston replied.

It was all in good fun. So what if Steve and I didn't share the same taste in music.

"How about just listening to the radio instead?" Steve suggested.

"Sounds like a plan," Preston agreed.

"Thank goodness that's settled," I said with a sigh of relief. Now if I could just get a moment alone with Steve. Was that so much to ask?

I got my wish shortly after when Steve and I found ourselves sitting alone at my kitchen table.

"Do you want to smoke some weed?" he asked.

My hesitant response screamed apprehension. I hung out with drinkers, not stoners.

"I'm sorry. It's just that everyone I know smokes pot. I assumed you did too," he said.

"It's okay. I don't usually smoke pot, but what the heck."

"All right!" he replied, as if the party was finally getting started. "Ladies first. You take the first hit."

"Thanks." Steve was not only cute, but thoughtful too! What more could a girl ask for? After finishing the joint, it was evident what more a girl could ask for. A lobotomy sounded appealing. Within seconds my sweet state of euphoria had transformed itself into a paranoid nightmare.

A couple of years had passed since I'd smoked pot. It became crystal clear why I usually avoided it. How could I forget those awkward, spaced-out moments in high school? Why would I get stoned just because a cute guy offered it to me?

Spooked by the Devil's Weed

In a span of a few minutes, Steve's angelic face had transformed itself into something strange. I had to get away from him, and quick.

"Excuse me for a moment. I have to use the restroom." I fled the scene. After a few minutes in the bathroom, I realized it was a less-than-perfect hiding place. What if he assumed I was going number two? How embarrassing would that be? So instead I made a quick dash to my bedroom, seeking refuge until my paranoia subsided, which could take hours. I couldn't successfully hole myself up in my bedroom without someone finding me. I lived in a one-story house, for goodness' sake! With minutes ticking away like hours, a knock beckoned from outside my bedroom door.

Reluctantly, I responded with a simple "Yes?" hoping the response wouldn't have a male voice attached to it.

"Shana, are you in there?" Melinda asked.

Relieved, I opened the door. "Hi, Melinda. Come in." I gestured, safely closing the door behind us.

"What are you doing in your room?" she asked. "Steve's wondering what happened to you."

"Oh man, Melinda, you won't believe it," I said. "I smoked some pot with Steve, and now I'm freaking' out!"

"Why did you get high with him?"

"I'd forgotten how bad it was, and you know, he offered it."

"So you're just really high, and you decided to lock yourself in your room?"

"See, the problem is that after I smoked the joint, suddenly Steve looked ugly to me." I shook my head in wonder.

"So now you don't like him?"

"Yeah. I guess it's the pot, because I looked at him, and he just kinda grossed me out," I replied.

"Shana, obviously it's the joint you smoked, you were just gaga over him half an hour ago."

"I know . . . I know!" I agreed. "Melinda, just stay in here with me for a while, please?"

"Okay, but eventually they're going to come looking for us."

"I know, but let's stay in my room until they do," I replied.

Escaping Steve's presence helped alleviate my paranoia. Now it was just Melinda and I hanging out, laughing hysterically over nothing. But inevitably, a male intruder disturbed our sanctuary.

"Hello?" Preston opened the door. "What are you two hens talking about for the past hour?"

"Hi, Preston," I greeted him.

"Ah, not to interrupt what I assume must be fascinating conversation, but I'm pretty tired, Melinda," Preston said. "And, Shana, what's up with you?"

"What do you mean?"

"You ditched Steve after you begged him to come here tonight," he said with a bewildered gaze.

"I figured you guys were talking," I fibbed. No way was I going to confide in Preston and risk Steve finding out I couldn't handle a few puffs of weed.

"I'll go talk to him." I quickly dashed out to the living room.

"Hi," I greeted Steve meekly.

"Hey, is everything okay?" he asked, sitting patiently on my living room sofa.

"Yes. Melinda and I were just laughing in my room about stupid stuff," I answered.

"I was a little worried, after we got stoned, you disappeared," he said.

"What a sweetheart." I sighed silently. He was worried about me! That must mean that he missed me too.

"I waited for you to come back, and you never did."

"I'm sorry," I apologized. He was waiting for an explanation I didn't want to give.

"That pot is pretty strong," he said, as if reading my dazed and confused mind. "I'm sorry if you got too stoned."

"No, it's okay. I guess it's because I don't usually smoke the stuff," I admitted.

"Are you okay now?"

"I'm fine."

After we resolved my unfortunate pot fiasco, I was anxious to find some dim lighting and call it a night. The perfect end to this complicated evening would be to turn the lights down low and cuddle up in my warm, cozy bed. This scenario would, of course, include Steve, who would definitely benefit from some mood lighting.

"I'm kind of tired," I hinted.

"Yeah, me too." He proceeded to lounge across the living room sofa.

What's he doing? I wondered. Didn't he realize this was his cue to follow me?

"Do you have an extra blanket?"

Indeed, his mother had trained him well, but this was not what I had in mind. He was regressing back into his introverted shell, which translated into me hugging my pillow.

"Steve, you don't have to sleep on the couch," I replied.

"It's okay. I don't mind," he assured me. "Your couch is pretty comfortable."

I wanted to scream, "Well, I do mind if you sleep on the

sofa! Are you nuts?" Instead I opted for more subtle coercion. "Why don't you just sleep in my room? It's much more comfortable than this couch." I turned in the direction of my bedroom and hoped he would follow me.

The next morning, I awoke to the most darling profile on planet earth. My sweet prince had returned.

I could have chatted over silly pillow talk for hours as Steve and I lay in my bed entangled like octopi. It was occasional moments of happiness such as this that made life worth living to me. Not to mention he was the perfect gentleman, one of the few guys who hadn't tried to have sex with me.

Alas, it was short lived. Preston burst through my bedroom door.

"Top of the morning, you two lovebirds," Preston said. "Sorry to interrupt this picture-perfect moment, but, ah, it's almost noon."

"And?" I wanted to scream bloody murder at Preston for disturbing such a lovely moment.

"And that means its lunchtime," he said. "I'm pretty hungry. Steve, let's fire up the barbie."

Gee, tell me something I don't already know, I thought cynically. When wasn't Preston hungry? He consumed food like the Jolly Green Giant, yet resembled Jack of the bean stalk fame.

Although grateful for Preston's assistance capturing Steve last night, he'd become a hindrance now, as I watched my cutie pie slip sheepishly from my bed and follow Preston to the kitchen.

"Why was I so insecure anyway?" I comforted myself. "It's not as if Steve had hopped into an idling car without saying goodbye. He's only a room away preparing to curb his appetite." So why then had my sunny disposition faded to a gray, overcast day? In the dark recesses of my mind, I knew this relationship would also be short lived. I hadn't been able to keep a guy interested long term. Would this shy guy be any different?

"Hey, Shana," Preston yelled, interrupting my contemplation.

"Yes?"

"What are you doing? Steve's making hotdogs. You want one?"

"I'm coming," I shouted from the hallway, quickly ducking into the bathroom.

First, I had to make myself look completely irresistible, which called for backup. "Melinda, could you please come here?" I whisper-yelled. Melinda was lucky. She had already captured Preston's attention for the long term. In fact, she was so comfortable in her relationship that she didn't even fuss with wearing makeup every day, not that she needed to.

"Where are you?" Melinda asked.

"I'm in here," I answered through the slightly cracked bathroom door. The last thing I wanted was for Steve to know that I was primping to impress him. He had just rolled out of bed without so much as a glimpse in the mirror. "I need your advice," I whispered. "Hurry up. Get in here."

"Why are you whispering?" Melinda asked.

"Shh, hurry up and close the door."

"Are you getting ready?" she asked.

"Yeah, and I need your help," I replied. "How does my hair look?"

"It looks good," she stated. "Are you going somewhere?"

"No, I'm just getting ready," I replied. "Do these shorts look okay with this shirt?"

"Yes, it looks nice," she answered.

"Does the back of my hair look flat?"

"It's a little flat," she admitted.

"Oh! Fix it, please?" I handed her a hot crimping iron, knowing I could spend an hour in the bathroom and still not be satisfied with my appearance.

"All right, I've had enough." Melinda abruptly set down the crimping iron.

"What's wrong?"

"Your hair is so thick. I've crimped the same piece ten times, and it is still straight."

"This crimper is crappy, but I'm too cheap to buy an expensive one." I critiqued the back of my head through a small hand mirror. "It takes me two hours to do a twenty-minute job!"

"What the heck are you two doing in there?" Preston asked from the other side of the closed door.

"We're coming." I opened the door so he would quit his persistent knocking.

"Geez, Louise, how much hair spray did you two use?" Preston asked through the plume of fumes. "Steve made hotdogs."

"I'm not hungry," I said. A huge lie. Regardless of how hungry I was, under no circumstance would I consume anything that required chewing in the presence of a guy I liked.

Realizing that he couldn't penetrate my taste buds, Preston directed his attention toward Melinda. "You'll have a hotdog, huh, Minda?"

"No, I'll probably just have some chips," she answered.

There was a huge difference between Melinda's appetite and mine. Melinda effortlessly nibbled her way through life on junk food. She had the perfect body and the ultimate restraint. She truly could eat just one potato chip, and after a handful, she would be completely satisfied. How lucky were the tiny fraction of women who had no concept of that dirty four-letter word, *diet*. The only time I could control my appetite was in the company of a cute guy, but those times were few and far between.

Worse still was the sinking feeling I had ever since Steve slinked out of my arms that morning. Yes, he was still physically in my kitchen, but I already sensed him slipping away, and by the time I reached my kitchen, fully primped, Preston delivered the bad news.

Chapter 18

SEEKING SOLACE IN A BAG OF CHIPS

"Hey, Shana, I guess Steve has band practice today, so he needs a ride home," Preston said, as if trying to gently break the news.

"Sure, when does he need to leave?" I asked in the nonchalant tone I had perfected over the years, but inwardly my heart was breaking. It was almost as if the night before hadn't even happened, and as usual I was determined to pretend that life was just peachy.

"He needs to leave now," Preston replied.

"Okay, sure, let me just grab my purse." I retreated to my bedroom. I needed a few minutes alone to gain my composure. *He has a prior engagement, that's all. Why am I so upset, just because he's leaving to meet up with the guys for band practice? If anything, I should be ecstatic that I hooked up with a babe who plays the drums in a band. Just think! I can get in free to all the clubs his band plays at! It'll be just like that book* I'm with the Band, *only we'll be in Seattle instead of LA. Then hopefully, Steve's band will become famous and we'll all move to LA! Well, maybe I'm getting ahead of myself,* I reasoned as I stole one last glance in the mirror.

"Hey, Shana, we'll be in the car," Preston yelled from my front door.

"Okay, I'm coming!"

I hopped into the driver's seat, confident I would see my sweet babe again. "Where do you need to go, Steve?" I asked as plainly as I would ask a waitress if they served lemonade.

"John's house in West Seattle," he responded. "Do you know where it is?"

"I know the vicinity. You'll have to direct me when we get near."

After dropping Steve off, the three of us returned to my empty house. It felt so great to feel all grown up with the house to myself for two weeks. The only unfortunate part was that Steve was far away at band practice. "What are you two going to do tonight?" I asked Melinda as she lounged across Preston's lap on my living room sofa.

"I don't know," she replied. "Where are all the cool parties tonight, Preston?" Melinda playfully poked him in the ribs.

"Knock it off, Minda," Preston replied, quickly wrestling her to the floor.

It was obvious, as I observed their affectionate tickle-fest, that any audible response to my question would be at least a shower's duration away. "I'm going to take a shower," I said. There was no chance I'd stick around to watch the two of them wrestle on the floor like a couple of cubs on TV.

Melinda, my high school friend, had a boyfriend, and I was left in the dust. We had been through so much together. Yes, I was excited for Melinda the night she'd hooked up with Preston for the first time. We were supportive through the ups and downs of our relationships. Good ol' Melinda was always there for me when I called crying for a ride home the morning after spending the night with yet another jerk who'd disappointed me. I could count on Melinda to not only be home but also to come pick me up when the guy I just couldn't resist, in my drunken crush, wouldn't even give me a ride home. Melinda was my rock, and now my rock had firmly planted herself in Preston's arms.

While I rinsed the shampoo from my hair, visions of Steve holding me tight danced through my head. Steve and I were cuddled up around a massive bonfire on Alki Beach. We watched the sun set behind the Olympic Mountains, and as the waves gently rolled onto the shore, he whispered sweet nothings in my ear. It was the ultimate contrived fantasy, the story of my life—90 percent imagined and 10 percent reality. I daydreamed my way through life. How else could I endure an eight-hour shift rubber-banding bundles of labels at the print shop? Risk-taking was not on my résumé, and truthfully I didn't even have a résumé. I didn't need one because from a young age, I had taken life's less intimidating road. My philosophy was to stay in the outfield, far from any obstacles, and instead of chasing that fly ball, I ran from it. That was how I ended up in a monotonous job, with the only thing excelling being my vivid imagination. *If just once my wishes could come true*, I hoped silently as I emerged from the bathroom.

"You took a shower?" Melinda remarked. "Going somewhere?"

"I don't know. Are we going out tonight?" I plopped myself into a reclining chair.

"Preston, where's all the cool parties tonight?" Melinda

asked again, poking him playfully.

"Knock it off, Minda!" Preston replied, wrestling her to the living room floor.

"Oh, my goodness! I must be experiencing déjà vu!" I exclaimed. *Am I losing my mind, or had this same scenario taken place thirty minutes ago?* I wondered. "Are you two ever going to answer me, or should I go take another shower?"

"Why are you taking another shower?" Preston asked, raising an eyebrow.

Preston was absolutely hilarious. His upbeat humor and quirky facial gestures demanded attention, and beyond the jealousy factor, I truly was happy for Melinda. Her boyfriend made me laugh, and in my eyes she was a lucky girl to have someone holding her. I just wished so badly that someone was holding me!

"Ah, Nana, are you nuts?" Preston questioned. "Didn't you just take a shower, like, two minutes ago?"

"Thank you!" I replied, which translated to "Finally, someone is listening to me."

"Nana, are you feeling all right today?" he asked, questioning my sanity.

"Hmm, funny you should ask. Now that you mention it, I guess I was feeling a little off today," I retorted. "I wonder if it could possibly be due to the fact that I have been trying to talk to the two of you for the past hour!"

"Minda, I think Nana's a little cranky," Preston replied through his nose, in one of his comical voices that resembled someone with a severe cold.

It was all so sickening. The three of us had already established pet names, Presto, Minda, and Nana. Like three peas in a pod, we might as well have purchased a house in the suburbs and painted the fence white.

"I think she wants to know what we're doing tonight," Melinda said on my behalf. Then, as if reading my tightly closed mind, Melinda suggested, "Why don't you give Steve a call and see where the parties are tonight? I'm sure he's back from band practice by now."

"Sounds like a plan," Preston agreed.

My prayers have been answered, I thought. It was a shame that I couldn't confess my true feelings to my best friend. Deep down I knew that I couldn't fool Melinda, and I feared that she could see into my soul. So I tried all the more to hide what was on the inside.

What if I revealed my true feelings for Steve and he rejected me? Then I would look like a complete fool. There was no way I wanted Melinda and Preston to feel sorry for me if Steve decided that he loved me not. Which, I had a sinking feeling was the case.

After a quick conversation, Preston returned with the verdict. "Well, I guess there's a big blowout at Tom's place in White Center. Steve said that he's pretty tired and he's going to stay home tonight."

"Are we gonna go to the party?" Melinda asked Preston.

"Sure, if that's what you ladies want to do, we're there!" Preston said.

"On second thought, I think I'll skip the party and hang out here tonight," I said. There was no way I could endure an evening of simulated happiness, and I wasn't the type who sought condolences on my best friend's damp shoulder. No way! My puddle of tears was as secure as the Hoover Dam, at least until I found solace alone.

"What are you going to do here by yourself?" Melinda

asked me.

"Yeah, Nana. Didn't you just take, like, twelve showers, and you're going to stay home?" Preston questioned.

"I don't get the house to myself that often, so I'd really like to savor this time alone," I lied.

"Oh, yes, like a finely grilled steak," Preston quipped.

"You must be hungry again," I pointed out, happy to change the subject.

"When isn't he hungry?" Melinda gently poked his belly.

"So, are you sure you won't join us this evening, Nana?" Preston asked.

"Yeah, you two go ahead," I replied.

What a relief. I sighed inwardly as I watched Melinda and Preston pull out of my driveway. At least now I could have my pity party alone. Why did I always have to chase after the cute ones? Couldn't I, for once, see past the guys with the oh-so-fine exterior and dig a little deeper? Why couldn't I opt for a less attractive, dependable guy? At least then I wouldn't be here all alone.

After about ten minutes of deep introspect, I found myself sitting in the kitchen munching on a supersized bag of freshly opened chips. Seeking solace by means of food was a habit I had adopted in my childhood years.

My first memory of this gluttonous form of eating was during my grade school years, and the event still burned in my mind. There I was on our family's two-tone brown velvet sofa, engrossed in an afternoon television program, wasting the day away by means of a few cookies. Then suddenly I realized the full package of cookies had disappeared to the innermost depths of my stomach.

Later that evening, my mother asked from the kitchen,

Seeking Solace in a Bag of Chips

"Shana, what happened to the package of cookies?"

"I don't know," I lied. I'd been caught and wasn't about to admit my shameful indulgence. It was the first time I had lied about a food binge.

"There was a whole package of cookies this morning when I left," said my mother from the kitchen. She was confiding in my father over hushed tones, but from my vantage point, I could make out what was said.

"Are you sure?" my father asked.

"Yes, I'm certain she ate the entire package of cookies and now she's lying about it," my mother said.

"Well, what do you want me to do about it?" Dad asked.

The discussion tapered off, but my secretive behavior had only just begun. A seed had been planted in my soul.

In the kitchen a decade later, I found myself in an all-too-similar circumstance. Polishing off the whole bag of chips, my compulsive eating habits from childhood had manifested into an actual disorder with a name. Mood eating had reached a whole new level since my adolescent years. The excess calories I consumed no longer evaporated into thin air. How could I continue to devour food when nervous or bored, yet still stay thin? I had developed a habit of emotional eating over the years, but now the habit had taken on a whole other side . . . and it was ugly.

"If I could only discipline myself," I agonized as I knelt on the bathroom floor to a position that had become all too familiar. This was the worst part of the binge-purge cycle. The binging was great. I could eat to my heart's desire. It was literally a food-induced numbing state of euphoria. All my problems seemed to diminish while I gorged on delectable delicacies. Anything that consisted of high fat or sugar was forbidden food as far as my butt was concerned. These taboo treats were strictly reserved for my binges, which were becoming more expensive the further my addiction progressed. Money was irrelevant in the current cloud of my perception, even if it meant spending much of what I earned on food, food that I had no intention of keeping down.

But there was a horrible downside to moments like this. There I sat on my bathroom floor, staring at the porcelain commode and wishing I didn't have to shove my finger down my throat. Sometimes the purging was relatively quick. It was dependent on the intake of fluid-to-solid ratio during my binge. Sometimes the food wouldn't come up, and that was when I really panicked. This was my deepest fear, that the thousands of calories I'd consumed would actually make their way through my digestive system. In my mind, this translated to colossal hips. It was imperative to purge every last morsel of food I'd taken in, regardless the extent of gagging that entailed. Not until I quivered from the bitter taste of acid from my stomach lining did the purging cease. Then I knew I was out of the woods, as far as the calories were concerned.

This particular day the chips made their way down the toilet bowl in record time. The hard part was over. Now all I had to do was brush my teeth and consume a ton of water to stay hydrated. Oftentimes, the purging drained me physically, and I had to sleep it off. I made my way back to the comfort of my bed.

If only Steve were here with me, the two of us cuddled up like kittens together. If I only had a boyfriend, I could beat this bulimia. A man in my life would definitely bring me the happiness and security I craved. If only Steve were here, I wouldn't have needed those chips to fill this emptiness inside me.

Seeking Solace in a Bag of Chips

My train of thought was diverted by the rapid pounding of my heart, something I hadn't experienced before. I was petrified I was having a heart attack. I'd read about a girl who'd died from a heart attack the first time she binged and purged.

Shortly after I discovered that I had what was defined as an eating disorder, I conducted a little research to find out exactly what the definition of bulimic was. I fit the criteria to a tee. The consequences were appalling: rotted teeth; raw, inflamed esophagus; electrolyte imbalances; and worst case scenario—spontaneous heart failure.

After absorbing the list of side effects, I vowed to never succumb to this heinous behavior again. I thought the research itself was enough to scare me straight, and it did for a few hours. Then it was right back to the same vicious cycle of gorging and puking.

Back on my bed, I sat there in silence, feeling the deep palpitation of my heart. Without hesitation I cried out to the God of my childhood, hoping He would answer my plea. "God, please forgive me for throwing up," I begged. "I don't want to die. I promise, if you save me just this one time, I'll never binge again."

I was so afraid. I felt completely isolated. Emotionally lonely and scared to death that I was going to die. When my heartbeat slowed down, I was relieved and thankful, as if God had heard my cry but as far as keeping my promise to never throw up again, that I couldn't do.

Chapter 19

BAREFOOT AND BUZZED

Alas, summer was coming to a close, and how I wished it could be an endless summer. I resided in the Northwest though, which meant warm, sunny days would soon put on their jammies and slumber for several months. There was one bright side. I was house-sitting for my sister. This meant a little more fun and freedom. Even better, Melinda and I had located a happening party just a few blocks away, so we hopped into my car with the music blaring.

Dressed like a sixties-hippy-chick-meets-Seattle-grunge girl, I felt like a million bucks. I opted for a vintage short-sleeved shirt full of vibrant floral colors and my favorite pair of jeans, which I'd cropped off with a pair of scissors just above the kneecap. They were perfectly worn out in all the right places, and finding a good pair of jeans was no easy task. As a part-time hobby, I spent numerous hours, usually with friends, combing the racks at various hole-in-the-wall thrift stores. It was fun, the feeling I got when I found another unique addition for my growing wardrobe, which I knew no other girl would have. My find that summer was a pair of men's jeans, complete with naturally frayed holes in the rear! It was my new weather-permitting look, and it made choosing an outfit pretty simple. All I had to decide on was a shirt, considering that beautifully barefoot was also part of my look. I thrived on being different.

Making small talk on the way to the party, I asked Melinda, "So is Preston going to meet us at the shindig tonight?"

"He said he would meet up with us after he watches Steve's band practice," Melinda said.

The very mention of Steve's name caused my eardrums to percolate, not to mention my pulse. Maybe Preston was getting a ride from Steve. He did just recently acquire a station wagon, albeit one of the funkiest vehicles I'd ever laid eyes on, yet functional. *Perhaps*, I silently wished. I'd been lovesick since hooking up with Steve while my parents were away. As my luck would have it, Steve and I never collided with a kiss again. I had seen him at parties, but that was the extent of it. Stolen glances across a crowded room. I didn't know what was worse, being treated like a doormat by Dillon or falling for a shy guy who wouldn't make a move. Either way I was left alone to hug my pillow while my friend Melinda had a boyfriend. Was it too good to be true, or could Steve really be Preston's chauffer tonight? My heart skipped a beat in anticipation, but I wasn't about to ask Melinda. Then I would surely look like a lovesick girl. I had to come up with another way to find out, something more subtle.

"Is Preston ever going to get his license?" I desperately tried to maneuver our conversation to reveal Preston's mystery driver.

"Who knows. Probably never, considering he has me as a chauffeur," Melinda stated.

Barefoot and Buzzed

Well, this isn't going according to plan, I thought. She just didn't seem to be taking the bait. "This is true, but you're not with him every day. It must be a drag taking the bus."

"Are you kidding?" Melinda laughed. "Preston is way too arrogant for that!"

Oh, my goodness, I marveled in frustration. This was harder than trying to crack open a can of soup without a utensil. I wanted to just scream, "So who the heck is driving Preston to this party tonight, since we've already established he is way to cool to take a bus?" *Maybe I should try a different approach.* My bare feet made their way from my carpeted car to the rocky pavement.

"Are you sure I'm parked okay?" I asked. "I don't want any of these drunks hitting my car!"

"Yeah, you're fine," she confirmed. "But aren't you one of these drunks?"

"Buzzed, not drunk. There is a difference," I assured her.

"Of course." she agreed with a smile.

And like a schoolteacher, I explained, "Just because I have one drink doesn't mean I am intoxicated."

"One drink?" She laughed.

As we made our way down the residential street, I realized that my clever conversation had been completely fruitless. *Only time will tell if Steve shows his sweet face at the party tonight*, I thought with an inward sigh.

"What's wrong?" Melinda asked abruptly, bringing me back to reality.

"What do you mean?" I asked.

"Well, you just sighed," she said. "Are you okay?"

I didn't realize when I was thinking about Steve that I'd sighed out loud! How embarrassing. I needed to come up with an excuse, and quick. "Yeah, I'm fine. It's just these damn rocks hurt my feet." I pointed at the rocks and hoped that Melinda would buy my excuse. Considering that Melinda was practically psychic when it came to reading my mind, I had to add a little limp emphasizing that, indeed, it was the rocks, not shy boy Steve who never called me, that caused me to sigh.

"I don't know why you just don't wear shoes," she said. "Is it so hard to slip on a pair?"

Whew, I diverted her attention back to my feet, I thought. But deep down I could feel my transparency. In fact, it was downright irritating that Melinda could read me like a worn-out book. Melinda and my mother were two people who could see right through me, no matter how hard I tried to conceal my feelings. And I'd perfected the art of concealing my feelings. If they issued a master's degree in the subject, I would have had one. For some reason, there were certain people in my life that I just couldn't fool.

"Are you ignoring me?" Melinda asked, bringing me back to reality again.

I had to get my mind off of Steve or blow my carefree party girl cover for sure, "I'm sorry. What was the question?"

"You were complaining about your feet, and I asked you why you don't wear a pair of shoes," she reminded me.

"Oh yes. Because it only hurts when I'm walking on rocks, and the rest of the time its fine. Hey, isn't that Preston over there?"

"I don't know. I forgot to put my contacts in," Melinda answered.

"Yes, it's definitely Preston!" We gravitated toward the music that blared from our destination's backyard. It was an outdoor house party, which I absolutely loved, especially on a warm summer evening with outdoor lighting illuminating the night sky and hordes of partygoers congregating on the fresh cut grass.

"Hey, Presto," I greeted.

"Hi, Nana," he replied in his usual nasal tone. "What took you two hens so long?"

"You know, Presto, I'd appreciate it if you wouldn't refer to us in such a derogatory manner," I replied.

"Oh, big words!" he teased. "Is it that time of the month, Nana? You're kinda cranky," Preston remarked.

"Just because I don't want to be referred to as a hen, doesn't make me cranky," I retorted.

"All right, that's enough, you two," Melinda refereed.

Preston was right. I was cranky. And it had nothing to do with being called a hen. It had to do with my question of the night finally being answered, and his name was Tom. Preston had gotten a ride from his friend Tom, not Steve. To think that I had gotten my hopes up and actually believed that Steve might go to the party with Preston, just to see me. What a joke. He wasn't as lovesick as I was, and once again I would be spending the evening alone.

"Nana, I'm sorry for calling you a hen. I thought you knew I was joking," Preston apologized.

"It's okay. It was my fault. Maybe I am a little cranky."

"We need a group hug," Preston joked as he squeezed the four of us together.

My night could have just ended at that. A few more drinks and then back to my sister's double-wide. But remarkably, it took an abrupt turn down an unexpected path.

"Oh my goodness, Melinda, that's Joel!" I exclaimed as I gazed upon his lovely face several yards away.

"Joel who?" Melinda asked.

"Joel, you know, the guy who worked in the record store at the mall," I reminded her.

"The one that looks like the guy from Duran Duran?" she asked.

"Yeah, when Duran Duran was in town, Lisa and I saw him on the metro," I replied. "He was sitting at the back of the bus on his way to the concert, and when he got off, all these girls were chasing him because they thought he really was in the band!"

"And you were one of the girls chasing him?" Melinda asked sarcastically.

"No. I was too shy. I just loved him from afar. Now Lisa, on the other hand . . ."

"I know Lisa wasn't too shy to talk to him," Melinda said.

Lisa, my fearless friend who wasn't the least bit shy around the opposite sex.

"Lisa even called him once at the record store he worked at. She told him her name was Martha. I can't believe her nerve." I laughed. Truly, I stood with jaw-dropped amazement by Lisa's boldness that day, fake name or not!

"Where's he at? I don't see him," Melinda stated, scanning the dimly lit yard.

"That's probably because you don't have your contacts in," I stated. "Okay, if you squint real hard, you might be able to make him out. He's standing right next to the preppy guy in the fuchsia shirt." I pointed. "Do you see him now?"

"There's a guy wearing a fuchsia shirt?" Melinda marveled.

"Forget about the guy in the fuchsia shirt. Anyway, I think it's probably hot pink. I'm not sure. My eyes aren't that good either," I replied.

"Is there a difference?" she asked in a sarcastic tone that was her trademark and usually made me laugh. Like any other time than when I was attempting to inconspicuously point out a babe at a party.

"Yes, there's a difference between fuchsia and hot pink!" I exclaimed. "How did we get on the subject of shirt color anyway?"

"Hey, you brought it up, talking about this guy's fuchsia shirt," she replied.

"All right, can we just forget about the shirt for one minute?" I asked. "Don't stare. Joel is walking our way!" I poked Melinda in the side. "Can you see him now?" I whispered.

"The tall guy, right?"

"Yes. Isn't he a fox?"

"Yeah, but he definitely doesn't resemble anyone from Duran Duran," she said.

"Well, that was, like, five years ago. Not to mention that people change. Regardless, he's still a babe!"

"Calm down. You don't have to get mad," Melinda replied. "Are you going to talk to him?"

"Well, what do you think," I replied with a tinge of annoyance.

"I don't think you have the guts to go talk to him," she answered.

"Precisely!" I affirmed. "For a minute there, I thought you had forgotten who you were talking to." Melinda knew I was a chicken. That was the only reason I drank in the first place, to acquire liquid boldness.

Melinda was lucky. She had a boyfriend now and no longer needed to be bold.

"You're just going to love him from afar?" she teased.

"The story of my life," I said with a sigh.

Just then Preston came back from his extended wait at the beer keg. "Jeez, did that take an hour or what? Consider yourselves lucky, girls, because the keg is officially empty," he said as he handed us both a full cup of foam. "What are you two hens whispering about?" Then catching himself, he added, "Sorry, Nana. If you would, please omit that last derogatory statement from the record."

"I will indeed. And for your information, I'm keeping a tab," I snapped in the snottiest voice I could fake.

"That would be beer tab, correct? Because I did pay for yours," Preston retorted.

"No, smarty pants. That would be my tally of derogatory statements that I've had to endure from you, probably since the day we met! And thank you for the beer."

"Speaking of beer . . ." Melinda interjected. "Is that what you're calling this cup of froth that you waited an hour for, Preston?"

"Melinda, he's standing right behind you!" I whispered as I nudged her in the side.

"Where is he?" she asked in midturn.

"Shh!" I hushed. "Don't turn around. He's going to know we're talking about him!"

"Who's going to know you're talking about him?" Preston interrupted.

"Please, Melinda, whatever you do, don't tell Preston what we're talking about."

"Tell me what?" Preston asked.

I locked eyes with Melinda, fearing the worst, that Preston would embarrass me in front of Joel.

"Melinda, please don't tell him. Presto's got a big mouth," I insisted.

"Hey, who you calling a big mouth?" Preston replied. "That's it. Put 'em up," he threatened as he lifted his fists for a mock fight.

"I'm going to go use the restroom," I replied. I could hear Preston clucking like a chicken as I scurried across the grass.

Once I reached the house, I located an empty bathroom to collect my thoughts. While I peed in privacy, I tried to determine how I could start up a conversation with Joel. After primping in front of the mirror for a second and determining I didn't look half-bad, I traipsed back to the crowded yard. Maybe I could accidentally bump into him. *No, that's the oldest trick in the book, not to mention I would feel like a complete ass.*

While I contrived a scheme that was no more believable than the latest Hollywood flick, I was suddenly deterred by a sharp pain. Some drunken jerk had stepped on my big toe. Looking up, low and behold, it was the guy in the fuchsia shirt.

"Oops, I'm so sorry!" he exclaimed. "Did I step on your foot?"

"Yes, you did." In any normal situation I would have been irritated, but as I was about to discover, this was far from any average night out. How could I be upset with this cutie pie with such a sparkling disposition, even if he was wearing that infamous shirt?

"Hi, I'm Jaxon," he said. "Is your foot okay?" His eyes glanced toward the ground. "Hey, you're not wearing any shoes."

"I like to go barefoot in summer," I replied.

"Man, that really must have hurt."

"It's okay. I'm fine," I assured him. Frankly, the pain had ceased the instant I laid eyes on his twinkling ones. Jaxon's name suited him to a T. He was this happy-go-lucky babe whose smile illuminated the night sky better than any tiki torch ever could.

"I'm sorry. I didn't get your name?"

"My name is Shana."

"Hey, Jax, where have you been?" a voice beckoned.

"Joel," Jaxon greeted. "I was just talking to Shana here."

My heart stopped. I couldn't believe it. I was actually standing in the presence of Joel.

"You look familiar," Joel said with a look of curiosity. "Have we met before?"

"No, I don't believe so."

"Didn't you used to come into the record store at the mall with your friend?" he pressed on.

"Yes," I replied hesitantly. *Did we used to come to the mall, he asked?* Duh, only every weekend for two years. Not to mention, Lisa's unabashed lingering in the record store as I tagged along. Even though many years had elapsed since our puppy dog crushes at the mall, it seemed Joel had an excellent memory.

"I remember you coming in with a girl . . ." he continued.

"Yeah, that was my friend Lisa." Why was he persisting in this embarrassing walk down memory lane? If it had been up to me, we wouldn't have even entered into Joel's presence as he manned the cash register in the midst of various lovesick teenage girls. Seriously, how many ridiculous questions could a girl possibly ask, weekend after weekend, without making a single purchase? But that was just me, shy Shana. I felt most comfortable in the store when Joel wasn't working, even though he was a fox.

"Didn't she go by another name?" Joel inquired, bringing my wandering mind back to reality. "Didn't she go by the name of Martha?"

Barefoot and Buzzed

Oh my goodness. Lisa's sly alias hadn't worked after all! Luckily, after insisting that Lisa wasn't the infamous Martha, Joel shifted the conversation to a more pleasing subject.

"This party is kind of lame," he said. "Would you like to leave?"

"Sure, but what about your friend?" I hadn't noticed Jaxon had wandered off.

"Jax has a ride. Let's go," he replied.

"All right, just give me a minute to go tell my friends."

The following afternoon I couldn't wait to ring Lisa with the details of my unbelievable night.

Chapter 20

PLEASE TELL ME
THIS IS A DREAM . . .
I'D LIKE TO WAKE UP NOW!

"Hello?" Lisa answered in a groggy voice.

"Hi! Sorry. Did I wake you?" Not that I remotely cared. This news was too incredible to wait for beauty sleep.

"Yeah, I didn't get to sleep until six a.m.," she replied. "Can I call you back in a couple hours?" she asked in a soft, sleepy tone.

"I'm sorry, Lisa, but this news is just too terrific to wait. I gotta tell someone!"

"Wow, well it sounds important. What is it?"

"You won't believe who I got together with last night!" I exclaimed.

"Who?" she asked in a just-had-a-double-latte voice.

"You'll never guess!" After all, I wasn't about to blurt out the answer. That was half the fun.

"Joel," she guessed.

"How the heck did you guess?"

"I don't know. I just thought of him for some reason," she replied.

"I can't believe you would guess it was some guy we were gaga over, like, five years ago!" I said. "Just out of the blue. You spoiled all the fun." I pouted.

"I'm sorry, Shana. I don't know. Maybe I'm psychic," she said. "So, are you going to tell me the details?"

"I thought you'd never ask!"

"Now that you woke me up, yes, do tell!" she insisted.

"I just got home from his apartment. He lives down by the waterfront with his friend, and no he's not cute."

"Damn!"

"Yeah, but he does . . . wait. I'm getting ahead of myself." I caught my breath, "Anyway, we met last night at a party right up the street from my sister's place. He had this cute preppy friend named Jaxon with him. I wish you would've been there. Maybe the two of you could have hooked up," I said. "Anyway, so Joel suggested that we ditch his friend and head over to his apartment."

"Well, of course, he wanted to dispose of the competition and have you all to himself," she remarked.

"Oh, you know I never thought of that," I replied.

"Are you kidding, Shana? You're so beautiful. I'm sure he was worried that you would go for his friend instead."

"Maybe . . ." I hesitated. "So, do you think he'll call me?" I asked in my familiar desperate manner.

"He'd be a fool not to. You guys would make such a cute couple," she remarked. "Just promise me that you'll introduce me to his cute friend if you two start dating."

I'd Like to Wake Up Now!

"Of course I will," I exclaimed. "Oh, and Lisa?"

"Yes?"

"He knows you're Martha."

"What?" she questioned in that I-feel-like-such-a-jerk-you've-got-to-be-kidding-me voice.

All I could muster was a meek "Sorry" and quickly said goodbye. Now that I had filled her in on all the excitement, I would let her go back to sleep. I could meet up with her later at the espresso bar she worked at and fill her in on all the juicy details while I munched on way too many chocolate-covered espresso beans.

My encounter with Joel could have ended right there. A one-night stand or maybe several nonconsecutive one-night stands. That had become the pattern ever since I had lost my virginity. It wasn't what I wanted. What girl ever dreamed of growing up and being swept off her feet by prince charming for a night, or better yet, three whole weekends in a row. Like it or not, I was used to the routine, and why would this one-night stand with Joel be any different?

As the weeks passed by after my giddy early morning conversation with Lisa, it turned out that this time was different. Joel had called, and I quickly fell gaga over heels for him. After five long years since my first school dance, I actually had a boyfriend to call my own. God had answered my desperate plea. Not that I spent much time praying to God, aside from a nightly "Now I lay me down to sleep" prayer that I had held on to since childhood.

I had grown up attending church as a child, and even cried one morning when I was too sick to go to Sunday school, but that seemed like a lifetime ago, and somewhere in the back of my mind, I never stopped believing that God still existed, and in times of deep distress, I would cry out to Him. I truly believed in my heart that God answered my prayer for a boyfriend by sending Joel my way. I was desperate to stop throwing up, and I was sure that Joel would fill all those ugly places inside me. No more detestable purging. No more living in fear of being found out. Everything would be better now. My prince had finally arrived in his Jeep to take me away from it all . . .

Many months had passed since Joel had officially spoken the three words I had spent my life longing to hear. And at first, "I love you" was enough to quench my internal thirst. Until reality set in.

As did the twenty unwanted pounds I had acquired while sharing an apartment with Joel. Who knew that living with my boyfriend would turn out so bad, and worse yet, that I would be hiding my eating disorder with the bathroom fan on while Joel sat stoned, fully engrossed in front of the television? Not to place the blame on my boyfriend, but he had turned me on to pot in the evenings. It was how we passed our time, eating and watching television. It seemed like a wasted life to me.

Basically, I was just getting through the days, numbing myself along the way. I hated it and myself. I hated my manual labor job. I hated that I didn't have the modeling career I secretly dreamed of, and now I even loathed the boyfriend whom I had prayed for. I wanted out, but I was helpless. Too afraid to quit my job and chase after my dreams, and now too afraid to move out of Joel's apartment, going it alone. I felt stuck, practically paralyzed. This didn't stop me from threatening to leave Joel a million times. He didn't take me seriously after I cried wolf one too many times.

I eventually mustered up the nerve to dump Joel after we had a horrid fight over one of his friends that I'd flirted with.

I'd Like to Wake Up Now!

Joel exploded when he realized our behavior had gone on right underneath his nose. Sure, it was rotten of me to even flirt with his buddy, let alone take it to the next level. Which I came very close to doing, until Joel discovered our motives.

That was the fateful night we broke up, and I left our apartment for a weekend of refuge at Emily's house. This was where a crystal ball would have come in handy. Maybe I could have seen the cliff up ahead, the one I was about to cascade off.

By the end of our weekend breakup, I sought a reconciliation. I should have known better when a mysterious female rang our apartment asking for Joel. If that weren't enough to send out a red flag, I should have known better when I found that same mysterious female's telephone number in Joel's pocket.

Of course, he denied any involvement, and I was too scared to leave our sedated nest for the insecurity of life on my own. So I opted for that river called "De-Nile" and elected to cruise downstream. This seemed to work for a season, until I was abruptly thrown out of my cozy basket midstream. It happened just after our return from a two-week trip to California, a last-ditch attempt to salvage our relationship.

My nightmare began just after waking up in an empty bed. Joel had already left for work, and being that it was the weekend, I was enjoying a leisurely morning. Until I felt a burning sensation around my bikini line. A tan bikini line that, to my shock, was now marred with blisters. I had never felt so panicked in my life. I dialed my sister.

"Hi, it's me," I said.

"Hi, what's wrong? You don't sound good," she replied.

"I'm not. I woke up this morning with these things all over me." My voice quivered.

"Things? Where are these things?" she asked.

"They're all over my, well, you know. Down in the female area."

"You must have contracted an STD?" she said in a stunned voice.

"I'm freaking out!"

"Okay, just calm down. I'll come pick you up and take you to the doctor."

"All right, and hurry, please!" I urged.

In an instant Debbie arrived. Thank God I had her to call. I didn't know what was happening to me. I didn't feel like I had anyone else to confide in, and Joel was at work. She quickly rushed me to the doctor, and I waited for a diagnosis. It was the longest wait of my lifetime.

"The routine pregnancy test came back positive," the doctor stated. "Did you have any idea you were pregnant?"

"No," I replied.

"Is this a desired pregnancy?" he asked.

"Definitely not," I stated.

"Your insurance covers an abortion procedure, if that is the direction you would like to take," he informed me. "But you will have to wait until you are a few more weeks along."

"Okay," I replied bleakly.

"You also tested positive for genital herpes, a sexually transmitted disease. The lesions should subside within a week or two. A warm bath will help soothe the discomfort. There is no cure for this STD, and outbreaks could occur at any time. It's an unfortunate virus that many people live with," the doctor said. "Do you have any questions I can answer?"

"No," I replied numbly. It was the only word I could muster.

Debbie drove me to my apartment in silence. I didn't feel

like talking, but I sure had plenty to say to Joel. I was armed and ready to verbally lay hold of him the minute he walked in the door.

How could I have contracted a STD? Sure, I'd been promiscuous in the past, but the last two years had been complete monogamy on my part. Maybe it was payback for all those girls' nights out with Lisa, flirting incessantly with the cute guys at the bar.

I'd collected phone numbers, received calls at my work, and even planned tentative rendezvous, but that was the extent of my unfaithfulness. I never followed through with it. Who could blame me? I was incredibly lonely, and in my eyes, Joel was to blame. Countless nights I had fallen asleep in an empty bed while Joel partied with his friends till dawn. It wasn't that he hadn't invited me to tag along, but I'd rather have eaten dirt than spend endless hours with his bachelor friends. The highlight of their evening was kicking back on their sofa with a doobie in hand and the TV blaring in the background. Joel never made it home until the following morning, just about the time I was waking up. It was a dead-end relationship that I should have exited a long time ago. Now to make matters worse, I was pregnant with an STD! Oh yeah, was I ever ready to lay into him the moment he opened the door.

"Hi," Joel greeted me at the front door.

"Hey," I stated glumly.

"What's wrong?"

"Well, I went to the doctor to find out what the heck all these sores are that I woke up with this morning," I stated angrily.

"And what did you find out?"

"That I have herpes!"

"Herpes?" he echoed.

"Yes, and obviously I got it from you, because I haven't been with anyone else for the past two years!"

"I don't have herpes, so there's no way you got it from me," he replied.

"Well, who else could I have got it from?" I retorted.

"I don't know, but you didn't get it from me," he insisted.

Playing the blame game was useless. There was no way I was going to get any confession from Joel.

"I'm sure it was that tramp that you slept with. She probably has herpes and gave it to you." Why did I bother? Joel had barely confessed to his one-night romp in the backseat of his car with this girl. Actually, I had ignorantly found out from the girl's best friend at a club one night. I felt like an utter fool when she coyly replied, "Oh, I thought you knew."

It seemed that all his friends knew about his one-night stand, everyone except me. He played off the telephone call and phone number I'd found as an unreciprocated crush. Supposedly she wasn't pretty and had taken a liking to him the weekend we had called it quits. We broke up for two days, and he'd managed to sleep with some girl!

"Well, obviously you are just going to deny it, so there's no point in talking about it," I retorted. "And that's not all, I'm pregnant, too."

"You're pregnant?"

"Yes, and don't try to play this off like it's not your fault."

"Why did you stop taking the pill?" he questioned. "We've been together two years, and you never got pregnant. I don't know why you quit taking the pill!"

"I quit taking the pill because our relationship has been over for a long time. You are just too self-absorbed to notice," I replied.

I'd Like to Wake Up Now!

"You can't keep it," he insisted while I stormed off to the bedroom.

A few weeks later I sat with Joel in the lobby of the abortion clinic. When the nurse finally called my name, I stood up and followed her without looking back.

"Is that your boyfriend?" the nurse asked me.

"Yes," I replied.

"Would you like him to be with you during the procedure?" she asked.

"No. I'm fine, thanks," I replied. It wasn't that I had planned to exclude Joel during the abortion, but I did want him to take the initiative. For once I just hoped that he would insist on being by my side to comfort me. Heck, and if it wasn't too much to ask, that he would even hold my hand. After two years of shacking up with a self-centered man, I naively expected that such a dramatic event would stir up some sort of emotion in him.

So that was that. I went through the abortion without Joel by my side. Which was fitting, considering that our relationship had finally reached its last legs. Chapter closed. Lesson learned. A boyfriend isn't the cure for an eating disorder, and casual sex can have dire consequences!

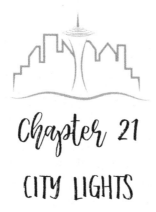

Chapter 21

CITY LIGHTS

It was a sunny, crisp day as I turned onto the tiny gravel alley-way that led to my new apartment in the city. It wasn't exactly the city, as in downtown Seattle, but it was even better! Just across Elliott Bay, a ten-minute drive from downtown, my new stomping grounds in West Seattle enjoyed a fun community with killer views of the Puget Sound and city skyline.

Restaurants, a theater, grocery stores, were all located within walking distance—more than a twenty-two-year-old newly single girl could want. It was far from the airport suburb I'd grown up in, and better yet, even farther from Joel's apartment. Two wasted years of arguing and television, cheesecake and pot! Finally, I was single and actually looking forward to it. At last I would prove Joel wrong and lose the twenty pounds of flab, the only thing I had to show for all that wasted time. I would regain my figure and snag a babe to call my own in this city. I was ready to fly solo, to soar up in the sky on my very own, for the first time in my life.

I easily climbed the four stairs to my tiny porch. I fumbled for my house key and swung the door open. I saw past the pooh-colored shag carpeting. In fact, I could overlook the tiny blah bedroom and the *don't turn around too quickly or you might hurt yourself* bathroom too. None of that mattered, because this was my very own apartment! I planned on spending all my time in the kitchen anyway, which would be decorated in shabby chic thrift store finds.

I envisioned myself sitting in the tiny dining alcove with a foamy latte in hand, staring out the bay window. Some might see the view as a nondescript gravel alley, but I saw it as hip city-girl living, with privacy to boot.

I checked the refrigerator. Knowing Sue, she surely left me a little apartment-warming treat. "Please, Sue," I whispered, "let there be something in the fridge!" Sure enough, I spied a large bottle of bubbly with a card attached to it. *Welcome, Shana, to your new home. Here's a little champagne to christen it with. I'm so happy for you! Love, Sue.*

What a wonderful friend I have. I watched the candles on my dining room table flicker and the bubbles dance in my champagne glass. If it weren't for Sue's generosity, I would still be living with Joel. Regardless of how many times I'd threatened to leave him, I would never have had the nerve to set out on my own.

But Sue was getting married, and she didn't need her apartment any longer. I had sat in this same apartment with Sue after she had finally found the nerve to leave her dead-end relationship.

I had shared in her joy, sitting in her new rental, drinking champagne and complaining about work. I loved getting together with Sue's friends after another monotonous day at the print shop.

City Lights

I had been happy to see Sue enjoying her newfound single life.

And to think, now this apartment was mine! While Sue was about to walk down the aisle, I was walking into her old apartment, the one I had admired. While Sue started fresh with her new husband, I started my big breakaway from Joel. Could life get any better?

Yes! I lost twenty pounds within a few weeks, and after over four years working at the print shop, my ship finally sailed in. It was a ship I had heard rumors about for weeks but didn't dare believe was true. Could the print shop really be closing its doors? I didn't want to get my hopes up. There was too much at stake. I had already spent so many years of adulthood making OK money at a job I hated. I had spent much of that time day-dreaming to pass the forty-hour workweek and binging during lunch to cope with my reality. After work I grabbed a copy of the latest tabloid and daydreamed that I was a celebrity plastered on the pages. It was the highlight of my day. Pathetic, I knew. I was stuck. A single girl with no marketable skills supporting myself, yet no matter how much I loathed my job, I was too frightened to leave my comfort zone. I didn't have the guts to quit.

The days crept by with my only hope being the coming weekend of reprieve, but the rumors continued on. My co-workers whispered about what they feared the most and I secretly hoped for. I downplayed my enthusiasm because they faced devastation. Some had worked at the company for many years during the prime of their lives. Others had families to support. But all I could think of was how much I wanted out.

The news came like a bright sunny day. Unfortunately for Sue, the one who delivered the news with tears in her eyes, it was more like a dark, thunderous downpour.

"Oh, Shana, have you heard?" she asked, red eyed.

"Heard what?" I questioned, trying to save face.

"They're closing the print shop. We're all out of a job."

"You're kidding, right?" I asked with dropped jaw. The news was too good to hope for. I didn't want to get excited until I knew it was true, and even then I would have to squeal in the privacy of my car.

"I know. Isn't it awful?" Sue shook her head in disbelief.

I wasn't a good liar, but that day I excelled at putting on a sour face around my grieving coworkers. Inside I jumped up and down with joy!

Drawing unemployment plus a small stash of cash in savings, my hopes were sky high as I embarked on my first weeks of waking when and if I pleased. "I will never throw up again," I assured myself with a sigh of relief. That crappy job at the print shop was why I had started purging in the first place, and being laid off would rid me of the shameful habit.

I was also thrilled about the new entrepreneurial business I'd contrived over a bag of weed one evening. I would sell restyled vintage clothes out of my apartment. I loved thrift stores and had frequented them since my teenage years. I also loved authentic clothing from the sixties and seventies. Occasionally I would sell some of my finds to a trendy clothing store downtown. The store wouldn't pay me much, but it was a little cash in my pocket and a sense of accomplishment. The only thing about vintage clothing was sometimes it was just a bit off, a little too dated. So I would alter it.

Once I found a somewhat hideous full-length peasant dress, lace and all. I liked the top, so I cropped it off at the waist and removed the long bell-bottom sleeves. I added some decorative trim, and voila, my new favorite summer shirt.

City Lights

Why waste all this talent? Why not market my redesigned clothes? I would sell my exclusive one-of-a-kind apparel at a high price tag by appointment only. I came up with a brand name, Cool Beans, and the catchiest slogan ever—"Reverse the signs of aging. Hang upside down in your Cool Beans!" Then I started sewing. The stitching part is where my business plan sort of flopped. I didn't own a sewing machine nor had the savvy to hire someone who did. Instead I hand sewed each new creation. It was clear that all my profit would be eaten up by endless hours of stitching.

The weeks sped by, and my dreams with them. Being an entrepreneur was too hard. I possessed the ideas but lacked the drive. My eating disorder returned with a vengeance, and it was difficult to attain my dreams when I spent much of my day throwing up and getting stoned.

After six months on unemployment, I felt the crunch financially. By the end of each month I was counting pocket change, even though my unemployment checks could have paid all my bills and provided some spending money too. If it weren't for the eating disorder burning a hole in my wallet—a habit I couldn't seem to kick—my only alternative was to move out of my apartment to a cheaper place. Did I really need an entire bedroom to myself? A studio would surely suffice.

My second rental was located in the hub of West Seattle, in the middle of the bustling Junction, a busy strip of town where the buses ran and people parked their cars and walked. In the Junction I could trade in my old CDs at the local record store, look for cool vintage clothes at two different thrift stores, buy my groceries, take my new cat to the vet, and grab some yummy Indian cuisine, all within walking distance.

I even experienced a close encounter with the one and only Eddie Vedder himself while browsing through an antique mall in the Junction. I couldn't believe my luck as I stole glances from the corner of my eye and pretended I wasn't madly in love with the famous rock star. That was also the day of my rude awakening. It seemed the rumors were true. Mr. Vedder had a significant other. How could it be? Didn't he realize I was to be his wife? Now there were two rock stars I could cross off my marriage list, Tommy Lee and Eddie Vedder! Oh well. I still had a cool studio in the Junction and hope for a bright future. At least until my unemployment checks ran out.

When life threw me a lemon in the form of a bicycle messenger named Jonathan, I didn't discard him. I made lemonade out of him, and boy did he hit the spot.

Chapter 22

SUPER-DUPER MODEL

But when the phone stopped ringing and my now empty glass of lemonade sat on the coffee table hopelessly waiting for a refill, I ended up with the worst case of lovesickness.

It started off all wonderful with butterflies fluttering around as I anticipated the next encounter with Mr. Wonderful or Mr. Take My Breath Away, I Could Inhale You Forever! Then the phone calls stopped, and I came down with the fever, the first telltale sign of lovesickness. After that came the heartache and the endless hours pleading with the phone. There was really no telling how long lovesickness would hang around. It could take weeks, months. (Heck, I even heard about a girl who had lovesickness for years.) No matter when I got it or how long it lasted, there was one thing for sure—*it stunk*!

Like a cool glass of lemonade in hand while swinging in a hammock on a hot summer day, Jonathan gave me a case of lovesickness that I'd never forget!

It all started when I answered an ad for "models wanted" at a clothing store in Seattle. Ever since junior high, I had secretly dreamed of being what I referred to as a "super-duper model." When I saw the ad, I picked up the phone next to my apartment's large open windows that overlooked the bustling Junction below. The store owner needed models for some print ads. The fact that he was not paying his models didn't concern me. I saw it as an opportunity to become famous in our city.

When I arrived, all a jitters, at the clothing store, I made small talk with a spunky girl named Nikki. She wasn't tall and lanky like supermodels, but rather petite and filled out in all the right places. What Nikki had that I truly envied was her attitude. She had no qualms perfecting her sultry pout for the owner as he snapped shot after shot of Nikki while a roomful of other wannabe models observed. Oh, how I wished I could be like Nikki, so free in front of the lens.

I was one of the last models left in the clothing store. I waited patiently for my turn in front of the camera. Unlike Nikki, I had popped some Valium, a.k.a. boldness in a bottle, to conquer my fear. I wanted to impress the owner with the ultimate shot that would end up in an ad. I wanted to beat out all the other models, even Nikki, regardless of how we'd hit it off as potential friends. Instead of feeling empowered behind the lens like the other girls seemed to be, I was shy. I couldn't do it sober.

A desperate girl seeking validation by means of fame, I thought if the world believed I was good enough, by plastering my image in full-color ads everywhere, that was all that mattered. All those years of slouching my way through school, wishing to be someone, all those wasted years would melt away. So what if I never hung out with the popular crowd or snagged the gorgeous guy in school that all the girls drooled over. None of that would matter anymore if I became a fashion model. I would finally be accepted and have the lifestyle I dreamed of. Because wasn't fame the single most validating thing there was?

I had *easy target* written across my forehead as the store owner directed his attention toward me and another male model, the only two left.

"I'm sorry. What was your name again?" asked Ricardo, the owner, as he threw an outfit my way.

"Shana," I replied, slightly intimidated and slightly high.

Ricardo was one of those self-confident people who aren't afraid to speak their minds, and oh, how those people intimidated me.

"All right, Shana, put that outfit on, and make it snappy. I've got to close up shop and get home." He pointed at his watch.

Not having a chance to look at the outfit, I said, "All right. Can you tell me where the changing room is?"

"Well, I guess if you're the shy type, you can change in the bathroom. But don't worry. I've seen it all."

Regardless if he'd seen it all, I changed in the confines of his closet-size restroom. After putting on the outfit, I perched next to the male model I would be posing with. Lo and behold, fear struck.

"All right, you both look great. Sergio, move a little closer to . . . ah . . . Shana?" Ricardo interrupted.

"Yes," I replied.

"Hon, you have to take the bra off. It's going to ruin the shot," he informed me.

"But my boobs will sag," I retorted. He surely didn't expect me to wear the black mesh top without a bra?

"Judging from my viewpoint, your breasts look great," Ricardo said. "Okay, so off with the bra so I can get home!"

Reluctantly I took my bra off, wishing I could disappear. Was this my dream? Even though the shirt was black and not completely see through, I felt uncomfortable. I was too insecure to put up a fuss, and desperate to see my dreams come true . . . for once.

After several clicks of his camera, the owner decided it was time to change clothes before we called it quits. I was relieved to change into a cute black skirt, complete with fishnet stockings and a full-coverage white top. I felt at ease, with another model by my side. This was what I'd always dreamed of, a real-live photo shoot.

Two weeks later, Ricardo called and asked if I'd be one of his models for a fashion show at a local club, to promote his clothing store. Even though, once again, there would be no pay, I jumped at the chance. Frantic to get my foot into the fashion industry, and I had finally been given my big break, pay or no pay.

When the night of the big fashion show arrived, I stood next to Nikki, trying to pretend I wasn't nervous. Luckily, Ricardo gave us all a glass of champagne while we waited backstage.

Nikki would go first, which made it a tad bit less intimidating. I had never walked down a runway before. What if I tripped? Too nervous to make small talk, I stood there adjusting the second outfit I had worn at the photo shoot. Nikki interrupted my jitters with a good-luck squeeze and a dazzling smile before disappearing behind the long black curtain.

I was next, and oh, how I hoped that I wouldn't fall. Without thinking, the instant I saw Nikki's smiling face again, I stepped onto the runway. My jitters melted away quicker than I could even say *runway*. I couldn't believe that I, shy Shana, maneuvered with such ease! Every eye in the dimly lit club was on me, and I felt like a million bucks. In fact, I was so confident under the bright lights of the stage that I was hesitant to leave. It was the first natural high I ever experienced, and I didn't want it to end.

After exiting the catwalk, I took my place next to Nikki, and all the models walked back onto the stage with the store's owner. Nikki and I then dashed for the changing room, since we unfortunately wouldn't be keeping the clothes.

I followed Nikki to the club's bar, where her husband stood waiting for her, grinning from ear to ear. He seemed quite proud of his young fashion-model wife.

"Shana, this is my husband, Trey, and his friend Jonathan," Nikki said. "Are you going to stay for a drink? There's an open bar for the models for an hour."

"In that case, yes," I replied with a smile.

Nikki's husband seemed just as nice as her. He had long brown hair and hazel eyes, like Nikki. He played in a band, and the two seemed like the perfect match. As for his friend Jonathan, the sugar hadn't been added to the lemonade yet. He was tall and lanky, with short caramel-colored hair and green eyes.

We gravitated to an intimate candlelit table to enjoy our drinks over some casual conversation. This was when I received my second natural high of the evening. I noticed that all the tables had a flyer promoting the clothing store, and I was elated to see my face in the middle of the flyer. The owner had chosen the shot of me and the male model to promote his clothing line, albeit on a photocopied flyer. But hey, a girl's gotta start somewhere, right?

I wasn't the only one who noticed my picture, for the first comment Nikki made was, "Wow. He used your picture on the flyer!"

"Yeah," I marveled, acting as if I had just noticed it myself, "and the picture isn't half bad."

"Didn't you know he was going to use it?" she asked with a curious look.

"No. He didn't say anything to me," I replied, unsure where Nikki was going with the question.

"He can't use your picture to advertise his clothing store without your permission," she stated indignantly. "I can't believe this guy. We're not even getting paid for this fashion show, and he has the nerve to plaster your picture on every table in this club."

I was secretly elated to have every patron staring at my face, but by the way Nikki acted, I didn't dare say a word.

"If I were you, I would make sure he doesn't use this photo in one of his print ads, without paying you a dime!" Nikki warned.

I knew Nikki was just looking out for my best interest, but seriously, I lost her after the words "print ad" spilled from her lips. While she fumed, I daydreamed of seeing my face all over Seattle. Could I seriously ever be so lucky? Surely I was on the brink of something big. Maybe my boring existence was coming to an end and a modeling career was actually within reach!

While I dreamed, Nikki continued to talk. "I only did the photo shoot so I could get free pictures to put in my portfolio. And his cheap ass doesn't even give me one picture! At the very least we should have been able to keep the clothes we wore tonight. Well, if he does use you in one of his ads without permission, sue him!" She laughed. "I would."

While Nikki was a sweet girl, it was evident she knew how to stand her ground. As the evening transpired, Nikki filled me in on all the juicy gossip of her life in LA as an aspiring actress.

She told me how difficult it was and that the competition was ruthless. To think it was a storybook ending, by Nikki's definition, was a joke. Then, as if that weren't enough to burst a starstruck girl's bubble, she revealed the misconception of dating a rock star.

"At first it was great. Traveling the world, flying in private jets, drinking champagne for breakfast!" She laughed, staring in the distance, as if reliving it. "But all the glimmer of living the high life in the Hollywood Hills came crashing down when I had to pry off these brazen women that would leech themselves to my boyfriend," she stated with her hands in the air to emphasize just how grueling it was to stand by her famous man. "Seriously, Shana, I just got so tired of having to either run from these crazy girls, or even worse, fight off a girl trying to make out with my boyfriend when I was standing right next to him! It was unbelievable and completely exhausting."

"Not worth it?"

"Not at all, at least not for me. I moved back up to Seattle, and shortly after that I met the love of my life." She smiled as she turned to look at her husband, who was engaged in a conversation with Jonathan, over the blare of the club's music.

After drink number three or four, not that I was counting, I warmed up to Jonathan, who had gradually transformed into a hot babe. My initial quick glance upon introduction had evolved with each drink, and poof, Jonathan was a babe I didn't want to take my eyes off of. Not to mention that with the club's music blaring, we both had to lean in close to hear each other talk.

I hung on Jonathan's every word while he filled me in on his dangerous occupation as a bicycle messenger on the busy streets of downtown Seattle. I was amazed by his tale of near-death experiences with moving vehicles, not to mention the endurance it required to scale the hilly terrain each day. It made sense why Jonathan was so lanky. He couldn't eat but a light lunch, and then it was back to his physical task of delivering on the congested streets. To top it off, he then rode his bike several miles uptown to the college district where he lived. He opened my eyes to a whole other world, one I had never realized existed.

I loved the way Jonathan grinned shyly when I mentioned him driving. "I don't drive. I ride."

He was strong physically, all man, but shy with the ladies. Just the kind of guy I could fall for and surely not the type who would stomp on my heart!

Back to reality. Nikki directed her attention away from her husband. "Shana, I guess we're going to take off now. Our sitter is probably wondering what's taking us so long. And truthfully," she said with a smile as she squeezed her husband's hand, "I miss our little girl."

"New moms!" Trey laughed. "But, yeah, Nikki's right. We'd better get going. Jonathan, you ready, man?" Trey shot him a sly grin, sensing the sparks flying between Jonathan and me. "Unless you want to stay awhile and catch a ride home with Shana?" Trey turned to me for a response.

"Trey, you're so rude!" Nikki snapped. "You brought Jonathan here, and now you want to make Shana take him home?" She shook her head. "I'm sorry, Shana. We'll take Jonathan home."

Thank goodness for mood lighting, because this beating around the bush was treading a fine line between comedic and downright embarrassing. It seemed that Nikki was the only one who hadn't a clue what was going on.

"It's okay, Nikki. I can drop Jonathan off on my way home," I replied.

"No, don't be crazy. It's totally out of your way," Nikki said.

"Uh, babe, why don't you just let Shana drop Jonathan off?" Trey hinted, nudging her in the side.

"Ouch! What are you poking me for?" she barked.

They made such a cute couple, even if Nikki had no idea that Jonathan and I didn't want the night to end.

"Oh, now I get it. And I thought I was the only one missing our little one!" She nudged Trey back in the ribs.

After a little coercion, Jonathan and I said our goodbyes to Nikki and Trey. In all fairness, it wasn't that Nikki was completely clueless. It was just that Jonathan had been transformed before my very eyes. He had turned into a sweet-'n'-tangy glass of lemonade, and Nikki had no idea that I had fallen for her husband's friend—and fall I did!

That evening, parked in front of Jonathan's rental house, I could have spent another twelve hours saying goodbye. And our first kiss! There was nothing sweeter than two sets of lips softly touching for the first time. I was sure Jonathan felt the same as I did when I finally pulled my car away.

Jonathan and I met up at many bars to start off our evenings together. We enjoyed each other's company and shared a mutual liking for microbrew, marijuana, and music. But we were both shy. An onlooker would surely shake their head in amazement, watching Jonathan and I each weekend. We started each encounter a mile away from each other. If we happened to be at his house, we sat on separate sofas. But once we had sipped a few drinks, we found ourselves lip locked again.

Jonathan was also a gentleman. No matter how many weekends in a row that I slept next to him in his bed, he never tried to take my clothes off. We were intimate to a point and only to that point.

My favorite thing about him was his new haircuts. His hair grew like a chia pet, and when he would get a fresh buzz cut, he looked like a babe. Our relationship never could get past the shy factor. Even though we would make out on his sofa with the soothing sounds of Nirvana's "Heart-Shaped Box" blaring on the stereo, in the morning it was awkward shyness all over again.

I was too scared to call him, so when the phone stopped ringing, the ice had melted, my lemonade was watered down, and our relationship had ceased to exist.

Jonathan inspired many pages in my journal. I was still unemployed and spent time alone in my apartment watching the cars in the Junction while I wrote my heart out. Pages and pages dedicated to Jonathan, with the journal's cover reading, *Occasional Moments of Happiness*. It was the only journal I had ever given a title.

Chapter 23

RUNNING AWAY FROM MYSELF

The worst night of my life started at a bar I frequented with friends. I naively thought it was OK to talk to any guy with a smile on my face. It was my trademark, a huge smile, often accompanied with a major buzz. What I didn't realize was that my happy-go-lucky-buzzed-girl demeanor might be perceived as an invitation by the opposite sex.

It was a common problem, and this night at the bar was no different. I always made small talk with a man, Jake, who worked there and also happened to be a part-time actor. When he hinted about a cast party, I took the bait, though I had no interest in Jake. If the two of us were on a deserted island together, I would construct a raft and try my odds out at sea. What was probably perceived as interest on my part was actually a young starstruck girl wanting to mingle with celebrities. When the invitation came, I agreed to attend the party with my much older date. In my mind it was never a date.

With stars in my eyes, I closed my apartment door, wearing the cutest nineties grunge-girl outfit I owned and stood on the sidewalk to be picked up. I couldn't wait to get to the invitation only party and catch a buzz. My quest was to meet a babe in the industry who would whisk me away from my boring life of unemployment and addiction, to a life of red-carpet premieres and mansions. All those years at the print shop had cultivated vivid daydreams that I was anxious to make come true. Otherwise, my life would be completely wasted. I had to use the looks that God gave me to make something of my life, since that was the only asset I possessed.

When we arrived at the party, I was extremely disappointed by the dismal showing. The few celebrities there hung out in their own cliques. So I did what I usually did when uncomfortable at a party—I drank. I was really skinny, drinking on an empty stomach, trying to feel comfortable. It didn't take long to realize the party was a bust, so just shy of an hour from our arrival, we made our exit.

Instead of taking me home, Jake took me out on the town. His side of town, that was. The bars he took me to were ones I had never been in and were filled with people I didn't know. My friends and I were into the grunge scene.

After at least three bars and who knows how much beer, my "date" said we should call it a night. Like the perfect predator, he took me to his house to sleep it off.

I woke with a dry mouth and an incredible headache. Unfortunately, I was not in my funky little studio overlooking the Junction. No, I was in an old and unfamiliar house. Dingy and cluttered. The word "pack rat" came to mind.

Opening my eyes and realizing that Jake lay next to me about stopped my heart. Not only was I lying in this man's bed, somehow my black tights had ended up around my ankles.

"Good morning," he greeted me with a smile.

"Why am I at your house? What happened?" I demanded.

"Nothing. You were pretty drunk, so I brought you back to my house."

"What happened? Why are my tights off?"

"Nothing happened," he assured me. "We were just messing around a little . . ." He hesitated.

I can't believe this is happening to me. "I want to go home, now!"

"Sure, we'll leave right now," he replied meekly.

I sat in silence for the duration of the car ride. All I wanted to do was escape this man's presence and forget the night ever happened.

As we approached my apartment, I flung open the door before his car came to a complete stop. Not looking back, I slammed the door with hatred and ran for the sanctuary of my studio.

"Shana, are you going to be okay?" he asked from his open car window. "Nothing happened."

This final plea was interrupted as I disappeared into the foyer of my apartment building and ran up the flight of stairs. Once inside I drew up a hot, sudsy bath to soak away my misery. Unfortunately, every candle in my house, along with K. D. Lang's *Ingénue* album, couldn't take away my mental anguish.

"You're going be okay, Shana," I whispered. "Just sleep it off." The walls closed in on me. I reached into the medicine cabinet and took out two sleeping pills.

The following morning I awoke to the same four walls and pit of despair, a sinking feeling I had never experienced before.

I decided I needed to escape my apartment. Maybe a little

fresh air would help clear out the crud in my mind.

I walked briskly through the Junction that Sunday morning. My feet came to an abrupt halt in front of a church. I had admired this beautiful brick church on many outings. It was a favorite of mine, with its lovely archway entrance and mounted lanterns, but on this morning the church's exterior meant nothing to me. I needed much more than stunning architecture. I needed God. Maybe He could take away this sinking feeling of despair that was so awful, I could taste it in my mouth.

Hesitantly, I opened the huge church door and snuck into a back-row pew. My entrance didn't go unnoticed as the hushed congregation turned to see who was late. *Thank goodness the church is dimly lit,* I thought, wondering how I could make a speedy exit. Trying to seek comfort in this church had been a big mistake. I was ready to leave the minute I sat down. I was out of place. I didn't belong there. I was a party girl who had screwed up my life with one too many parties. It seemed like a lifetime till I mustered up the nerve to sneak past the usher guarding the exit door.

I wanted to run away from myself, but how in the world could I run away from me?

I had plenty of time to ponder life's letdowns as I packed my belongings. I was moving. But this time it wouldn't be down the street. I would move to the east side of Seattle in an attempt to escape my mess of a life, which I had screwed up single handedly.

Being lovesick over Jonathan now seemed to be the least of my troubles. I had already learned the art of fishing for pocket change. Now I was literally counting pennies by the end of each week's unemployment check, I threw up in excess of four times a day. On a good day I consumed nonfat lattes that I made on my small espresso machine, Granny Smith apples, and white rice drenched in soy sauce. On those days I walked five miles and capped another lonely night off with a few beers.

Bad days were a shameful, familiar scenario of spending the bulk of my unemployment check on beer, food, and pot, with the majority going to my addiction to food. As if that weren't enough baggage for a twenty-four-year-old girl, I carried a lingering sick-to-my-stomach feeling as I attempted to push the memory of "that night" out of my mind. I couldn't erase the scene, and my only viable solution was to move far away from the memory.

Chapter 24

GROOVY SUMMER PAD

"Wow, I'm impressed, Matt!" a woman exclaimed as she quickly grabbed a kitchen towel to dry off her damp hands. Matt, my tour guide, and I had just entered the kitchen of the two-story groovy summer pad I would soon be calling home.

It hadn't taken long to make my decision after a five-minute tour of the lofty, rundown house. Cobwebs and all, I was willing to look past things that could be eradicated with a mop and disinfectant. I focused on the view of Lake Washington, the sprawling blackberry bushes in the driveway, and the cute little herb garden someone had planted right outside the kitchen door.

"Hi, I'm Sofia, but you can call me Sofie," she said, extending her thin olive-skinned hand.

"This is Shana. She's going to be renting the room," Matt replied with a wide grin.

Matt, my glam-meets-grunge-rocker new roommate, was well aware of Sofie's outnumbered status. She was the only female in the house. At a ratio of four to one, not including her male cat, the odds were finally changing in her favor.

"It's nice to meet you, Shana," she said with a warm smile. "I thought for sure Matt was scaring all the female applicants away."

"Excuse me, Sofia, but the last female vacated because of your cooking," Matt teased.

This remark brought instantaneous laughter from Sofie, causing her to double over as she gestured to the garlic press in her hand.

"The smell of my cooking does not inflict grown women with pain," Sofie replied, trying to keep a straight face.

I was clueless at the inside joke. I smiled, directing my attention to the hummus Sofie was stirring. The cutting board in front of her held fresh vegetables, and she poured olive oil into her bowl of ingredients. My eyes darted like a ping-pong game from Sofie's tall, lanky frame to her never-ending bottle of olive oil.

"You're probably wondering what we're laughing about," Matt said, pulling me out of my calorie-counting trance. "The last female roommate here constantly complained about Sofia's cooking. She said that she got a migraine every time Sofia got near the kitchen."

It seemed that Matt liked to tease Sofie, and from the looks of it, she didn't mind. They both appeared to be laid back, hence the title Matt had chosen for the ad, "groovy summer pad." It was just what I needed, a breath of fresh, laid-back summer air near an enormous lake. It was far from the memories that my studio in the Junction conjured up.

I couldn't wait for the change, and to have a female roommate to talk with seemed all the better. No more hanging out in my apartment alone, thinking way too much.

"Sorry to run, but I have band practice." Matt said. "And, Sofie, please try not to scare our new roommate away."

"Funny you should say that," Sofie retorted. "I was just about to ask Shana if she would like to stay for lunch." She laughed, motioning to the fresh assortment of raw vegan cuisine.

Saying our goodbyes, I turned toward Sofie. "I'd love to have lunch. All I had was a latte," I replied, taking a seat at the dining room table.

"Oh, a true Seattleite!"

"What about you? Did you grow up here?"

"No, I'm from the East Coast. But it was love at first sight the first time I saw Seattle. The streets sparkled. They were so clean," she said, smiling.

"Wow, that's one way to look at the rain. I guess I don't appreciate it because I've lived here my whole life," I replied.

"And how long is that? Eighteen years?" Sofie teased.

"Actually, I just turned twenty-four. How about you?"

"I'll be forty next year," she stated proudly.

"You've got to be kidding me! You don't have any wrinkles, and you're so hip!"

Sofie had the most beautiful olive skin. She wore no make-up. She didn't need it; she had dark lashes and brown eyes that stood out all by themselves. Her long brown hair was in dreads, which she wore atop her head in a large hair band. Pebbles meets hip Rastafarian chick was my impression. She also wore long cotton men's pajama pants with chunky sandals and a T-shirt. She had her own style, and I found her intriguing.

"I think slumber keeps a woman youthful. I take a nap with my cat every afternoon," Sofie confided, passing me a large ceramic platter filled with fresh hummus, tabbouleh salad, and salsa. The aroma permeated the room, and I felt as if I had been swept away to a different country.

"Well, whatever your secret is, I hope I look that good when I'm thirty-nine," I replied.

As the summer heat intensified, so did my friendship with Sofie. Not only did I have a new friend to hang out with, I had a mentor teaching me holistic nutrition. Her approach was simple, her lifestyle laid out before me. And the best thing? She knew how to make use of a teachable moment with humility. Even when I offered her a cup of instant sugar-free artificially flavored coffee.

She smiled, directing me to the back of the label.

"I do not consume anything I can't read."

"Interesting," I said, taking note of the ingredients for the first time. "The only thing I ever look for is fat content."

With an enthusiastic smile, Sofie asked, "Do you like blackberry smoothies?"

"I've never had one, but it sounds delicious!"

Turning on her bare feet, Sofie directed me past her tiny herb garden to the blackberry bushes next to the garage. With colander in hand, we picked berries until our fingertips had turned a deep purple.

"I love the red ones," I said. "They're sour."

Back in the kitchen, Sophie brushed tiny pebbles off the bottom of her feet, then showed me how to make a blackberry smoothie. As I sipped the icy beverage, I all but forgot about my instant coffee waiting patiently on the counter.

"Bon appétit!" She raised her decorative glass for a toast.

Our pad was a block up from Lake Washington, in one of the many picturesque communities surrounding the lake.

Groovy Summer Pad

My new stomping grounds were a favorite spot for cyclists and joggers. Many rode in from miles away to weave through long stretches of lakefront with unobstructed views. Countless homes were perched on hills so steep one could almost fall backward while walking up. It was great for the glutes, especially considering my only mode of transportation were my legs. I had sold my car shortly after moving closer to the city. Why did I need a car when I could take the bus or walk? At least that is what I assured myself. Even though deep down, I knew it was the eating disorder I battled. No matter where I lived, it just wouldn't seem to go away.

Some of the best spots in my new neighborhood were tucked away, mere feet off the beaten path. These secluded parks were full of old-growth trees that intertwined overhead to form a natural canopy. They came in handy when a tepid summer rain snuck up on me during one of my afternoon hikes. Afterward, the peaceful scent of evergreens permeated the air.

Still unemployed, I walked for miles each day that summer. Every afternoon I would grab my favorite woven bag—which my parents had picked up on their trip to Africa—slinging one leather strap over each shoulder to form a makeshift backpack. With the Beastie Boys blaring through my headphones and a fresh-packed pipe for the road, I was off on another stoned adventure without a care in the world.

Some afternoons Sofie would accompany me across the floating bridge to a waterside park or down past the neighborhood watering hole, where schoolchildren swam all summer long. More often than not, I traveled solo, while Sofie took her midday nap.

In the evening, Sofie and I would take an occasional jaunt on four wheels. Sometimes we'd stop at the local co-op, Sofie's favorite place to shop. I was enamored the first time I stepped into the organic marketplace. Our first stop was the bulk-food aisle, which housed a hundred different dry goods in a vast assortment of transparent bins. Who knew the infinite possibilities one could create with a large scooper and some water? I'd grown up on sugar-coated cereal, fast-food lunches, and home-fried dinners. My eyes were like saucers the first day at the co-op. I was in an overzealous frenzy with a basketful of grains, lentils, and spices.

Sofie was taken aback as she observed my compulsiveness. "Are you stocking up for winter?"

"No." I took note of Sofie's empty basket.

"How many nonperishable items can you consume in a week?" she asked with wide eyes.

"I'm not exactly sure, but I'll tell you what," I began, gesturing for her to hand me another bag. "I had no idea you could make a burger without meat! Is that possible?" I scanned the bin label.

As if Sofie was contemplating whether or not she'd just stepped into a twilight zone, she calmly asked, "You've never been to a natural-food market, have you?"

"Precisely!"

"Ohh . . ." Sofie nodded, as if it was all finally making sense.

"That's right. You've created a monster!"

"I can see that, and we haven't even gone down the produce aisle yet."

When we weren't shopping for groceries, Sofie and I often hit up a local thrift store. It was there that I witnessed my new friend handpick unlikely ensembles, yet exit the dressing room looking like a dream.

Groovy Summer Pad

"How in the world can you combine two completely different patterns and look so great?"

"You want to know the secret?" Sofie replied with an enticing smile.

"Yes." I hung on her every word.

"The patterns don't have to match. The colors do."

"Hmm, interesting," I agreed, perceiving that Sofie could wear a gunnysack and look great.

Of all the firsts I experienced that summer with Sofie, including a failed attempt at piercing our bellies with a safety pin, my favorite was our trips to the Ethiopian restaurant near our house.

The spicy veggie combo accompanied with fermented flat bread was her go-to meal. On any given day, this cozy family owned restaurant was sprinkled with an eclectic mix of Seattle-ites, all savoring the exotic cuisine.

I was thoroughly convinced that my taste buds would have missed out terribly if it hadn't been for Sofie.

Chapter 25

PRETTY MODEL

*E*ven though my first attempt to be plastered all over Seattle, posing for Ricardo's clothing store had fizzled, I was still hopeful. A local radio station had announced they were searching for several girls to represent them. The winning contestants would carry the prestigious title of Rock Girl. There would be lots of public appearances and promotional events—even autograph signings!

The following day I was at the post office bright and early to mail my entry to the radio station. During my short stint working for Ricardo, I had been introduced to a middle-aged photographer named Paul. He was tall and skinny with wild jet-black hair. I had Paul to thank for landing me my first paid modeling job. It wasn't much, enough to buy a shopping cart full of groceries, but it was significant in my world. Unfortunately, in the end, the owner of the clothing store selected his wife to represent his company.

The next day, Paul took me down to the arboretum, dockside, for a photoshoot. It was my consolation prize. No tears were shed on my part though. The final result was the cutest picture I had ever seen of myself. I wore a sleeveless black dress that hugged my lean frame, complete with black tights and shoes. I was the epitome of Miss Grunge America, all smiles with my long dark hair framed around my face. If it weren't for Paul, I wouldn't have had a picture to send to the station.

In an uncharacteristic move on my part, I was so excited about the prospect that I told Melinda and Preston over a twelve-pack one evening at their apartment.

"Guess what, guys!" I set down my beer bottle.

"What?" they asked in unison.

"I'm gonna be a Rock Girl," I stated confidently.

"Hematite. Malachite. Carnelian . . ." Preston mused aloud.

"You know I'm not talking about precious stones!" I slapped him on the arm.

"She's talking about the radio station contest," Melinda pipped in.

"The calendar girls?" Preston cocked one eyebrow.

"I don't know about the whole 'calendar girl' thing, but I do know they represent the station at major events around the city," I said. "Don't you think it sounds fun?"

"What I think, Nana, is you're going to need a new wardrobe," Preston hinted.

"From Fredricks of Hollywood." Melinda rolled her eyes.

"You might want to supplement your income. How much are you making on unemployment, Nana?" Preston asked.

"Preston Allen, I'm livin' off pocket change! Why do you ask?" I snapped.

"You're definitely in trouble now. She called you by your full name." Melinda locked eyes with Preston.

"Sorry, Nana. I know it sucks to be unemployed. But in

all seriousness, I hear Fredricks of Hollywood can get *pretty* pricey." He chuckled.

"That's the last time I tell you anything!" I bopped him on the arm again.

"You know I'm kidding. We wish you the best of luck," Preston assured.

"Melinda, I don't know how you put up with him." I sighed, picking up my beer bottle.

Later, I sat in my room sheltered from the late-afternoon heat with the radio on and my door closed. Soon the moment I'd been waiting for would happen. My name would be announced live. I would be crowned a Rock Girl! My heart raced in anticipation. What would it feel like to win? In the grand scheme of life, that was. To be chosen. Not like PE class, where I was always passed over, or more accurately, purposely avoided. What would it feel like to stomp on all the broken dreams and rejection of my past in triumph and finally be deemed good enough?

I stared at my Smurf wind-up clock ticking away on my dresser. Time stood still. After much anticipation, the first name was announced, then the second. I chewed my nails. *Please let my name be next.* The third, the fourth, the fifth. I laced my fingers together behind my back and paced the room. *A Rock Girl needs to have nails!* A sea of names were announced—Becky . . . Annabel . . . Stacey. But not mine. I hadn't been chosen. I wasn't good enough.

I boarded a bus near my house, destination unknown. With music blaring through my headphones, I sat at a window seat. I stared out at the lovely view as the bus weaved along the lake. It was evening time, and the daily commuters were already at home eating dinner. For most of the ride, it was just me and the bus driver announcing stops. I tried to mend the wounds of my broken heart by tuning out the world.

Why had I been foolish enough to tell Melinda and Preston? As I blankly stared at my passing surroundings, I recalled an event in grade school. An unpopular boy had invited the whole class to his house for a juice and cookies party. There was a dance contest. I danced my butt off in an effort to win. Even though I wasn't popular, neither was the boy hosting the party. For once, it felt like an even playing field. But I didn't win. I was shocked. I'd really thought I'd had a chance. This memory left a lasting impression. It's best not to confide my hopes and dreams to others—they might not come true. Rather, better to keep things a secret and not feel like a fool.

I rode that bus for well over an hour when it finally looped back to the same stop I had boarded at. I exited the bus, packed away my dreams, and returned to my groovy summer pad.

Model

Oh pretty model, as you start to pose
You better look perfect, baby, or you won't get chose.
Oh pretty model, you didn't get the prize;
Poor lonely model with the tears in her eyes.

Chapter 26

A CUP OF CHAMOMILE TEA

As the summer wound down, so did my finances. I needed a job, and quick.

After spending a week house-sitting at my parents', I returned to a pitch-dark and chilly summer pad. "Autumn is just around the corner," I said, wondering where everyone was.

For the first time in months, I needed a warm sweater, but first I had to find one. Somewhere between my navy polyester flares and black slip that I wore as a minidress, I found a thick, clingy knit.

Perfect! I thought, walking toward the living room. *If only the rest of my life fit as snug and toasty as this sweater.* I noticed the moon illuminating the night sky.

From the living room's large windows, I could see forever. The midnight blue waters of Lake Washington danced around the twinkling lights of Mercer Island in the distance. The perfect setting for contemplating one's life.

The large, rundown house was silent. Not a roommate in sight, except a sound in the distance. Voices! But I thought no one was home.

I stood there motionless, slowly turning my head, trying to discern where the curious sound was coming from. I noticed the side living room door that was only used to access the deck. With much trepidation, I tiptoed to the door to investigate.

The voices grew stronger as I stepped outside onto the large open deck that overlooked the yard below. In the distance, under the moonlight, I saw flickering candlelight and people chanting.

I ventured out farther to the deck's ledge. Several people in the yard below were dressed in long hooded robes. I couldn't discern the faces, except that of my roommate, Damien, the most elusive of the three male roommates. He had offered me a book about his religion a few weeks before. Curiosity had gotten the best of me.

For the first time in my life, I'd come in contact with people who didn't believe in the God of Christianity, the only God I'd ever known, although my knowledge was limited. Somewhere between "Jesus Loves Me" and becoming a teenager, I'd forgotten everything I'd ever learned about God in Sunday school.

The night Damien gave me the book, I had just finished watching a movie with a couple of my male roommates. In my stoned stupor, I accepted it, wondering what else the world had to offer. I proceeded upstairs to my bedroom and set the book on my nightstand. I would read it another day. Just before sunrise, I awoke from a nightmare. My heart was pounding out of my chest. I sat up in my bed and recalled the dream. I was in total darkness, surrounded by a bone-chilling presence. I couldn't see anyone or anything, but I could feel this unseen realm. They were closing in on me, and there was no way of escape. I cried out, "Jesus!" It was the only word I uttered in my dream.

A Cup of Chamomile Tea

I took one look at the book Damien had loaned me, still lying on my nightstand. I knew I had to get it out of my room and back to its rightful owner. Unread, I wasted no time. I tiptoed down the stairs at the break of dawn and returned the book while he was fast asleep.

That was the extent of my exploration into alternative religions. I felt like God had drawn a line in the sand that night, a line that I was not to try and cross again. It was my nightmarish wake-up call, and I was so thankful for it.

On the deck that evening with the dream fresh in my mind, I took one last glance at my roommate in the yard below. Damien stood with the others. The full moon shone down on them. He was fully engrossed in something I dared not look upon any longer.

I slipped back into the house, sensing my roommate was caught up in something very wrong.

"You look sad," Sofie noted as I entered our cozy kitchen the following morning.

I quickly grabbed my usual spot atop the counter, with my legs dangling over the side. Sofie looked beautiful, as usual, not a stitch of makeup on.

"I'm a little bummed." I found it hard to muster up a smile.

Sofie and I were in the same boat. We had both enjoyed a lazy summer and were in need of a job.

Sofie set her teacup down and gave me her full attention. It was that time again. The time I would try to conceal what was bothering me. I had been elated just days earlier at a rekindled romance with Steve. Sofie, who had a boyfriend, was overjoyed to see I'd found somebody too. Only I knew that it was over already.

"Don't worry. I'm sure your mood will liven up once you find a job." She tried to cheer me up.

"I know. I just need to snap out of it."

"How about a cup of chamomile tea? It will calm your nerves."

"Maybe I should move back home," I blurted, jumping off the counter.

This out-of-the-blue statement took Sofie by surprise. Standing eyeball to eyeball, she looked at me intently. "Are you sure that's what you want to do?"

Through the dead silence, I replied, "No, but my finances are low and my options are slim. Considering my situation, I think it would be the smartest thing to do."

After a relaxed conversation over a warm cup of tea, Sofie and I concluded that moving back home was my best option. Sitting together at the dinette that overlooked her herb garden, we watched the September rain moisten the ground. The summer sun had turned into a foggy gray. We sat there listening to the pitter patter of raindrops.

With unspoken words, we exchanged warm smiles, knowing this would be the last cup of tea we would share together in our groovy summer pad.

I left the pad and headed twenty miles south to the home I'd grown up in. My old room had already been renovated into an office. The only visible reminder of my youth was the mid-eighties black carpeting I'd picked during my all-black stage. Not that I wanted to take up residence in my old room across the hall from my parents. It was already a humbling experience, being in my midtwenties and giving up my freedom to move back home, regardless of how temporary.

A Cup of Chamomile Tea

I set up shop in our family room, located at the far end of the house. I used my futon frame as a makeshift wall/wardrobe rack for my vast assortment of thrift store clothing and set the mattress on the plush carpet. The only thing left was to fire up the woodstove and call it a night. Life wasn't so bad. Things could always be worse, right?

Chapter 27

JIGSAW PUZZLES AND TV DINNERS

"What is that smell?" my mother questioned with a look of bewildered disgust. It was a crisp autumn evening, and she had just finished a walk, with my father trailing close behind.

"I don't smell anything." I arduously continued my workout.

"How long have you been working out?" she asked.

"About twenty minutes," I replied, short of breath.

With flared nostrils, my mother slowly approached me, sniffing all the way.

"What's wrong?" I hopped off my mother's stationary bike.

"Have you been cooking something?" she asked.

"No, I made some hummus, but that doesn't require any cooking," I replied.

"What did you put in it?" she asked with a suspicious glare.

"Boy, I feel like I'm being interrogated!" By this time my mother had already followed me into the kitchen to see with her own eyes what concoction I'd been cooking up. "I made it from scratch. Sofie taught me!" I proudly displayed my bowl of hummus. "And don't worry. I cleaned up my mess."

Viewing the immaculate countertop, my mom asked, "And the utensil on the counter?"

"The garlic press? Isn't it cool! I bought it a couple months ago." I beamed, proudly displaying my new best friend.

"Exactly how much garlic did you press?" Mom questioned with a stern look.

Thankfully, the phone rang, interrupting her interrogation. "Hello?" I answered.

"Shana, it's Sue."

"Hi, Sue. Just a sec. I'm headed to my room so I can hear you."

In the background I could hear my father ask my mother in a concerned tone, "Do you think something died underneath the house?"

"Sorry, Sue. I couldn't hear you that well. How have you been?"

"Great. Hey, I got a job for you if you're still looking."

"Are you kidding? I'm desperate for a job!"

"My cousin just moved here and is in need of a technical assistant."

"Ah, Sue," I uttered in disappointment. "That sounds like it requires a college degree."

"You'll be fine. Can you start tomorrow?"

"Sure, but I don't have a car," I replied.

"It's okay. He'll pick you up. Just listen for his horn."

"Will do! Thanks, Sue. You've saved my butt!"

"You're welcome. Just make sure you dress that butt of yours in some warm clothes. You'll be working outside, or did

I forget to mention that little detail?" She laughed.

"At this point I could care less if I sell ice cream in Alaska. I can't wait to tell my folks!"

"Anything I can do to help a friend."

"Sorry to rush, but I need to go check on my folks," I said.

"Is everything all right?"

"Oh, my parents are fine. I just found out that my mom has an aversion to garlic, especially when it's oozing out one's pores!" I laughed.

"Sounds like an inside joke. Call me tomorrow and tell me how your first day went."

"Of course I will, and thanks!"

***

"Hi!" I greeted my parents. It was another crisp fall night in the beautiful town of Sea-Tac. After a chilly wait at the bus stop and a long walk up the hill, I was more than thrilled to be inside my folk's toasty home. Especially considering that my new job was in the great outdoors, setting up and disassembling cones on the side of the road behind my boss's work truck—all day long. Yes, it felt good to be home.

"Long workday?" Mom asked over a piping-hot TV dinner. It seemed my mother had tired after years of cooking the family meal. She and my father now opted for a large veggie salad and whatever cuisine that could be heated in five minutes or less.

"Work ended hours ago. Actually I was at church. They have an evening service," I replied nonchalantly, quickly plopping down into an empty recliner. After a few short weeks, I'd grown accustomed to life back in the family nest. I enjoyed kicking back with my mother, watching TV and commenting on the latest Hollywood celeb's attire.

My dad was another story though. He was a great father, but I didn't understand his fascination with jigsaw puzzles. Night after night he could be found in the same spot, wearing his glasses.

"Shawn, would you come over here and tell me whether this piece is black or dark green?" he beckoned.

Jumping to my feet, I approached the card table my father sat at, complete with fold-out chair. I stood there slowly shaking my head. "Dad, they all look to be the same shade of blackish green."

"Thanks, Shawn," he replied, looking up briefly. "You were at church?"

"Yes. The big church down on the highway. It's great. I love it!"

"Isn't that the church your sister attends?" my mother asked.

"That's how I found out about it. The music is cool, and the pastor is really funny, and look, I even have a Bible now." I held it up proudly.

"That's really neat," my father said.

It had been over a decade since I'd attended church on a regular basis, and those memories were of utter boredom. Once I graduated from children's church, I had to attend church with the adults. I sat next to my mother, not having a clue what the pastor was talking about. In silence I would doodle, waiting for the service to end so we could go out to eat.

One of the restaurants we frequented sold books for avid readers like myself, but my favorite restaurant had been a buffet. They had the best hot apple crisp, which I'd topped with a ton of soft-serve ice cream.

By the age of twelve, old enough to stay home alone, I opt-ed out of attending church. I was enjoying my new freedom, with two less siblings in the house.

When I was fifteen, I was top dog. Three out of four kids had left the family nest, and I loved it. I could party the week-ends away with friends and wake up just about the same time my parents were returning from Sunday morning service. This went on for several years, my life of leisure.

The fact I was attending church with a shiny new Bible in hand must have been a shocker, yet my parents simply smiled and encouraged me.

The weeks passed, and I continued to attend church. I also read my Bible, even though I found it difficult to understand. I had a hunger for it. I wanted to know more.

Just weeks into this new journey, my desire to know more about God was granted. There, in a Wednesday night service, the pastor explained the concept of salvation. He said that we must be born again. I was perplexed. Wasn't growing up in a Christian home enough? Didn't this make me a Christian? It seemed the answer was no.

There, in a dimly lit sanctuary I sat alone, yet surrounded by many people. All eyes were fixed on the pastor as he softly called all those who wanted to accept Jesus as their Savior. One by one people stood and made their way down the aisle to the front of the church. The pastor greeted everyone with an encouraging smile while he continued to address the congrega-tion. He said no one was good enough to make it to heaven by their own effort. That Jesus died on the cross for every single person in this world. The words he spoke resonated inside me, as if God were calling me by name.

Without hesitation I stood to my feet. I joined so many others who felt the same way I did, that they needed Jesus too. We recited the sinner's prayer in unison, and afterward I met with a prayer partner.

I had accepted Jesus Christ as my Savior. The easy part was over. Now I was faced with a difficult choice. Would I give up the parties, the club scene, and my perpetual search for male companionship in all the wrong places? Would I give up the lifestyle I'd become accustomed to and follow after my Savior?

"Hi, long time no see," Melinda greeted me over the phone while I spent another evening hanging out in front of the television with my folks.

"Hey, how's it goin'?" I asked.

"Great!"

"Wow, sounds like you're in a good mood."

"Guess what?" she asked.

"You're getting married!" I blurted.

"All right, let's be realistic!" Melinda said.

"Um, okay, let's see . . ."

"Preston found a house for us!" she exclaimed with the enthusiasm of a Lotto winner.

"Really?" It had only been two months since they had decided to start looking for a place. "That was fast."

"Well, you don't sound too enthused," she commented.

"No. I'm just shocked it happened so quickly. Is it in West Seattle?" I asked, thinking there must be some sort of catch.

"Of course. You know Preston would never leave West Seattle." She laughed. "Anyway, we can go see it tomorrow after you get off work if you want."

"Of course I want to!"

"Good. For a minute there I thought you were backing out on us," she remarked.

"Are you kidding? Do you think I want to live with my parents forever?"

"Cool beans! I'm so excited. Can you borrow your parents' car and meet us at our apartment after you get off work?"

"I will be there with bells on," I confirmed, hanging up the phone. Once again freedom was knocking at my door. I would be living the young and single life, out on my own again. I had tasted this sweet life for several years, and then to have to abruptly move back home with my folks—how humbling. But the funny thing was, I had gotten used to living with my parents. Even though there was a bittersweet tinge to it all, my friends were calling. In fact, West Seattle was calling again, and I wasn't about to let my friends down.

The following day flew by as I anxiously awaited the viewing of our prospective rental. After meeting up with Melinda and Preston, we all piled into her car. It was just a short distance up the hill from Melinda and Preston's beachside apartment to what would, hopefully, be our new rental.

As we slowly approached the house, Melinda and I noted the quiet neighborhood setting. "So far so good!" I said.

Turning into the home's narrow driveway, Preston announced, "Here we are, ladies."

Whatever the house lacked in curb appeal, it more than made up for it with a garage, basketball court, swing set, and deck. I imagined how many cool barbeques we could have during the summer and the flowers we could plant in the yard. Until, that was, I discovered where my bedroom would be.

"Melinda, I thought you said it was a three-bedroom

house?" I questioned after viewing the entire first floor.

"Indeed it is," the landlord replied. "Don't worry, dear. We're just getting started. We've yet to see the downstairs rooms, fully equipped with washer and dryer." She smiled.

"Downstairs?" I nudged Melinda's tiny frame.

"Ouch!" She gave me a stern look. "What are you poking me for?"

"Ladies? Is everything all right?" questioned the homeowner.

"Yes." Melinda replied as she pinched my arm in her defense.

"All right then, shall we view the downstairs rooms?" She pointed toward the stairwell.

"Yes, ma'am, we're right behind you," Preston replied.

"Geez! You two hens!" he whispered with a perturbed look. "Could we save the bickering for later? If the two of you want to have a fistfight outside, let's wait until after we sign the lease!"

"But—" I interjected.

I was interrupted by Mrs. Landlady ascending back up the stairs she'd just gone down. "I thought you were all behind me. Don't worry. I will show you the backyard after we see the basement," she informed us.

"Yes, ma'am," Preston replied. "You'll have to excuse the ladies. They were just taking a look at the pantry. They love to cook," he added, not wanting to appear as if we were immature young adults playing house.

"Melinda, I told you, I don't do basements," I said in my most adamant hushed voice.

"It's not really a basement," she replied, grabbing my arm and ushering me down the stairs.

"Oh, great! We all made it," the landlord said, then began

her tour of the downstairs living area. "This is the family room, and here is bedroom number one. On the other side we have bedroom number two," she continued. "Now I assume you will be staying downstairs?" She directed her question my way.

"Yes," I replied, with a plastered-on smile.

After viewing the rental, the lady finally left us alone for a minute of decision-making. Preston asked, "So what do you ladies think?"

"Are you kidding?" Melinda replied.

"I know," Preston agreed. "I can see the Miata parked in the garage already."

"And where are we ever going to find rent this cheap, splitting it three ways?" Melinda questioned.

"I can see it now," Preston dreamed out loud. "I'll invite the guys over to shoot a few hoops, and you two hens can have a siesta on the patio."

"I know! Can you believe how big the deck is?" Melinda gestured, and in unison we all turned to look at it.

"What about you, Nana?" Preston asked. "You're pretty quiet."

"She doesn't do basements, Preston," Melinda replied.

"Oh, come on, Nana, you could get lost down there. You'll have so much space to yourself, not to mention the wall-to-wall carpet!"

Preston made it impossible for a person to be irritated in his presence. He'd coaxed a smile out of me.

"Well, are you going to come downstairs to kill the humongous spiders that lurk in basements?" I asked in a dramatic fashion.

"For you, anything, Nana," he replied.

"In that case, I guess the answer is yes. I mean, who could

say no to their very own spider catcher?"

"This calls for a group hug," Preston proclaimed.

"Roomies!" Melinda and I exclaimed in unison.

It was the start of the next chapter of my life. One that would begin with saying goodbye to my parents' and packing up everything I'd ever owned, again. Hopefully, it would be a more long-term residence. Once again I would be moving away from our airport suburb. No more watching TV with my folks in the evening. No more of my mom spraying air freshener to mask the smell of garlic or my dad asking me to discern various shades of puzzle pieces.

There would also be no more attending Wednesday night church. Instead I would tuck away my new Bible among my decorative trinkets and keepsakes. Who knew when I would pick my Bible up again and how much dust would it collect.

Chapter 28

ITALIAN LEATHER SHOES AND EUROPEAN COLOGNE

Snow

My man I will have in time to play in the snow.
A new home I have, a new life to go.
A few weeks I will wait, what it takes, but in time I just know
Together we'll be with love that will grow
Into the spring, we'll emerge all aglow,
Tumble in the grass, but first let in snow.
Winter lovers that snuggle together when it's cold,
Or just whenever, it's a pleasure, being together—
We're in love, or did you know?

"Ahh . . ." I sighed aloud. "Another lazy winter day. What shall I do?" I asked, ascending the stairwell to our kitchen. It was nearly noon, and I was still in my pajamas. From the large French doors that overlooked the backyard, I observed the melting snow. Because of the inclement weather, I'd received four weeks paid leave, but by the looks of the slushy mess outside, it seemed my vacation would soon be over.

I would have to pull on my trusty snowsuit, paired with my bright-orange vest. Unsightly? For sure! Nevertheless, the ensemble kept me piping hot out in the elements, as well as safe. It also beat doing jumping jacks to keep warm. Was I still thankful to Sue for saving my butt and getting me the job? Of course, but did I love the job? Definitely no.

"Yep, it looks like work is just around the corner," I confirmed with every drip that cascaded off the roof. Then turning my bare feet 180 degrees, I exclaimed, "This calls for a latte, double shot extra foamy!" This wasn't the life I'd imagined for myself, but nonetheless it was my life. A quick hit off my pipe for its numbing effects and caffeine to keep me going. Add mood music, and I was set!

On this day it was Tony Bennett's Christmas album, thanks to my roommate Preston's exquisite taste, but with all these externals, my life was still a far cry from what I'd dreamed it would be as a child.

In the fifth grade I'd imagined myself swept away by the cutest guy in school, living in a faraway land. Sometimes I'd envisioned a thatched-roof cottage in the middle of a forest.

Each morning I would awake to the sound of birds chirping at my open-shutter windows, and in the evening I would sweep the tiny cobblestone path leading to the cottage entrance.

Other days, I would be swept away to an ancient castle complete with drawbridge and moat. I would take long walks by day over the green mossy hills to watch the ocean waves crash against the rocky cliffs below.

By nightfall, I'd returned to the castle, illuminated by torches, lanterns, and candlelight.

Italian Leather Shoes and European Cologne

After supper, I would ascend the dark, flickering stairwell, my long velvet robe trailing in my wake. I would then retire to my sleeping quarters, lit up solely by the moon's light.

I was a dreamer. I had been one since I could remember, wishing my life was a fairy tale. And in my fairy tales I would be loved, happy, and secure. There would be no need for alcohol or drugs, and certainly not an eating disorder. No. In my daydreams I would have the perfect figure and be forever young and disciplined in every aspect of life.

In reality I was faced with the fact that I had, once again, a job I loathed. Yes, I had a generous, alcoholic boss who footed the bill after work for food and many cocktails at nice restaurants, but that, if anything, was a hindrance. Little did my boss know that after dropping me off at the house I rented with Melinda and Preston, I would immediately leave to go out in the bitter cold in search of food.

Still buzzed, I would walk several blocks through my neighborhood to the nearest convenience store. After selling my car, I had survived quite well on public transportation and hoofing it. It was an urbanite's way of life. But having to leave my warm rental on a cold winter night, that part I loathed, yet I was driven by this incredible force. Truly this eating disorder was controlling me, and like an obedient pet on a leash, my sickness led me as far as it needed to go in search of food.

Once I reached the store, I would load up on forbidden junk food, as much as I could get my frozen hands on. Then it was back to the chilly streets, where I would binge from a large paper bag that concealed my deeds. By the time I reached home, I'd already consumed the contents of the bag and disposed of the evidence. I wasn't a litterbug by nature, but bulimia had made me one, always careful to cover my trail.

233

To avoid my roommates, I would enter via the side door that led to my downstairs living area. There in my own private bathroom, I'd rid myself of every last morsel. Finishing off the binge with a hot shower, I returned to the land of the living, spending the rest of the evening upstairs with my roommates.

We watched TV together, then Melinda and I congregated in the kitchen. Although we rarely cooked, we spent many hours there talking. This hang-out time only occurred after my necessary binge though. Inside me was this need to release all the stress of the day, and to cope with frustrations I didn't know how to verbalize or control, with food. It was as if the entirety of letdowns were wrapped up in a delicious burrito, and I shoved them down bite by bite. My way of coping was unfortunate, but it was the only way I knew how. I hated it—oh, how I hated it—and I hated myself, but I was stuck, with no foreseeable way out.

By spring I had stopped working. It seemed my boss was in love with me, or so he said, and couldn't bear to see me day after day. I, on the other hand, was still pining over a short-lived winter romance with a tall, dark, handsome man. He'd had everything a girl could want: a gorgeous face, cool accent, and cologne that lingered even after he'd left the room, yet I'd known, deep down, I couldn't trust him with my heart. Feeling uneasy, I broke it off. Even though, all the while, I secretly wished he would come chasing after me. Yet instead it turned out he'd been chasing after a green card. To say that I had dated the most gorgeous guy would be a true statement, but if I couldn't trust him to be faithful, all those looks weren't worth it. But still, I was lovesick again, and oh, how I loathed being lovesick.

So I focused my attention on our backyard instead. Summer was just around the corner, and boyfriend or not, I wanted a cool place to hang out with friends. I enlisted Melinda to help me in my Operation Beautification Spring Project.

The first thing on our list was flowers, a must for any backyard. With Melinda by my side and shovels in hand, we braved all the creepy-crawlies that lurked in the earth's soil. It was our first attempt at gardening. We were novices with visions of wildflowers and sunflowers dancing in the night.

Number two on our list was a large hammock, which we attached to our deck.

Third, strategically placed tiki torches were sandwiched between the sunflowers.

Then a mai tai bar decorated with hand-cut and dried pampas grass, which I had snipped from a neighbor's yard under the cover of night. It would be the perfect summer hangout, just in time for my birthday.

"Hi, Melinda! You're looking way too comfortable," I said, plopping into a lounge chair on our deck. It seemed that Melinda had wasted no time breaking in our new hammock as she gently swayed back and forth. After a hard day's work, it was the perfect spot to soak up the warm afternoon rays.

"You're looking way too happy to be unemployed. Did you find a job?" Melinda asked, sitting up to make room for me.

"How'd you guess?" I said with a huge grin.

"Cool beans!" Melinda exclaimed. "This calls for a celebration!"

"Definitely," I agreed, "but we don't have any alcohol."

"We'll have iced lattes instead." Melinda jumped to her feet.

"Great idea!"

"Yeah, you can tell me all about your new job while you make them." Melinda laughed.

"Since I'm the one that landed the new job, shouldn't you be making the lattes?" I joked as we made our way to the kitchen.

"Only because you're so good at it," Melinda replied.

"Either that is a sincere compliment, or . . ."

"Or I just don't want to make them?"

"Exactly! So anyway, about my new job." I grabbed the milk from the fridge.

"Yes, do tell." Melinda took a seat at our kitchen table.

"So, the temp agency called me out of the blue yesterday, and I was totally happy because, as you know, I'd already quit my job at the deli."

"The deli that you worked at for three whole weeks just wasn't cuttin' it?" Melinda asked.

"Actually, I didn't mind so much slicing tomatoes. It was just waiting on the customers that I didn't like," I admitted.

"Yeah, if it weren't for those pesky customers . . ."

"I know. If it weren't for the customers, I could have retired there." I laughed, realizing how ridiculous I sounded.

"So, about the job?"

"Yes, the temp agency called in the nick of time and offered me indefinite employment at a bank downtown," I boasted. "Not to mention that it's a high rise with a view of Elliott Bay."

"And you could probably hitch a ride with Preston in the morning so you don't have to take the bus," she replied.

"That would be amazing! Riding in the Miata, with the top down!"

"Your hair all windblown," she added.

"Now it totally makes sense why women wore scarves in all those old movies," I said. "Anyway, there's more!"

"Wait. Before you say anything more, let's cheers!" She

raised her decorative crystal glass complete with blue umbrella straw. In unison, our glasses chimed.

"Here's to your new job with the cool view!" Melinda said.

"And here's to Preston's sporty new convertible!" I added. Then setting my glass on the kitchen table, I continued in a calm voice. "I met someone downtown today."

"Who'd you meet?" she whispered.

"His name is Francesco. He's Italian, and why are we whispering?"

"I don't know." She giggled.

"He just moved here from New York, Manhattan to be exact, and he works at a hotel downtown," I said, trying to sum him up in one breath.

"And what hotel does he work at?"

"Oh please, Melinda, you're not the only one who can read minds around here," I replied, rolling my eyes for effect.

"What?" she questioned innocently.

"I know what you're thinking, and no, he's not a bellhop at some shady establishment," I said sarcastically.

"Hey, I was never insinuating that the hotel wasn't nice," she replied in her defense.

"I'm just kidding, but seriously, it's a five-star hotel, and he works at the front desk."

"He checks people into their rooms."

"I don't know if he checks people in or if he's a concierge. He didn't elaborate, but who cares. He's a babe," I replied.

"What's this new obsession of yours with foreign men?" Melinda asked.

"I don't know. They're so exotic," I stated dreamily.

"Hmm . . ."

I could tell by Melinda's tone that she was concerned. After nine years of friendship, Melinda was well aware of how impulsive I was. I had moved several times since leaving the family nest, and I was already on my third job of the year. What could I say? In my defense, I loved the scenic roads of life and had all of the scrapes to prove it.

Melinda was just trying to protect me from myself basically. She knew me too well.

"He has an olive complexion and—"

"And dark-brown eyes, the kind a girl could get lost in?" she guessed.

"That too! But what I was going to say is, he has the cutest accent," I purred.

"Just be careful."

"I will," I agreed, trying to gloss over her concern with a smile. *Geez, she hasn't even met him and she already doesn't like him.*

"So when are you bringing him over?" she asked.

"Soon." I concealed my disappointment with a smile.

Why was I disappointed? I had just met a mature and distinguished import to spend the warm summer nights with. I could already picture us walking hand in hand along Alki Beach at twilight, barefoot, with the Seattle skyline illuminated in the distance. My perfect dream come true!

But Melinda's subtle apprehension had struck a chord of fear in me. We'd been friends since high school, nearly a decade, and if there was one thing I knew about her, she had killer instincts. Just like my mom, she could smell something fishy a mile away. I hoped that this time the trail wouldn't lead directly to my new man.

Chapter 29

TWO FERRIES PASSING IN THE NIGHT

"Hi, Melinda!" I greeted her from my favorite spot on the deck. She had just arrived home from work, and I was elated to be sharing the hammock with Francesco on a warm, breezy evening.

"Hello," Melinda said, noticing my guest swaying in step with me.

"Melinda, this is Francesco," I introduced.

"It's a pleasure to meet you," Francesco said, extending his hand for a formal introduction.

"Nice to meet you too," Melinda replied.

"We just got back from the beach. Would you like some fish 'n' chips?" I asked with the kind of grin that only a new romance could bring.

"No thanks. I'm going to wait for Preston to get home. We'll probably go get some pizza," she said.

"What is it?" I questioned, noticing the puzzled look on Melinda's face.

"Are you eating olives?" she asked.

"Yes, Francesco bought them at a market in the city. They're marinated in olive oil and garlic. You know I always hated olives, until today."

"Okay . . ." Melinda hesitated.

I knew what she was thinking. I could sense it from the moment I introduced her to Francesco. Melinda didn't like him, and frankly, I hated her for it. Oh, not *hate*. She was my dear friend, the one who'd stuck by my side through thick and thin. I just hated her impeccable judgement of character. It was as if her little radar detector was buzzing. *Run, Shana, he's not the right guy for you.* And that was what made me so mad.

Even so, I glossed over what I perceived as her disapproval. I told myself I didn't care, and why was it so wrong to want someone to hold me through the night, just like she had in Preston? I was tired of being alone, of various addictions being my sole comfort. I wanted to be happy too. Was that so much to ask? And I wasn't about to let Melinda spoil my budding relationship, whether she was right about Francesco or not.

Breaking the awkward silence, Melinda said, "I'm going to give Preston a call. It was nice meeting you, Francesco. You two enjoy your evening." Then turning toward the French doors, she disappeared into the house.

We swung gently, like two lovebirds, as the sun set. It was the perfect night. I could have sat there forever, but when I looked into Francesco's eyes, I knew he had more on his mind. "It's getting a little chilly. Shall we go inside?" He rubbed my arms to warm them up.

"Sure. I'll show you my room downstairs."

Once inside my bedroom, Francesco didn't waste any time. He never did. Since our first date, it was clear that our relationship was based on sex. That was never my motivation. But at least I had two strong arms holding me.

Francesco never spent the night. He seemed to always be in rush. It was as if he were going to turn into a pumpkin, and this night was no different. After what seemed like only an hour in my room, we walked hand in hand to the bus stop two blocks from my house. I slipped my arms inside his suit jacket and clung to him tightly while we waited. I had never dated anyone like Francesco before. He was so sophisticated, and he always smelled like expensive European cologne. Even though I had never seen the high-rise apartment he lived in, smack dab in the heart of downtown Seattle, I knew it must have been equally as charming as he was. I wished that Francesco could have held me there on the sidewalk forever.

The tender moment was interrupted by the glare of head-lights in the distance. The best part of my evening was now over. I stood silently and watched Francesco board the bus. He sat down in a window seat and waved goodbye with a dazzling smile on his tanned face. I walked briskly back to my house, feeling the chill of the night air. I would comfort myself with sweet dreams of my new man.

The following day I couldn't wait to get to work and chat with my new coworkers at the bank. We had a great time, the four of us girls, passing the day away with much conversation.

"So how did your date with that handsome man go?" Deidre asked with a curious smile.

"Yes, do tell," Ann added.

"You already had a date with the guy you met?" Joan asked in a surprised tone.

"They've had three. Not that I'm counting!" Deidre said.

"Geez, will you two ladies quit talking and let her get to the details." Ann rolled her eyes.

"It looks like someone had too many lattes, and it's only eleven o'clock," assessed our manager, Joan, staring directly at Ann. Being the youngest, Ann definitely had an abundance of energy and sassy remarks.

"For your information, I only had one latte. You ladies are just too old. I can't help it if I'm only twenty-one and still have an abundance of energy," she bragged.

"Oh, please, Ann, you're only four years younger than me," Deidre said in her demure voice that fit her petite frame so well.

"Yeah, whatever!" Ann replied, unfrazzled.

"So how was your date?" Deidre reiterated, ignoring Ann.

"It was great," I replied dreamily.

"Did he bring you flowers?" Joan asked, not waiting for an answer. "Oh, I remember when William used to bring me flowers," she continued as she strolled down memory lane. "He was so sweet, and shy too."

"Will you please let the lady talk!" Ann exclaimed.

"I'm sorry, Shana. I just love new romances and the feeling of being swept off your feet!" Joan gushed.

"And all the butterflies . . . there's nothing like it in the world." Deidre sighed.

"Enough gabbin', ladies. Let's cut to the chase. I don't have all day." Ann snapped her fingers. "Forget about the flowers. What restaurant did he take you to, and more importantly, how much did he spend?"

"He took me to a couple of restaurants down at the Pike Place Market. The first one was so cozy, like a little hideaway. Oh, and the view of the Sound was incredible, at twilight, my favorite time. After that we went to this really crowded Italian restaurant for a drink. It was dimly lit, with candles on all the tables." I tried to sum up all the details before lunch break.

"Oh, it sounds like a dream," Deidre cooed.

"Whatever. So are you going to call him, or are you the type who just waits for the phone to ring?" Ann asked, once again cutting to the chase.

"Geez, Ann," Joan remarked, "haven't you heard of chivalry?"

"Well, actually . . ." I hesitated. "I don't really have to worry about calling him since I don't have his number. He calls me."

"And what lady"—Deidre glared in Ann's direction—"calls a guy she just started dating? He is supposed to woo you, not the other way around."

"Deidre's right! He'll probably call you when you get home tonight. I'm sure he doesn't want to bother you at work," Joan assured me.

"Wait a minute, ladies. All this sappy romance stuff is messing with my hearing. Did you just say this guy didn't give you his number?" Ann asked with a smirk, directing her attention at me.

"Well, I mean, he didn't give it to me and I didn't ask. Besides, I don't call guys anyway. If he likes me, he'll call me," I replied, now on the defense. Of course, knowing Ann, she wasn't going to let this inquiry go.

"All right, so did he, by chance, give you any way of reaching him?" she asked, seemingly knowing my response.

"Well . . . I know where he works," I replied.

"He's got a girlfriend!" Ann blurted out, pointing her finger at me for added effect.

"Don't listen to Ann. She doesn't know anything," Joan replied.

"I can't believe you said that to her, Ann! You haven't even met him!" Deidre gave Ann a death stare. "Shana, don't pay any attention to Ann. Three years ago she was still in high school. She has no idea what she's talking about," Deidre said with a reassuring smile.

"Sticks and stones, ladies, sticks and stones. Listen, I know what I'm talking about." Ann stared at me like a detective. "What did you say his name is?"

"Francesco. He's Italian," I answered, knowing she would most likely use my response against me.

"Then I was wrong," she responded with a clever grin, as if she had something up her sleeveless dress.

"See!" Joan and Deidre exclaimed in unison.

"I told you she didn't know what she was talking about," Deidre glared at Ann.

"Actually, that's where you're mistaken." Ann fixed her eyes on Deidre. "I said I was wrong because I didn't have all the facts. He doesn't have a girlfriend—he has a wife. And Shana, you've just unwittingly become his mistress!" Ann snickered. "You ladies really need to lay off the romance novels and get a clue."

"Oh, Ann, go to lunch!" Joan exclaimed.

"Yeah, quit scaring her," Deidre barked. She defended me like a mother bear would her cubs.

"Bet you a hundred bucks!" Ann grabbed her designer handbag off the desk. "Well, I'd love to stay and chat, but it's lunchtime." She added, "Shana, its summertime. Check his ring finger for a tan line."

Two Ferries Passing in the Night

"Married?" I echoed with disbelief while I primped for my date with Francesco. "No way, that's just way too soap opera-ish," I reassured myself. *But maybe I should ask him.*

Shaking my head, I reasoned, "Am I seriously going to let a twenty-one-year-old girl ruin my brand-new relationship? Surely Ann doesn't have a clue! But then again, what if she's right?"

I took one last twirl in front of the mirror, quadruple checked my figure, and tried to push the worrisome thoughts out of my mind. There was no time to recheck my hair or worry whether Francesco was married. It was late. I needed to catch the bus or miss my date entirely. Which was another ugly reminder of what Ann had observed—he hadn't given me a number to reach him. I had two minutes to sprint three blocks or be a no-show for our date.

Once inside the bus, I would have plenty of time to resume my obsessing. *Is he? Isn't he?* By the time I reached the pig at Pike Place Market, a prominent meeting spot, I would have rehearsed the nasty little question I knew I had to ask. But first I had to catch that bus.

I stood next to Rachel the Pig on a somewhat chilly summer evening. In no time I had spotted Francesco's distinguished face among a slew of tourists, locals, and vendors. One could easily get lost in the sea of faces that crowded the sidewalks and cobblestone streets. But Francesco stuck out. His dark wavy hair was pulled back from his chiseled face. He had just gotten off work, still sporting a silk suit and Italian leather shoes.

Good thing I didn't wear jeans, I thought, catching his eye from a distance. He had a warm smile and luminous tan. Oh, how I hoped beyond hope that he wasn't married.

After a lingering hug and gentle kiss on the lips, Francesco and I walked hand in hand through the quaint little alleyways of the marketplace, past the espresso stands and tiny sidewalk restaurants, around the outdoor fountains and down the sweeping stairway that led to a waterfront park. The aroma of dozens of food vendors and fresh-cut flowers filled the air. The sound of drums could be heard in the distance. The smell of salty water wafting off the Puget Sound permeated the evening air. We were in the heart of downtown. Everything that Seattle had to offer encompassed us, yet it all seemed secondary to the simple touch of Francesco's hand.

It wasn't until dark had fallen and the city lights were already reflecting off the water that I mustered up the nerve to ask about Francesco's marital status. It was such a simple question, yet way out of my league.

I'd dated wannabe grunge rockers and bicycle messengers with buzz cuts and tattoos. I hung out in circles where the question of the week was, "Who's playing at what club?" We revered microbrew, blended cocktails, and the latest episode of *Friends*. We lived for the moment, and the last question on our minds was marriage. It was an elusive thing our parents had done, and our generation would probably do, eventually, someday.

I never fathomed that I would have to ask that question.

"Francesco?" I looked into his eyes.

"What is it? Are you still cold?" he asked.

"No. Your jacket is quite toasty. Sorry," I replied with a chuckle.

"There's no need to apologize," he said, taking me in his arms. "I would lend you my jacket anytime."

"Thanks," I replied, staring deep into his eyes once again.

Then as if Francesco could read my mind, he asked, "Is

something troubling you tonight? Please tell me what it is."

"Are you married?" I queried, amazed that the words actually fell from my lips. With my eyes fixed on Francesco and our arms still intertwined, I felt him gently release his grip.

Francesco's warm smile faded. The same smile that made me feel as if I were the only girl within a hundred-mile radius was replaced with silence. Still acknowledging my presence, he turned briefly away toward the moonlit waters of the Puget Sound. Then turning back, Francesco quietly replied, "Yes."

A huge sigh filled the air. It was the kind of sigh that precedes only the most solemn conversations. This time I turned away, staring out into the distance. There I noticed two ferries passing in the night. They were both illuminating the dark waters, yet each headed in an opposite direction, like the perfect depiction of Francesco and I, passing in the night.

He explained that his life was complicated and that he hadn't expected to meet such a wonderful girl like me.

I replied that under no circumstance would I ever date a married man. The conversation continued well into the night, back and forth like a ping-pong ball. The distance between us diminished with each word we spoke.

What am I doing? I questioned. This was the part where I was supposed to call him a jerk and go hop on the closest bus! Amazingly I found myself inching my way closer to Francesco. Staring intently into each other's eyes, our conversation was now only a gentle whisper. How had I become such a desperate girl? Weren't there enough single guys out there? Was I seriously going to continue dating a married man? This was not the Shana I knew, but then again, I had never been faced with this problem before.

My conscience was screaming, *Please reconsider what you're about to do! There is still enough time for you to walk away and catch the next bus home.* But I didn't listen. My need to be and feel loved overrode my conscience. Not that Francesco seriously loved me. Ann was right. I had unwittingly become his mistress, minus the penthouse and expensive gifts. Whether our relationship was based on sex or not, I couldn't resist his touch and the sweet words he whispered in my ear that blanketed me in goosebumps.

Instead of vowing to never see him again, by the end of the night, I found myself back in his arms. I knew it was wrong. I knew it was a dead-end relationship. I knew I would eventually have to muster up the courage to walk away from Francesco . . . just not this night.

Mask

I used to want to have you
Now I wish I'd never met you.
You make me sick, you treated me like shit
All I want is to forget you; yes, forget you.
So now I have to see you, the weekends coming and I'm going to see you
I wish you'd go but no you won't.
So we'll have to compromise
I'll wear a mask so no one can see me and remember the past.
 Alas, I wish there was no past
I'd start all new and no one could touch me.
I wouldn't let anyone touch me
No, not you; especially not you
Not here, not there, not anywhere.
No hurt, no pain, no memories
But what's the most pain?
That I am all to blame.

Chapter 30

WISHING LIFE WAS A HALTER TOP AND AN ORANGE POP

"Geez, what happened to you?" Preston questioned, greeting me at the front door.

"It's called not having a car," I replied, standing in the entryway.

"Melinda, grab a towel. I think I'm going to need backup!" Preston yelled, trying to hold back the laughter.

In a flash Melinda had joined Preston at the front door and was now shaking her head with the same perplexed expression as Preston. "You're drenched! What did you do, walk home?"

"Pretty much," I replied, peeling off my soaking shoes.

"You're kidding, right?" Melinda asked.

"Geez, Nana, you should have called us," Preston said.

"Today has been the worst day of my life, thus far. I'd have a drink, but there's no time. I stayed late to finish drilling holes into a million stacks of paper and still didn't get it all done. When I left work, I just missed the bus. So I started walking, figuring I'd see a bus along the way. But no such luck. Then it really started to rain and I'm still walking, and guess what?" I tried to catch my breath.

"No bus?" Melinda answered.

"Bingo!"

"You should have called. We would have picked you up," Preston said.

"Well, let's just say there weren't too many cars out on the road either," I said.

"I know. It's a bad storm. They've been showing footage on the news all night. There's record winds"—Melinda hesitated—"which you obviously are aware of."

"I'm not kidding! A huge metal sign came crashing down onto the sidewalk and then flew across the street. I could have been killed!" I exclaimed.

"Boy, you did have a rough day," Preston said.

"That's not all," I said, taking a seat near the fireplace.

"Oh no, maybe you should have a drink?" Melinda joked.

"It seems that my lovely new coworkers at the print shop devised a plan to put ink in my pop can while I was in the bathroom. I guess they thought it would be simply hilarious to see ink stains all over my mouth!" I exclaimed.

"So what happened?" Melinda asked.

"An informant told me the plan. Now I take my pop with me to the bathroom," I replied with a sigh.

"Poor Nana," Preston said in his comical nasal voice.

"And now I've got to go to bed. I have to get to work early and finish punching holes into a billion stacks of paper before my super-scary boss arrives. Why did I leave my job at the bank?" I questioned, standing back on my sore feet.

"I don't know. It seemed like a cool place to work, with a great view. We toasted to it," Melinda replied.

"We sure did," I said, nodding in remembrance.

Wishing Life Was a Halter Top and an Orange Pop

"Cheer up, Nana. Maybe it's not too late to get your old job back. It's only been a couple weeks since you left," Preston suggested.

"Trust me—it's too late." I knew what terms I had left my job at the bank. They were details that I hadn't disclosed to Melinda and Preston, details I hadn't disclosed to anyone.

"Speaking of the bank . . ." Melinda hesitated, knowing it was a touchy subject. "A girl called from the bank. She said you still have her bus pass."

"It's Savannah. She loaned me her bus pass while she was on vacation. I have to return it to her." I dreaded the thought.

"She said she needs it right away," Melinda said.

"I'll take care of it tomorrow after work, if I make it through another day." I sighed. Just when I thought the night couldn't get any worse. After saying good night, I walked downstairs to my room. I now had two things to worry about. First, I had to face another eight hours with my intimidating new boss and spiteful coworkers. Then I had to figure out how I would return the borrowed bus pass.

The next night I sat alone in a small pizzeria, downing a glass of microbrew and nervously eating a slice of pepperoni pizza. Darkness had already fallen on the streets of downtown, and there was a bitter chill in the air. I wasn't looking forward to heading back out into the elements. Usually not having a car didn't bother me, but on this evening, it sure would have come in handy. What did bother me was the fact that I was still out at such a late hour. I should have been long since home, watching TV with my roommates, next to a warm fire. Instead I was clutching a borrowed bus pass in one hand and attempting to conjure up enough liquid bravery to return it.

"Why had I left the bank, just walked out? Why had I been

such a coward?" I asked myself. After four months of low pay, working as a temp at the bank, I'd finally been offered a permanent position. Everyone had been so excited for me. My manager Joan had put in a good recommendation. Deidre and, yes, even Ann was thrilled that I would soon be hired, even if it was in a different department. When I told my mother I wasn't sure if I wanted to accept the job, she thought I was nuts. That was easy for her to say. I had always envied her administrative abilities.

Like a little kid, I was scared to death. I didn't like the new position they were training me for. I didn't know any of my new coworkers. Even the title itself intimidated me: online banker. I didn't believe in myself.

I had no computer experience, so I didn't believe I was qualified for the position, regardless of what my superiors thought. Just like Natural Helpers Camp, it was the same mental dilemma, just a different setting. I didn't think I belonged and felt out of my comfort zone. I saw myself in a certain light and wore that label through life.

I shamefully ran, just like I had tried to leave camp undetected, yet this time I succeeded. I showed up for work on that infamous day, mentally prepared to accept the job. But then I clammed up. I was down in the basement with a handful of new coworkers, who all seemed to know what they were doing. I felt so out of place.

So I grabbed my purse, walked out the door, and didn't say a word to anyone. I stepped onto the elevator, walked past the security guard, and exited the bank's high rise for the last time. I didn't know how to honestly share my feelings with people. I acted like all was cool, when it wasn't. I was a runner and had never jogged a mile in my life. Instead of admitting my feelings, I ran like a coward. If only I hadn't borrowed Savannah's bus pass, then I wouldn't be in this mess.

After finishing beer number two, I stood to my feet. With one hand on the door, I said a quick "thanks" to the man behind the counter and exited the pizzeria.

Back on the streets of downtown Seattle, the business district, I prepared myself for the task at hand. After a short brisk walk, I reached the corner and came to a silent halt.

Just across the street was the bank's towering high rise. Even though it had only been a couple weeks since I had seen the building by the light of day, the once familiar setting now seemed unrecognizable. It was dark and desolate. There were barely any cars on the street. The espresso stand where Ann and I grabbed our morning lattes was tightly shut up for the night. The crowded sidewalks Deidre and I walked down at the end of a summer workday were empty. The umbrellas and outdoor seating were put away, only to return in the spring. All that was left were memories.

"Here goes nothing," I said, taking in a deep breath. It was reminiscent of jumping into a cold swimming pool. Even with a slight buzz, it took all the gusto I could muster as I sprinted across the street and down the alleyway.

My destination was the bank's loading dock. I knew the mailroom was located on the same floor. If I could catch an employee's attention from down on the loading dock, I would be home free. They could deliver the bus pass for me, and I would never have to face Savannah. I was sure she had already been filled in on all the gossip of how I'd just disappeared.

Once I returned the pass I could go home and sleep peacefully, knowing that via interoffice morning mail, the pass would be reunited with its rightful owner. It was the perfect plan for someone who didn't want to endure the shame of facing disappointed former coworkers. It was the perfect plan for someone who held people at arm's length, who didn't place any value on relationships, who could work side by side, day after day, with people and never even say goodbye. It was the perfect plan for me.

"Hey, another late night at the office?" Melinda joked, greeting me as I walked in the door.

"Actually, it's more like a factory," I said, dropping my backpack on the living room floor. It was late. I was exhausted, but at least I didn't have Savannah's bus pass anymore. All had gone according to plan.

"You look tired, Nana," Preston said from his spot on the living room sofa. With remote in hand, he turned to Melinda and asked, "Do you think now is a good time to tell her?"

"Tell me what?" I plunked down on the couch next to Melinda. It was an all-too-familiar setting that I'd grown accustom to over the past year. After a hard day's work, the three of us gathered together around the television. It was our time to unwind and laugh together over the latest hit sitcoms. We couldn't get enough of shows like *Friends*, *Frasier*, and *Seinfeld*. It was always tinged with sadness, though. I loved Melinda and Preston. They made a great couple and were dear, trustworthy friends, but, oh, how I despised being the third wheel.

I was always the one that outdrank, outsmoked, out-what-evered my roomies, perpetually attempting to fill the void within and never feeling satisfied.

"Are you going to tell her, or should I?" Preston asked.

"Why don't you tell her? You seem to be bursting at the seams." Melinda laughed, shaking her head.

"You know how you wanted to find a place closer to work, Nana?" Preston began.

254

"Yeah?"

"Well, you've got thirty days to do so," he said.

"Excuse me?"

"The landlord called. She's selling the house," Preston replied.

"Wow. I knew the lease was up soon, but that definitely took me by surprise. I guess I will be moving closer to work . . . either that, or Atlanta," I said, still shocked.

"You're joking, right?" Melinda questioned.

"No, I've been considering an out-of-state move," I said.

"To Atlanta? Do you know someone who lives there?" Preston queried.

"No," I said.

"Have you even been there?" Melinda asked, just as stunned.

"No, but I've been to Iowa," I replied, laughing.

"You do know that Atlanta is like a billion miles away from here?" Preston questioned with his trademark brow lift.

"Yes," I affirmed.

"So how did you get the idea of moving to Atlanta? Did you just pull it out of a hat?" Melinda wondered.

"Pretty much. Either that or Las Vegas. Who knows. Maybe I'll just get a place near my work," I said.

"I hope so. We'd miss you, Nana," Preston said.

"I'd miss you both too," I replied. "And Melinda, if I do stick around, would you please not give Francesco my number . . . in case he calls, that is."

"Of course," she replied.

I didn't let on that I knew she smiled inwardly.

"Hello?" I questioned, approaching my new rental located in Ballard. The kitchen door was wide open, and a spicy aroma filled the air. Technically, it was my second rental since saying goodbye to Melinda and Preston. We were still friends but I now lived much farther away, within walking distance to my factory job.

On the front porch sat an adolescent girl with a deep summer tan and contrasting golden highlights in her loose curls. Her nose was sprinkled with freckles, and her face beamed with happiness. She had the kind of smile that brought back memories of my own summer breaks as a child in grade school.

I hadn't a care in the world then, just lazy, warm days where my sole purpose was to chase after the ice cream man before he got away. After catching up to his truck, I'd return to my front porch with a red, white, and blue Popsicle that dripped down my arm onto the hot cement.

"Hi, I'm Kristi!" the girl said with a bright, cheery smile.

"It's nice to meet you, Kristi," I replied. Darling little girl, but who the heck was she?

"What's your name?" she asked in a sweet seven-year-old voice.

"Shana," I said hesitantly. Was I at the wrong house or something? I scanned my surroundings. The large trampoline I had admired the day I came to see the rental still sat in the backyard next to the modest-sized vegetable garden, complete with a white picket fence.

Whew. I breathed a sigh of relief. I was at the right house.

"Sunita, you've got company!" the young girl said from her spot on the porch.

Within seconds a petite young woman with dark skin and dark eyes appeared. She opened the screen door to welcome me. "Hello, it's so nice to meet you. My name is Sunita. Please come in," she said, gesturing with her hand.

Talk about a strange day. I had left the deposit and rent check with my new landlady just a couple of weeks ago. I only spoke with her once, but we hit it off right away. She said I seemed like a strong, independent woman, and considering that I worked swing shift, that I would be the perfect fit for a roommate. By the time I got home from work each night, she and her son would be fast asleep. But Nancy and her son, Gavin, who seemed to be about the same age as the little girl on the porch, were nowhere in sight. Either I had the correct house, or Sunita was the friendliest homeowner I had ever met, randomly welcoming in strangers.

"I just finished making lunch. Please have a seat. Do you like Indian food?" Sunita asked.

"Sure, um, I rented a room from a lady?" I said, scrambling for words.

"Yes, she's on vacation with her son. She told me all about you," Sunita replied, full of smiles.

"I can't believe he left for an entire month. That's practically the whole summer," Kristi complained from the front porch while she bounced a ball.

"Gavin is her best friend. She misses him so much," Sunita informed me.

"Of course, Gavin! I met him the day I came to see the rental." Finally a name I recognized.

"Nancy was so kind to let me stay here while she's gone, on such short notice. I just moved here from Nepal. My parents sent me to study English at the university, but there was a misunderstanding with my housing arrangement," she informed me.

"Wow. You came here all by yourself, and your English is so good!" I marveled.

"That is very kind of you to say. We have many American tourists that come to my country. They come to climb the mountain," she said.

"Mount Everest?" I questioned.

"Yes, this is what the Americans call it. My family are merchants. We have a store and sell goods to the tourists," she said.

"You're very brave to travel all that way by yourself," I replied.

"Thank you. Please have a seat," she said, gesturing to the kitchen table. "Lunch is ready."

"Thanks. It looks delicious," I said, pulling out a chair.

After a brief moment of prayer, Sunita began to eat. But she wasn't using a fork or spoon. Instead, her hand was fully immersed in her food.

I paused. This was a strange day indeed.

Sunita looked at me curiously, "Is there something wrong with the food?"

"No. It looks delicious. I just . . ." I scrambled for words. "Is all the silverware in the dishwasher?" I glanced toward my plate, and then to hers.

Breaking the silence, Sunita laughed hysterically. "Oh, you're wondering why I am eating with my hand!" she said. "This is how we eat in my country. Try it. You will like it."

"All right," I replied, immersing my clean hand into the food on my plate. "Oh, my goodness! It's delicious!"

"Thank you. You are very kind. I am pleased that you like it," she said.

"Like it? Are you kidding? So how long did you say you'll be staying here?"

Wishing Life Was a Halter Top and an Orange Pop

"Until Nancy and Gavin return. I will teach you many things about my country while I'm here," Sunita promised.

"I can't wait!"

During the next few weeks Sunita kept true to her word and taught me about her Nepalese culture. Aside from instructing me on the art of preparing Nepali cuisine, Sunita also taught me how to say "namaste" and wear a saree. I loved learning about different cultures. It was all so intriguing.

My favorite part was when Sunita opened her large duffel bag full of goods she had brought with her from Nepal. It was loaded with intricate silver jewelry and colorful textiles that she sold at summer festivals in Seattle. I was in awe that at the age of eighteen, Sunita supported herself in an unfamiliar country solely by the contents of this large bag. How brave she was to cross continents, and yet I was afraid to move to another state.

On our trek to the Pike Place Market, we dressed in vibrant sarees. We walked for miles through the crowded streets on that sunny day.

My biggest challenge was keeping my saree intact. It was also the source that brought the most hysterics. I lost count how many times we had to sneak into alleyways to rewrap my unraveling saree.

"Sunita, I should have worn some clothes under this outfit!" I said nervously. With visions of public nakedness dancing through my head, all I could do was laugh. "How come your saree isn't coming off?"

"Because I have more curves for it to cling to. You are so tall and thin," Sunita marveled, retucking my saree for the millionth time.

"Who cares about being tall and thin. I'd just like to be dressed at this point," I said, trying to cover my midriff.

"No, no. Your stomach is supposed to show," Sunita said, pushing my hand out of the way. "You're perfectly fine."

"Easy for you to say! You've been wearing sarees your entire life!" I said. "And here I am, completely clueless and at the mercy of one long piece of fabric."

"Shana, you worry too much. You look beautiful," Sunita assured me.

"Thanks, but to tell you the truth, I'll be happy when we get home so I can change into a pair of shorts!"

There were many differences between Sunita and me. Aside from culture and age, the biggest difference was lifestyle. Sunita had kept herself pure. She didn't drink. She'd never done drugs, and she was still a virgin. Her life contrasted to the lifestyle I was accustomed to. She was also a Christian. That was how my roommate was introduced to Sunita. Nancy was at church one Sunday and found out that a young woman from Nepal was in need of temporary housing. Was it a coincidence that I was surrounded by Christians at my new rental? Or was God calling me back once again?

I wished I could respond to that call from God. I wished I could lay down my bag of weed and leave the pitcher of micro-brew at the bar. It was an admirable life that Sunita lived, not worrying about hangovers, unwanted pregnancies or STDs, not having her heart broken in a million pieces by the guy from the night before who promised to call but never did. There was such a part of me that wanted to live the life that I knew was right, yet the emptiness inside me outweighed my willingness to follow God. So instead I put on a good show.

Sunita and I went to church together and spent Friday nights at home. We slept underneath the stars on the back-yard's giant trampoline, ate munchies, and talked about cute guys. I lived a double life with Sunita that summer. And for those thirty days it felt like I had returned to the innocence of my childhood, prior to the eating disorder, substance abuse, and promiscuous living, when life wasn't complicated, and way before cellulite. Back to my adolescence, when life consisted of a halter top and pair of shorts on a hot summer day.

My favorite mode of transportation back then was a set of three plastic wheels and pedal power. I thought I was so cool with my tiny radio and favorite can of orange pop. Indeed, life was simple back then, and those four weeks hanging out with Sunita were reminiscent of my youth.

Chapter 31

NEPALI MATCHMAKER

It wasn't long, though, before my roommate returned with her son from their vacation, and Sunita found a house near the university she would be attending. It was just a block off fraternity row and was filled to the brim with foreign exchange students from around the globe. Being subsidized by a Christian organization, everyone in the house shared the same faith.

On Friday nights, instead of bar hopping on the Ave, a group of thirty or more students would congregate in the large house for Bible study.

Being an avid partier, I was reluctant when Sunita called with an invitation to join her at one of these Friday night get-togethers, but I agreed, curious to see how my new friend was getting along.

After a long bus ride and brisk walk through the University District, I arrived at Sunita's new home away from home. She introduced me to a packed room of students she'd so easily befriended.

My initial assessment was that of disappointment. I should

have gone clubbing with Jenna! Instead, I made small talk with Sunita's roommates and pretended to enjoy myself. Until Yusuf walked into the room. Although he wasn't tall, he was definitely dark and handsome. He had dark-chocolate eyes and hair. His skin was a luminescent olive tone. Across the crowded living room I snuck peeks at him while he spoke Arabic with a friend. He was exotic, he was gorgeous, and he was single.

"Do you know that guy, Sunita?" I whispered.

"Yes, his name is Yusuf. He is very handsome. Would you like me to introduce you?" she asked.

"Not really," I replied.

"Oh, don't be shy. He's very nice." She grabbed my hand.

Within seconds I found myself swept away from my comfortable spot on the sofa. I was on the other side of the room, stuck to Sunita's side. And Sunita was standing next to Yusuf.

At this point I was cleverly trying to figure out how a five-foot-eleven-inch chicken could hide behind a five-foot matchmaker from Nepal. Luckily, I didn't have much time to stress as Sunita began the introductions.

"Pardon me, Yusuf. I would like to introduce you to a dear friend of mine." She smiled in my direction.

A casual "Hello" was all I could utter. I felt so transparent. Surely Yusuf knew that I was gaga over him.

"It's nice to meet you, Shana?" Yusuf replied, clarifying my name.

"Yes, it's nice to meet you too," I said, shaking his hand. The touch of his hand was electrifying. I would have loved to hold on to that hand forever, if it weren't for the fact that I was petrified. I was painfully sober and could not rely on my usual flirtatious smile and buzzed small talk. The kind that began at drink number two with the perspective babe an arm's length away and ended at 2:00 a.m. with the two of us snuggled up together. I was out of my element and had no idea what to say after the words "Nice to meet you too" had fallen from my lips.

Luckily, our introduction was interrupted by the group leader's announcement.

"Thank you all for coming tonight. It looks like we have a great turnout. If everyone will please take a seat or grab a spot on the floor, we'll begin with worship. Afterward, we'll split up into individual study groups," he instructed.

Whew! I could now return to the safety of the couch with Sunita by my side and continue to steal glances of Yusuf from across the room. Not as exciting as standing right next to him, but a lot less stressful.

No sooner had it started, than worship time ended. The leader put away his guitar and circled the room, giving each person a number between one and six.

"Sunita, I'm number three. What does that mean?" I asked.

"That means you're in group number three. There are too many people for us all to be in the same group."

"You're number two. That means we're not in the same group," I said, disappointed.

"Don't worry. Everyone's very nice, and look"—she motioned across the room—"Yusuf is in your group too!"

"What are the chances of that?" I asked, more terror-stricken than before.

"One in six," she replied.

"Great math skills, but that's not helping! I need you," I whined.

"I'm sorry. I have to go now. My group is meeting in the dining room," she said, standing to her feet.

"I'm scared," I admitted, nervously catching a glimpse of

Yusuf from across the room.

"Don't worry, Shana. You will be fine. Now hurry up so you can get a seat next to Yusuf!" she whispered with excitement.

Sunita dashed away before I could say another word. I had no choice but to walk slowly toward my group. After taking a seat on the floor, I realized why I was so afraid to be in Yusuf's group. He was not only the leader of our small group, but we would also all take turns reading the Bible aloud. Terrific . . . not.

"Shana, would you please read, starting at verse fourteen?" Yusuf asked, looking directly at me.

"Sure, but I didn't bring a Bible." Maybe I wouldn't have to read after all.

"That's okay. You can use mine," he replied, passing his Bible in my direction.

"Great! Love to." *Not!* I thought as I watched Yusuf's Bible approach. *What are the chances I can sneak away through an emergency exit?* I wondered, staring down at Yusuf's Bible. There it laid in front of me, opened to the exact chapter and verse.

I began to read aloud, and things transpired from bad to worse. The passage was one that I vaguely recalled hearing as a child in Sunday school. It was a familiar story to many, but it eluded me as I stumbled aloud through the text and then, the clincher, to mispronounce a name! Not just any name either. A well-known biblical name. If I wouldn't have been gaga over Yusuf, it wouldn't have been a big deal. After being kindly corrected, under normal circumstances I would have finished reading the passage and returned the Bible to Yusuf. The incident would have been chalked up as a humorous mistake, something to laugh about.

Nepali Matchmaker

Instead, my little error spoke louder than any name I could mispronounce. Yusuf was very different than the guys I was used to hooking up with. I sensed that he wasn't on the prowl for some pretty girl to hang out with. It was crystal clear that there was a reason Yusuf was single. He was looking for someone who shared his passion for God. Even though the chemistry between Yusuf and I was tangible, he was playing on a different field than I was. He was a man of integrity who wasn't willing to compromise. Those few minutes reading his Bible spoke a million words. I wasn't close to God. That was evident. We weren't on the same page. In fact, Yusuf and I were not even reading from the same book.

Chapter 32

A NEW YEAR'S RESOLUTION

It was New Year's Eve 1996, and I was stuck at a dark, cold, and crowded bus stop in downtown Seattle. There I stood and waited, and waited, in the midst of a torrential downpour. Oh, where was a bumbershoot when you needed one?

By the time I reached my comfortably warm rental in Ballard, it was well after 9:00 p.m., and the New Year was just a few hours away. Soaked from head to toe, my newly cut short hair dripping wet, the last thing I wanted to do was party in the New Year.

Regardless of whether the wet look was in vogue or not, I'd had enough of the gloomy northwest weather, which was exactly what I told my friend Jenna when she called that evening.

"Would you like me to come pick you up?" she asked in her sweet, could-pass-as-a-sixteen-year-old voice.

"No thank you!" I replied adamantly.

"Are you sure?" Jenna was the perfect combination of strong independent woman, yet total girly girl. She had mid-length dark-brown hair and big brown eyes.

I could just picture her on the phone, eyes wide open like saucers, as I refused her offer. I rarely turned down a chance to go clubbing with Jenna. We shared the same love for music, microbrew, and boys in bands. After a long night of partying, we'd occasionally finish the evening off with some breakfast food at a crowded neighborhood hole-in-the-wall. At least if we didn't find cute guys to hook up with, we could go home with the comfort of a full belly, even though I didn't keep mine down.

Jenna was shocked when I told her I was going to stay home on the most celebrated night of the year. "Jenna, I'm so tired of this town and its weather."

"I know it rains a lot," she agreed, "but just be thankful we don't get three feet of snow."

"I just spent an hour waiting for the bus, and I resemble a drowned rat!"

"It's okay. The wet look is in. Think of all the mass babes you'll be missing out on. I sound so totally eighties!"

"Yeah." I laughed. "You do have that Motley Crüe groupie thing going on."

"I wish. I'm sorry, but Tommy Lee is such a babe!"

"Speaking of which, are you sure you don't want to move to the sunshine with me?" I asked for the hundredth time. Jenna had moved to Seattle from the Midwest, and regardless of how much she loved Los Angeles too, she didn't want to move. She actually loved our rainy city.

I, on the other hand, was growing tired of waiting for someone to move out of state with me. So out of the blue, I exclaimed, "You know what, Jenna? I'm just going to move! I've saved enough money. I'm going to do it! Forget about ringing in the new year in this soggy town. I can't get a boyfriend here anyway. I have made up my mind. This year's New Year's resolution is to leave Seattle for good. I'm not going to sit around waiting for someone to hold my hand!"

"Are you sure? Maybe you should get a car instead. Then the rain won't bother you so much."

"No, I've made up my mind. I love to walk. I love not having a car. I am going to walk my butt off in a sunny state!"

"Wow, I'm impressed. I moved to Seattle with a friend, but you are going to move by yourself? You're so brave. What part of LA are you moving to? Malibu, the Hollywood Hills?" Jenna asked dreamily.

"Sorry to burst your bubble, Jenna, my budget doesn't include star-studded hills and sunset beaches. But two things are for sure. I am moving and there will be sunshine!

"You're so brave."

Jenna's words echoed in my head. It had been three days since I'd hugged my sweet friend goodbye. She was the last person I'd seen before climbing into my rental truck with my elusive cat. Well, and a small baggy of weed. I had vowed to start a new life in Vegas, free from drugs and eating disorders. Yes, I wanted a cute boyfriend and awesome job that I actually enjoyed, but I mainly wanted to be a whole person. I intended to find a support group when I reached Las Vegas. I would attend meetings without fearing that someone I knew would see me. I also needed to be far away from any source that would sell pot to me. I wanted a fresh start.

What solitude, I thought as I began my final ascent through the desert. I calculated the number of miles to my destination. Las Vegas wasn't my dream, but I had a plan. Or at least I thought I'd had a plan the day I packed up and left Seattle.

So what was my plan? I questioned myself, now unsure of

my impulsive move. *Oh yes*, I recalled with confidence. I had seen a job listing a few weeks ago for big bucks in the casinos. I could save up cash in no time. Tons of people from LA visited Las Vegas year-round. I would establish contacts quickly. Then I could move to LA. This confidence had filled me when I'd left Seattle. Only now my baggy of weed was empty, and I was unsure.

"Oh, thank goodness you're up," I said, though not expecting a response from my feline companion. It was twilight, my favorite time of day, and the barren desert highway was sprinkled with patches of Joshua trees. It should have been a picture-perfect moment. Instead, I wiped tears from my eyes.

The numbing effects of pot had evaporated. What on earth had I done? In exchange for a clear head, all confidence had disappeared. I wished I had just a little more pot to encourage me.

"Curious, where is this town?" I asked, nervous. "I don't see anything but desert!" What was I thinking, leaving the only family and friends I'd ever known?

I'd been filled with such excitement leading up to my departure. My father tried to explain that February wasn't a good time to be traveling over the passes. I didn't care. I had money, a vehicle filled with all the contents I'd ever owned, and a small baggy of weed. I planned to drive at a leisurely pace and stay the night at roadside motels. I didn't have a care in the world. But that was all past tense now.

"Curious! You know I could use a little companionship!" I blurted out to my cat, who'd retreated to her favorite hiding spot under the seat. "Where is this place?" *Does it really exist?* All I could see was empty desert.

Just as I was about to freak out a little more, I was interrupted. "Curious, I think we've found home," I said, amazed. In the distance, I caught my first glimpse of Las Vegas. Under a blanket of darkness, it looked like a neon oasis surrounded by a million flickering lights that extended across the entire valley below.

"Wow" was all I could say.

My first couple of days in Las Vegas were a blast. I found an apartment I could rent weekly, returned my rental truck, and took in the sights of the bustling boulevard on foot. Though alone, I consoled myself with the facts that I had enough cash until I landed a job and could sit at the nickel slots for hours, raising my hand for a free cocktail every time the server breezed by. After the beautiful sunshine had set in the desert sky, I trekked to my apartment and watched TV. Though lonely, I was determined to make it work.

Early in the morning on day four, I headed to Caesar's Palace.

"Excuse me. Can you tell me where I can find a cigarette girl?" I asked a casino attendant.

"I can page one for you," she answered.

"No, that's okay," I said, scurrying away. I didn't want the attendant to page a cigarette girl, because I wasn't in need of a pack of smokes. I had an entirely different agenda—to find out what my new uniform looked like. If I was going to be a cigarette girl, I wanted to work at the Palace!

Filled with curiosity, I finally spotted a cigarette girl in the distance. From my vantage point, she was a visual blur. To get a good look at her uniform, I would have to follow her. And this girl could walk! She obviously knew the ins and outs of the casino floor as she maneuvered effortlessly through the crowded slot machines and past the roulette tables.

At least I'll get plenty of exercise, I thought, determined to catch a glimpse of the elusive woman.

"I could use a pair of glasses right about now!" I whispered under my breath, continuing my pursuit.

I thought the casino floor would never end, when the cigarette girl came to an abrupt halt. Finally, I caught a bird's-eye view of her uniform.

With my jaw hanging open, I gawked at my second major shocker since viewing the light-studded Las Vegas the night I'd arrived. It wasn't the heavy illuminated black tray resting against her hip, or the colorful lighted yo-yo she flung with her one free hand, or the clear plastic heels she must have snagged from a sleeping princess. Nope, it was her backless purple minidress.

Did the seamstress run out of material? I wondered, shaking my head. *What happens if she drops something off her tray? Does she call it a loss or have to wait for a passerby to pick it up?"* How could I possibly wear an outfit that I would never be able to bend down in, if need be.

My first night working at a casino—Harrah's, not Caesar's Palace—invigorated me. A mixed bag of emotions for a tattooed, belly-pierced girl from Seattle now wearing a tiny black minidress and carrying a tray full of cigarettes, cigars, and souvenirs resting on one hip. I couldn't believe shy Shana traipsed around, beckoning "Cigarettes, cigars" in a loud voice to row after row of patrons entranced by the slot machine in front of them.

The loud atmosphere was punctuated with innumerable dinging slot machines and tables where dealers dealt out cards, rolled dice, and spun roulette wheels. I loved the sound of my pager blaring with yet another call from a pit boss needing cigarettes for one of his patrons. If the gamblers spent enough cash, their cigarettes were complimentary, which meant a tip for me, in the form of casino chips, simply for handing them a pack of smokes. In awe, I quickly grew accustomed to my ten-hour shifts.

The first pit boss I befriended was a tall, balding man named Tom, who oversaw the baccarat tables. I loved receiving a page from this high-stakes area of the casino, as that often ensured a generous tip. Tucked away from all the noise, it was a more intimate setting.

I handed a pack of cigarettes to a patron. The man extended a five-dollar chip in my direction, not taking his eyes off the table. I walked over to the pit boss and found a spot to rest my tray.

"Hi, I'm Tom. You must be new," he said, extending his hand for an introduction.

"Nice to meet you. Yes, last night was my first shift."

"How do you like the job so far?"

"I love it!"

"Good. We're happy to have you." He scribbled a quick signature and handed me a comp slip.

"Thanks."

He squinted down at my name tag that listed my hometown. "You're from Seattle."

"Yeah, I couldn't handle the rain anymore. So I flew south."

"It's a beautiful city though. I have a cousin that lives there. Did you find a place yet?" he asked.

"Well, funny you should ask. The apartment thing has turned out to be a bit of a bummer. At first it seemed like a decent place, during the day, that is. Then strange things started to happen. Like confrontations . . ." I explained, my voice trailing off. I was in denial and didn't want to face my apartment situation. Moving again translated to more work for me.

"Really, what kind of confrontation?"

"These security guards were in hot pursuit of some guy, running at top speed through the apartment complex. It freaked me out. So, I asked the lady next door, who happens to be eighty-years-old, if it's a safe place to live. She told me she's been there for years. She must be hard of hearing." I shook my head.

"Did they catch the guy?" Tom rapidly tapped his pen on the podium in front of him.

"I don't know. They disappeared behind one of the complexes. I felt like I was watching an episode of *Cops*!"

"Geez, what part of town are you in?"

"On Swenson, near Desert Inn," I replied.

"Sure, Swenson and DI. That's what the locals call it. It was a really nice area twenty years ago," he said.

"And now?" I sensed his reply.

"Well, it's a weekly, right?"

"Yeah, how'd you know?"

"Most people stay at a weekly when they first arrive in town. Once they start working, they figure out what part of town works best for them. There's a whole world out there. Just think of it this way—you girls only work four days a week, so that gives you three days to look for a place. You should try Green Valley, where I live. It's beautiful and a pretty short commute into work." Tom's eyes crinkled in a smile.

"I don't have a car though. I have to live close enough to walk," I replied.

"Wait a minute. You work the graveyard shift. You have to walk through that area at night?" He set his pen down and shot me a stern look.

"Precisely, and that's not the half of it." I picked at my nails.

"What? Did something else happen?" His voice held genuine concern.

"Not exactly," I said. "Luckily, this lady dropped what I'm guessing was a crack pipe in the middle of the road. She had to turn around to retrieve it, and by that time I was able to run past her to my apartment. In fact, it happened right across the street from my new place."

"Back up please, did you just say a lady was chasing after you?" He was trying to make sense of the conversation.

"Yeah, I've had a couple of women call me by different names. It's like they think they know me. One of them was calling me Sheri. She said, 'Is that you, Sheri?' It's weird. I don't know these women at all."

"So where do you see these women?" Tom raised an eyebrow.

"They hang out at this rundown apartment across the street from mine." I shrugged.

"Oh yes. I know what it is," he assessed calmly.

"What?"

"The ladies are trying to recruit new girls. They probably get paid by their . . . well, let's just say boss."

"Lovely," I replied sarcastically.

"You'll be okay. At the end of the month you'll move into a better apartment in a nicer area. Just do me a favor and take a cab into work from now on," he said.

"Cigarette girl to the party pit. Cigarette girl to the party pit," my pager blared.

"Sorry, I gotta run." I turned on my plastic heels. "It was nice meeting you, Tom."

"You too, and, Shana, take it easy," he said with a kind smile.

"I will," I assured him, knowing I would be facing several more shifts of walking into work after dark and trying my best to avoid any unwanted company along the way.

Days later, I was hunting for an apartment the old fashioned way, on foot. I'd been in Las Vegas for a few weeks and wasn't familiar with many streets. I headed up Sahara for several blocks. It was exhausting, but how could I find an apartment riding the bus?

I could see it now. "Excuse me, Mr. Bus driver, could you please stop here? I just saw a super cute apartment!" As that wasn't an option, I was on foot, about midway in my climb, when I heard my name.

"Shana"—*beep beep*—"Hey, Shana," the voice beckoned.

I was leery of answering any unfamiliar voices on the streets, especially female ones.

"Shana, its Penelope!"

"Oh! Penelope! I'm sorry. I didn't recognize you out of uniform and in your car, for that matter!" I said, walking toward her.

"Do you need a ride?" she asked.

"I would love one, but actually, I'm out looking for an apartment. I moved here in a rental truck. Where I'm from, people take the bus into work, or ferry for that matter, but I'm beginning to realize nobody really walks in Las Vegas," I explained, catching my breath.

"I must say, you are an ambitious lady! Now I know why you're in such great shape." She gave me an admiring glance.

"Thanks. I love walking. I'm still trying to get used to a Vegas block, though. What are they, a mile long?" I laughed. "I will never complain about waking up to sunshine every morning though."

A New Year's Resolution

"I'm in total agreement, but it looks like you've had your share of sunshine and exercise. Hop in. I can show you some apartments near work." She reached across her SUV and opened the passenger door.

"Penelope, not only do you have a sparkling disposition, you're also a lifesaver." I smiled, recalling how I'd instantly hit it off with Penelope the first night at the casino.

"You're sweet. I'm just thankful to be able to help you. It must be exhausting, searching for an apartment without a car?"

I closed the door, and she made a U-turn at the intersection.

"It wouldn't be so bad if I knew where to start, but I don't know this town very well, and I don't think I'm going to get to know it without a car. If I don't find a place soon, I will have to endure another month at my weekly," I confided.

"I know exactly what you mean. I lived in the most awful weekly when I moved here. But no worries. I know of a few studio apartments that are very reasonable."

"How can I ever thank you?" I sighed inwardly with relief.

"Don't mention it. Anything for a friend," she said with her trademark brilliant smile.

By the end of the day, I was thanking Penelope once again, as I signed the lease on a cute studio apartment, complete with exercise room and outdoor pool. Finally, with a permanent job and my very own studio, I felt like I was a resident of Las Vegas and not just passing through.

Chapter 33

AFRICAN CABBIE

At the end of my long graveyard shifts burning up the casino floor, I enjoyed relaxing cab rides home. I afforded myself the luxury only after a lucrative night. What I didn't expect, on another warm Vegas sunrise, was to encounter such a friendly cab driver.

"Good morning, young lady. Isn't it a glorious day!" the African cabbie said, opening the car door for me.

"It sure is," I agreed a little less enthusiastically. I took a seat in the back of his cab, rubbing my aching feet.

"My name is Hayle," he said after climbing behind the wheel.

"Hi, I'm Shana." I extended my hand over the seat.

"Nice to meet you. Where are you headed?"

"Sierra Vista Drive."

"Terrific." He pulled away from the curb. "Do you work at the casino, Shana?"

"Yes. I just started a few weeks ago. I'm a cigarette hostess," I said.

"I've given rides to a few hostesses. So where are you from?" He continued out of the casino parking lot and onto the street.

"I'm from Seattle. I just moved here . . . with my cat."

"Wow, you are a brave young lady to move here all alone . . . with your cat. Do you attend the university?" he asked.

"No. I don't go to college."

"Working in the casino is a hard life. Would you like to go to college?" he asked.

"I never really gave it much thought. Most of my friends attended college after graduating high school, but I started working right away." I fished through my oversized purse, in search of my wallet.

"A lot of young women your age go to UNLV. An education will give you a better future." He pulled into my apartment complex.

"I suppose so, but I have to work. I have to support myself." I grabbed some cash from my wallet.

"Many college students work and attend the university part time," he said, smiling from ear to ear as he opened the car door for me.

"I don't know. I just moved here. I don't know anything about the college here." I gestured for him to keep the change. If there was one thing I had learned since working in the casinos, it was how to tip.

"I can take you to the university and help you fill out the enrollment application. Since you work night shift, you have time to stop by the college during the day," he suggested.

"Well . . . I guess I could go to the college with you." I hesitated, amazed by his persistence. I was used to guys trying to pick me up—unfortunately they were never my type—but this cabbie seemed interested in my life, not my body.

"Shana, do you know Jesus?" He looked at me intently as he stood outside his cab.

"Well . . . yeah. I mean, I grew up going to church." His question caught me off guard. It wasn't every day that someone asked me if I knew Jesus.

"So you are Christian?" he asked with a beaming smile.

"Yeah, I'm Christian." I nodded. I'd asked Jesus into my heart, and I'd been to church plenty of times over the years. That meant I was a Christian, right?

"Praise the Lord, sister!" He shook my hand with enthusiasm. "My wife and I would love to invite you to our church, if you don't already have one that you attend."

"Sure . . . I mean, no, I don't have a church I attend. I haven't been to church for a while." I felt awkward. It was so weird, a seemingly nice married man so interested in extending an invitation to someone he'd just met.

"I can't wait to tell my wife all about you! May I have your phone number? That way I can call you before I come pick you up to take you to the college. I will also give you the address of our church." He reached into his cab and grabbed a notepad and pen from his visor.

"All right," I agreed, not knowing what else to do. This cab driver was not giving me the option of saying no.

"It was so nice meeting a sister in Christ today. I will be in touch with you in a couple of days," Hayle confirmed.

"It was nice meeting you too." I shook the hand he held out.

"You take care of yourself, working in the casino. Soon you won't have to," he said, waving goodbye.

Standing outside my apartment, the morning sun shining brightly on me, I wondered what the heck just happened.

What was the motivation for a cab driver to want to change my career so desperately that he was willing to pick me up and drive me to the college?

In the days that followed, Hayle was true to his word. He drove me over to the college, and we picked up an enrollment application. He also introduced me to his beautiful Ethiopian wife. The two of them took me to a church picnic in the park and to the buffet at a nice casino on the Strip. I was amazed by their kindness and generosity. Having no children of their own, they treated me like family and were motivated, it seemed, by a desire to show me another path in life. Hayle didn't think the casino was a good environment and continued to encourage me to attend the university.

But I wasn't ready to embrace Hayle and his wife with the same enthusiasm. My big plans to attend a support group had fizzled. I still drank, binged, and threw up—even throwing up the entire buffet dinner they had treated me to. I was living a lie, pretending to be this nice Christian girl around Hayle and his wife but knowing deep down I was far from it.

It seemed there was no place for me in life. I didn't fit in with the churchgoers on Sunday, yet at the same time I hated the addicted lifestyle that I was trapped in. Despite Hayle's best efforts, I kept my distance, not realizing the truth to his words, that the more time I spent immersed in the casinos, the more jaded I would become.

Chapter 34

SOMEONE TO SHARE THIS NIGHT WITH

Because I worked nights, I slept odd hours. The ringing of my phone jarred me awake one late afternoon. "Hello?" I answered with a groggy voice.

"Sha-na?" Jenna questioned, uncertain if she'd dialed the correct number.

"Jenna?"

"Sorry. Did I wake you?"

"It's okay. I have to get ready for work soon," I said, rubbing my eyes.

"I'm calling to let you know that I was able to take a few days off. I told my boss that I really want to visit you in Vegas, and she said yes. Is it okay if I make the reservation?" Jenna asked.

"Are you kidding? Is the sky blue . . . ah . . . let me rephrase that. Is the sky in Vegas blue?" Happiness surged through me like a double shot of espresso.

"I can't wait to see some blue sky. I'll call you back with the itinerary," Jenna said.

"I'm so excited to show you around. We're going to have a blast!" I exclaimed with the enthusiasm of a little kid in a candy store.

"Me too. I can't wait!"

"Call me as soon as you find out the dates!"

"I will!" she promised.

After hanging up the phone, it occurred to me just how lonely I'd become since leaving Seattle. Aside from casual chit-chat at the casino, I was utterly alone. The girls I worked with were nice, but I saw them only at work. I missed hanging out with friends and couldn't wait for Jenna's visit.

The next night, a breezy evening in late March, I tooled around the boulevard, alone. It was my night off, and since I didn't have any friends yet, I entertained myself on the crowded Vegas Strip. My usual routine was to grab a cheap slushy margarita and then proceed to a happening casino. Being the ever frugal gal, I only played the nickel slots, with high hopes to win big. This never happened, but it provided entertainment and free drinks.

After playing the slots for an hour, I strolled through my favorite cluster of casinos, taking in the sights with thousands of strangers.

First I hit the Palace, the place, alas, I still dreamed of working at. My favorite walk-by was Cleopatra's Barge. I never tired of looking at the Egyptian-themed floating bar. My next favorite spot was the Forum. I loved the open-air feel, admiring the painted ceilings and melodic fountains, the sheer decadence.

After exiting the Palace, it was back onto the crowded Boulevard for a short jaunt to my next stop, the White Tiger exhibit. What beautiful creatures! After a few oohs and aahs, I took off for an evening stroll through a lush tropical rainforest. It reeked of ambiance, for an ambiance kind of girl.

Before leaving the Mirage, I stopped at the hotel lobby and checked out the tropical fish. Then having my fill of interior beauty, I hit the bustling sidewalks to take in the next volcanic eruption.

After the spectacular display of lava and waterfalls by night, I finally drifted to my last stop, Treasure Island. I sandwiched myself between hundreds of excited tourists and awaited the battle. I loved the feeling of being swept away to a mysterious land of pirates. Intricate ships, moored in a man-made lagoon, commanded every tourist's attention as we all vied for the best spot. I was more enamored with the rustic setting, the creaking sound of wooden planks below my feet, and the flickering lanterns hanging in the desert night, than the actual show itself. I loved the melodic waves as they splashed against the ships.

If only I had someone to share this night with.

"Excuse me. Could you please tell me where the Stratosphere is?" a male voice asked.

I had just finished watching the pirate ship battle and was making a speedy trek home along the Boulevard. Although Penelope had helped me find an apartment, my new neighborhood, located off the main road on a less crowded side street, still lacked in the safety factor at night.

I glanced over to the voice and immediately recognized the pricey sports car. The car had passed by only seconds earlier, made a U-turn, and snuck up behind me. Now the car obstructed the sidewalk in front of me, which stopped me dead in my tracks.

"Excuse me. Could you tell me how to get to the Stratosphere?" the male passenger asked again.

"It's right there." I pointed straight ahead. These two guys were in serious need of some glasses.

"Oh, I can't believe I didn't see that!" the passenger exclaimed, noting the towering casino in plain view.

"Don't worry. It's a common mistake," I replied sarcastically.

"My name is Darius. I'm sorry—I didn't get your name?" he asked politely, then jumped out of the car.

Oh no! It's a pickup! Why hadn't I seen this coming? How naive was I, thinking that these two guys were seriously asking for directions?

"My name is Shana." *If I keep the conversation brief, maybe they will move on.*

"Shana. What a beautiful name. Do you live here?" Darius engaged me with a brilliant smile.

"I just moved here from Seattle." Brief wasn't working. They weren't moving on!

"I heard it's beautiful there." He inched closer to me.

"It's beautiful, if you like the rain." I glanced down at the make-believe watch I neither had on my wrist nor owned. "But actually I'm kind of in a hurry to get home."

"Have you had dinner? My friend and I were just on our way to a great Italian restaurant. Would you like to join us?" Darius stared at me intently.

"You know, I really appreciate the offer, but I'm going to have to decline," I replied.

"I can see that you are in a hurry to get home, and you're walking, which can be a little unsafe at night," he began, as if trying to sell me a car.

"Why would it be unsafe?" I questioned, knowing he'd set a trap for himself.

"Because of guys like Darius!" His friend laughed, reading my mind.

"Whose side are you on?" Darius tossed a frown at his friend.

"So tell me again, why it would be unsafe?" I directed my attention at Darius.

"In my defense, it's not every night that I see a supermodel walking down the Boulevard," he said, trying his best to charm me.

"You really need to work on your pickup lines, and you also pretty much ruined high heels for me," I replied with fiery sarcasm.

"Okay, ouch. That hurt my ego! And how could I have ruined high heels for you? We just met," Darius questioned with an unquenchable smile.

"If wearing high heels is going to get me this kind of attention, I'm better off in flats!" It was beyond me how this stranger had lured me into continuing the conversation.

"Come to dinner with us. It's the least you can do after insulting me." He put his hand on his heart.

"My mother warned me about guys like you, especially about getting into cars with guys like you." I stepped backward.

"Your mother taught you well, but I bet she didn't say anything about walking. It's a beautiful night for a walk. And the restaurant is only a couple blocks away. After dinner I'll pay for your cab ride home," he insisted.

"Where is the *exact* location of this restaurant?" I had lost the battle. He was persistent but defiantly harmless. He had a genuineness about him.

"Treasure Island." He pointed ahead.

"Treasure Island? That's where I just came from!"

"Perfect."

"Perfect what? That I have to walk back in the direction I just came from?" I shook my head.

"No, it's perfect that you know where the restaurant is. That way I won't have to give you directions." He gently nudged me to get my feet moving.

"Okay . . ." We walked side by side along the Boulevard.

"So how long have you lived in Vegas?" Darius asked.

"Two months," I replied, careful to keep my hand from brushing his.

"I've been here three," he said.

"Have you made many friends?" I asked.

"Not really, just a few coworkers."

"I know. Me neither. I mean, the girls I work with are really nice, but we don't hang out together outside of work. I don't know. It's kind of lonely," I said, finally taking note of my companion for the first time.

He had dark brown eyes and matching thick lashes. His hair was mostly pepper with a dash of salt sprinkled throughout. His skin was a deep golden brown.

"Well, I'm glad we met," he said.

"I know. Now we can be lonely together," I joked. "But what about your friend? Doesn't he live here?"

"Matteo's just here for the weekend, he's lives in LA," Darius answered.

"Are you from LA?" I was suddenly interested.

"Yes. Do you like LA?"

"Are you kidding? Warm sandy beaches, the smell of salty ocean air, palm trees, and sunset nights driving along the Pacific Coast Highway with the top down," I cooed.

"Wow, you really do like LA. Are you sure you're from Seattle?" He laughed, a lilting sound.

"Born and raised." I sighed. "But ever since I was a teenager, I dreamed of moving to LA." We stepped into the casino and were immersed in a sea of people.

"What part of LA do you want to move to?" a voice behind us asked.

In unison, Darius and I turned around to see his friend trailing us.

"How long have you been following us?" Darius asked.

"I know. He just kind of appeared out of thin air," I noted.

"I didn't want to interrupt what seemed to be a fascinating conversation," Matteo said, joining us as we zigzagged through the busy gaming area.

After being seated, Darius took advantage of the crowded atmosphere and sat close enough that I could smell his cologne—European cologne. With one whiff, I was transported back to a warm summer night swinging in a hammock with Francesco. The memory brought instant goose bumps. I didn't want to look conspicuous, but I had to do it—I had to look at his shoes! Designer, yes. Italian leather, no. I breathed an inward sigh of relief.

"You have goose bumps." Darius glanced down at my arms.

"They keep it so cold in these casinos." I rubbed my arms, as if trying to keep warm.

"I'd offer you my jacket, but it's Vegas."

"I know. I think my jacket is still packed away." I smiled at the thought. The last thing I needed was for this persuasive stranger to drape a suit jacket over my bare shoulders. I rarely thought of my adulterous summer fling with Francesco anymore, and I wanted to keep it that way.

Our one-on-one conversation lingered throughout dinner,

his friend playing the part of the dreaded third wheel. A role I was quite familiar with but glad I wasn't starring in this night. Darius asked me about life in Seattle, and in turn I asked him about life in LA. He told me that he'd moved to Las Vegas to help his boss set up a small computer business. I told him that I was "escaping the rain." I left out that I had run away from my hometown in search of a new version of me.

We skipped dessert, and by the time Darius handed his credit card to the waitress, I felt a little guilty. I wasn't looking to be wined and dined. Yes, I enjoyed having someone to talk to after so many weeks of feeling isolated outside of working hours—but it wasn't a date. It just wasn't for me. In my mind I chalked the evening up to a delicious meal and conversation. The first time this uncultured girl from Seattle dipped French bread into a balsamic–olive oil mix.

I was ready to hail a cab and never see Darius again. But he was tenacious. How would I evade his attempts to charm me?

After dinner I walked in step with Darius through the casino and headed toward the valet. It was now time to say good night. They would hop in their sports car, and I would catch a cab back to my apartment.

"I live just a few blocks away. Why don't we stop by my place for a little while? The night is still young," Darius suggested while we waited for the car.

"I know according to Vegas time it's still early, but I think I should be heading home," I said.

"What are you going to do at home?" he asked, placing a hand on my arm. "You live alone."

"I have a cat." I plunked a hand on one hip.

"It's Friday night and only eleven o'clock." Darius didn't back down.

"Hey, you two, the car's ready. Let's make up our minds," Matteo interrupted.

"Come on. Let's go for a ride. I live right up the street," Darius insisted.

"I just met you," I said, trying to reel him back to reality. In his eyes he acted like we had known each other for years.

"Yeah, and I just met you too. For all I know, you could have gotten kicked out of Girl Scouts," he joked.

"Oh, please." I rolled my eyes.

"Shana, you couldn't be out with a nicer guy." He grinned.

"I just don't get it. You even say my name like we've known each other for years."

"Exactly, so you know you are safe with me!"

"The car only has two seats," I said, standing next to the passenger door.

"You can have the front seat all to yourself. Don't worry about me." Darius held the door open.

"Yeah, we'll strap him to the hood." Matteo guffawed.

"I can sit here right under the dash," Darius said, pointing to the passenger side floor.

"We're holding up the valet. Let's make a decision." Matteo revved the engine.

"Okay, okay, you win," I replied, barely able to shut the car door.

Within seconds it was zero to sixty racing through Vegas side streets, leaving the neon lights in the rearview, Darius and I sandwiched in the front seat. Once again I could smell his cologne.

What was that intoxicating fragrance? I wondered, but didn't dare ask. Darius didn't need any encouragement.

I had to admit, it was fun speeding around the moonlit

oasis with the Pet Shop Boys blaring on the car stereo. Within minutes we arrived at Darius's apartment, located just blocks off the Vegas Strip.

Once inside, I was put on the spot when his friend turned to me and asked, "Do you smoke pot?"

"Yes," I replied without hesitation. Inside, I cringed. It was like going on a diet and then being offered a slice of decadent chocolate cake. So much for the pact I had made with myself after leaving Seattle. I'd truly believed that a geographical move would resolve all my problems. But one by one, the ugly habits and addictions reared their heads. I worked at a casino with a fully stocked employee lounge. Inside its four walls converged all the free food a bulimic girl could dream of. Now pot would be the next to defeat me.

I hated myself.

Darius's ears perked up, as if he had met his match made in heaven. "Did you say you smoke pot? Why didn't you tell me earlier?"

"Probably because you didn't ask her!" Matteo jabbed him in the ribs.

Handing me a joint, Darius smiled. "Ladies first."

"Thanks," I replied meekly, knowing full well the road I was heading down. On the outside, I was smiling as I inhaled slowly, but on the inside, I was dying.

Chapter 35

JENNA

"Cigarette girl to the dollar slots," blared my pager. It was 3:00 a.m., and I was working my umpteenth graveyard shift. Although most people from my hometown would have been tucked safely in their beds at this hour, I was burning up the carpet in my plastic heels, among a full house of casino patrons.

"Cigarettes? Cigars?" It was the usual guessing game as I sashayed through the crowded slot-machine aisles in search of the patron who'd requested the services I rendered.

"Cigarettes? Cigars?"

"Sugar, I'll take a pack of cigarettes," a voice called.

Turning, I asked, "Ma'am, what can I get you?"

"Hon, I'll take a pack of Carlton 100s," the woman replied, turning to reveal her face.

"Jenna?" I exclaimed in disbelief.

"Shana!" Jenna said in her darling little girl voice.

"When did you get here?" I wanted to drop my tray when I saw Jenna's sweet face, the first familiar face I'd seen in months.

"I just got here. I wanted to surprise you!" She laughed.

"Well, you did!" I hugged her with my one free hand.

"Shana. I can't believe that dress you're wearing!" Jenna giggled.

"I can't believe it either!" I smoothed my hand over the thigh-high hem.

"I mean, how do you . . ." Jenna swept a hand toward the floor.

I read her mind. "How do I bend down?"

"Excuse me, ladies. This sounds like a fascinating conversation, but I paged a cigarette girl an hour ago," interrupted a woman sitting at a slot machine nearby.

"I'm so sorry, ma'am. Just a minute, Jenna. What would you like, ma'am?" I tilted my tray toward her.

"Virginia Slims Ultra-Light," she replied.

"Here you go, ma'am." I handed her the cigarettes like a seasoned pro, telling her the cost.

"What?" she responded with serious sticker shock.

It was something I had grown accustom to since working in the casino. The convenience of not having to get up from a slot machine to purchase a pack of smokes had a high service fee attached to it.

"You ought to be ashamed of yourself, young lady," the woman said.

"I'm sorry, ma'am. I don't set the prices. My boss does."

"Well, tell your boss to stop ripping people off!" She handed the cigarettes back.

Under normal circumstances—not that living in Vegas could be considered normal—I would have been irritated by a page that didn't result in a sale, but tonight was not a normal evening. My friend Jenna was in town, and nothing could wipe the smile off my face.

"Boy, it looks like someone is on a losing streak," Jenna assessed with a hushed chuckle.

"I know. You can always tell which ones are winning. They're happy go lucky, tossing money around like it's a board game."

"Really?" Jenna questioned in disbelief.

"Oh yeah. I have to empty the coins off my tray periodically throughout the night. They weigh me down. Not the chips though. They're light!" I said, showing her my tray.

"You're so lucky, Shana. I can't believe you moved to Las Vegas, and look at what you're wearing. I've got to get a picture," Jenna said.

"Come on. I'll show you around the casino, and when you get tired, you can grab a cab to my apartment." I motioned her to follow.

"Actually, I already lost twenty on the dollar slots," Jenna informed me.

"I know. Those dollar slots burn a hole in your pocketbook fast. I'm cheap. I only play the nickel slots. Basically, I just play for the free drinks, and it passes the time. Well, I guess you probably just want to sleep then. I forgot that it's so late," I replied.

"When do you get off?"

"Six thirty, but I have to do inventory and cash out my chips," I said.

"Okay, I think I'll go to your apartment then," Jenna agreed.

"All right, here's the key. Just give the cabbie this address. I'll see you later. I can't wait till we can go have some fun!"

Although I thought my shift would never end, the sun finally rose, and before I knew it, I was knocking on my front door.

"Good morning. Sorry. I was zonked out on your trampoline," Jenna said in a groggy voice as she opened the door.

"I'm glad you like my bed. I wasn't sure if you'd find it comfortable." I kicked my heels off by the door.

"Shana, you crack me up. I can't believe you're living in Vegas, sleeping on a trampoline that takes up half your studio, and walking around the casino in that tiny dress." Jenna plopped into one of two beanbag chairs on the floor.

"I know. It's totally surreal. I can't believe it myself. The first night I worked, I just kept walking around the casino swinging my lighted yo-yo, thinking to myself, *I can't believe I'm doing this.*

"You're so brave. You moved here by yourself, and you have a fun job with your own apartment. I'm proud of you," Jenna gushed.

"Thanks," I replied with a sigh.

"So have you met any babes yet?" Jenna wiggled her eyebrows.

"Unfortunately, no. Hello! I'm like the plague here. I moved over a thousand miles away and still can't get a date?" I said, flopping into the other beanbag chair. I didn't tell her about Darius, since our relationship consisted only of pot and MTV. What else was there to tell? Besides, Darius was a few inches shorter than me. I would never be able to wear heels again, and our first kiss? It would have to take place on a stairwell, me perched on the bottom step!

"Are you kidding? With all those guys at the casino, you haven't met anyone yet?" Jenna grabbed a hairband and put her hair in a ponytail.

Jenna

"Well, there is this one guy at the casino. He's really cute. He's older though."

"How old?" Jenna asked with her trademark eyes the size of saucers. Surely she thought he was going on sixty, by the expression on her face.

"I don't know. I shouldn't even be talking about him. He's probably in his late thirties. Who knows? He may even be in his mid-forties," I continued.

"Mid-forties?" Jenna gasped.

"Maybe, but he's really good looking. He has dark hair and eyes, with an olive complexion," I elaborated.

"Sha-na," Jenna said.

The way she drew out my name cracked me up. She put so much emphasis into those two syllables, only the way a close friend could.

"I'm telling you, he has these muscular arms, and he wears these tight black T-shirts!" I fanned my face with my hand.

"So, have you talked to him?" she asked, knowing my answer.

"Of course not! Only when he pages me to his pit for cigarettes. He's got to be either married or have a girlfriend."

"You should talk to him, Shana. You never know until you ask," Jenna suggested.

"Maybe. I don't know, but I'll definitely show you who he is when we go to the casino. Which reminds me, I probably should get some sleep," I said.

"Me too."

Jenna and I awoke midafternoon to hit the pool. Since my apartment complex was so small, we brazenly donned our bikinis and enjoyed the seclusion of our little oasis in the desert. The swimming pool was set among towering palm trees and provided ample afternoon rays. It was the perfect day, sipping microbrews poolside.

What a difference it made to have someone to hang out with! After we had tanned under the desert sun, we primped in front of my large bathroom mirror until we were finally ready to hit the Strip.

"Let's take a bus. It's only a block away," I said. "And then we'll catch a cab on the way home."

"All right," she agreed as we both took one last look in the mirror.

During Jenna's three-day stay in Vegas, we played the slots until the wee hours of the morning or danced till dawn, enjoying nonstop fun hanging out on the Vegas Strip. Yet my fondest time with her was our twenty-minute wait at the bus stop.

We sat there at the corner of DI and Swenson Street in the warm Vegas twilight, just two friends chitchatting. Nothing so special on the surface, yet I knew it would be a lasting memory. It was like a mural on a wall that I wished I could jump into. Or an old familiar song that took me back to a place in time that I'd love to recapture. It was the most precious twenty minutes of my life, a lonely girl spending time with a friend.

Unfortunately, moments like these were fleeting, and before I knew it, Jenna was catching a red-eye back to Seattle, which left me more lonesome than before. I didn't want to let go of my friend, but had to. It was time for me to make friends of my own in the state I now called home. It was time to find another friend like Melinda who I could sip iced lattes with in the Vegas heat. And another Jenna who loved boys in bands and microbrew.

Chapter 36

FRIENDSHIP AND SUSHI

"**D**ude, she must not be home," Darius's friend said in a hushed voice.

At least his friend was attempting to be quiet, although I could still make out their conversation through the locked front door of my apartment.

"No, she's home. The lights are on," Darius insisted. He knocked fervently on my door.

"Dude, you're waking the neighbors. Let's just go. We can catch her another time," Guy suggested.

"No. I want you to meet her. Believe me—she's home," Darius insisted. Rat, tat, tat, tat.

Oh my goodness, I thought while seeking refuge in my bathroom. Darius wasn't going away, and I was in no condition to answer the door.

My one-room apartment resembled a war zone, with every square inch of kitchen countertop space occupied. I had been binging on my second consecutive night off from the casino. An array of empty junk-food wrappers were strewn about, and two frozen pizzas that I was anxiously waiting to devour. No way could I open the door. He would know I was binging! I'd just have to wait it out like a prisoner in my own apartment.

It wasn't the first time I'd crouched in silence, waiting for an unwelcome visitor's departure. Over the last eight years since my binging had begun, I'd had a landlord, ex-boyfriend, and friends bang on my door. Sometimes I actually crawled on my floor, not wanting to be seen through an open curtain. There was just no way, during a binge, that I would allow anyone in.

Usually, my stomach was bloated beyond recognition, and I never stopped until I got my fill. Regardless of who it was, no one was going to interrupt my binge, and especially not the purging that always followed.

But this evening was different. Darius wasn't giving up.

"Dude, she's not home. Let's go!" Guy said.

Clearly Darius's companion had enough sense to realize that by now the neighbors were irritated.

"I'm sure she's home," Darius insisted, as he continued to knock with the persistence of a three-year-old child.

"Maybe she's with someone, dude, and doesn't want to be disturbed," his friend suggested.

"She wouldn't be with anyone. She's not that kind of girl. She's probably just in the shower." Darius knocked yet again.

"Oh yeah, she's probably just blow drying her hair." His friends words were full of sarcasm.

Although I'd known Darius for a short time, I'd never met anyone like him. He had such persistence, the kind I dreamed of in a man. He was like the prince in one of those bedtime stories, who would chase after the princess with unrelenting pursuit. He never, ever gave up. But Darius and I were just friends, and this friend kept knocking on my front door.

Friendship and Sushi

In my paranoid state of seclusion, I felt I must make a move. I could either open the door for him or wait until a neighbor finally called the police.

"Darius?" I cracked the door just enough to see his face.

"I knew you were home. Good thing you finally answered the door—I was about to call the fire department," Darius joked.

"I wasn't expecting you." I pulled my door open halfway, using my body as a barricade.

"This is my friend, Guy. We were in the area. I hope you don't mind," Darius replied.

"Yeah, I'm sure she loves pushy guys dropping in on her at eleven o'clock at night. Pardon me—it's nice to meet you. Please excuse his lack of manners," Guy apologized.

"It's okay. Come in. You'll have to excuse the mess. I've been kind of busy lately," I replied, allowing my guests into my trash-ridden studio.

It didn't help that the smaller the living space, the messier it appeared.

"I see you've been doing a little spring cleaning," Darius assessed.

"Ha-ha, yes. I took everything I own out of the cupboards, cleaned them, and now I'm in the process of putting everything back," I replied with equal sarcasm.

"For a minute there, I thought you were in the process of moving out," Darius said, poking fun.

"Actually, I was waiting for an inconsiderate guy to come pounding on my door and help me clean up this mess." I pointed to my kitchen.

"What you need is a bigger apartment. I have plenty of extra space. And please, call me by my nickname," he replied.

"I hate to burst your bubble, but you haven't reached nickname status. I've told you this a hundred times," I assured him.

"Since when?" Darius rubbed his chin, as if trying to recall the conversation.

"Since the night we met!" Oh, how I wanted to bop him on the head.

"I can see you two are well acquainted. You're like a couple of old married folks," Guy gestured to the two of us.

"Hey, don't scare her off," Darius said.

"Buddy, if you haven't scared this young lady off yet, there's nothing I can say that will," Guy said. "So, let's cut to the chase. We're on our way out to have a couple of drinks and would love for you to join us."

"I don't know. I would have to get ready first," I replied with hesitation. Translation: I would have to use primping as an excuse to rid my stomach of the countless calories I'd already consumed prior to my unexpected guests arrival.

"No problem. We can wait here while you get ready," Darius said.

"I don't know," I replied.

"Dude, I think she wants some privacy," Guy said.

"That's not a problem. We can come back to pick you up in, say, twenty minutes?" Darius tapped his watch.

"Okay, that sounds good," I replied, relieved they were leaving.

Just when I thought I was out of the woods, ushering the two of them toward the door, his friend asked, "Hey, is that pizza I smell?" He wasn't the shy type either, stopping dead in his tracks.

The frozen pizzas were fully cooked and the aroma permeated my tiny apartment.

Friendship and Sushi

"Yes, would you like some?" My heart pounded.

"Sure, if you have an extra slice," he replied.

I had to come up with some excuse before they discovered that I, indeed, had plenty of slices to spare.

"Actually, I made two, so there's definitely enough to go around. It's easier to cook two. That way, when I want a quick slice, I can just pop it in the microwave." I hoped they would buy my lame excuse. I felt like a deer caught in a set of high beams.

It was all too reminiscent of a similar experience at a fast-food restaurant years earlier. That time it involved a one-night-stand I hadn't seen for months. In the middle of lunch hour, I had run into him with a family sized to-go bag full of food and only one, equally large-sized soda. It took only a millisecond for him to notice the enormous bag. The look on his face said it all. In my shame, I tried to play it cool, explaining that I was picking up lunch for the girls at the office. I knew he didn't buy my excuse, giving me a once over. I'd lost twenty pounds and looked great. It should have been a sweet revenge moment— look at me now. Instead his eyes had conveyed pity. I'd quickly said goodbye and rushed for the door.

Fortunately, Darius and Guy didn't give my explanation a second thought.

"We should go, dude, so she can get ready," Guy said, taking a bite of pizza.

"Okay, we'll see you in twenty minutes," Darius said.

"All right then, I'll see you in a bit."

"Oh, and thanks for the pizza. I was starving!" Guy waved his slice at me as I closed the door behind them.

It was 6:30 a.m. and I had just ended a long graveyard shift. Kicking off my plastic heels, I set my tray down and prepared for the tedious task of shift change. After so many hours on my feet, all I wanted was to find out how much I'd made and head home for some much-needed sleep. But first I had to count lighted yo-yos, jewelry, cigarettes, and cigars.

"Don't you look cute in your crop top and short hair," a new hostess said. "I'm Sheila."

Taken off guard by her enthusiasm, I simply smiled. "Thanks. My name is Shana."

"So, tell me, how is the money here?" she asked as I counted aloud.

"It's pretty good," I replied. "Some nights are crazy busy and some nights are slow, but the tips are usually great. I guess it depends on how good you are at sales."

"Oh, I plan on selling all right! And these uniforms, who designed these?" She held up the black minidress with the green sash.

"I know. It's not the greatest outfit I've ever seen." I glanced up to notice her boldly dressing in full view. Not only was this new hostess outgoing, she also had a perfectly tanned, toned body, the kind that looked good in a thong. Boy, did I feel inferior.

"I know the dress code calls for nylons, but I can't stand wearing them. They're too scratchy. I'm not going to wear them." She tossed them in the trash.

"You're very brave," I replied, amazed by her confidence, but who wouldn't be confident having a perfect hourglass figure.

"So how do I look?" She turned left, then right.

"You look great," I said, "but I can't believe you have the

nerve to wear that dress with no nylons. Let's hope you don't drop anything."

"Actually, it's better if I drop something off my tray." She giggled.

"How so?"

"That way, like a damsel in distress." She batted her eyes for added emphasis. "I can ask a handsome man to pick it up for me and sell a cigar to him at the same time. I don't know about you, but I'm here to make money, period."

"Wow!" I marveled. "I know it's only your first day, but I can already tell that you are going to make an awesome hostess."

"Thank you." She smiled. "It's showtime!"

"Have a nice shift. I'd wish you luck, but it doesn't seem that you need it," I said, watching her saunter out the door.

In the weeks that followed, Sheila and I clicked. Since she had lived in Vegas for several years, she knew the ins and outs of the city and all the bars and dance clubs, plus she had a car, which made going out on the town convenient.

We were an unlikely pair. I usually wore something new paired with an eclectic thrift-store find, with my dark super-short hair slicked back. She dressed in tight-fitting suit jackets with matching miniskirts and high heels.

At twenty-one, she presented herself with an air of composure well beyond her years. She always had a fresh mani-pedi and salon highlights.

Sheila was the only female friend I had in Vegas, so mismatched or not, we ended up partying many Vegas nights together. Our trips to the sushi bar were the most memorable. Not only did she introduce me to chopsticks, dragon rolls, and warm saké, she also amazed me by her way with men.

While I sat at the table calculating how much we both owed, including tip, my new friend was graciously thanking a young man with our bill in his hand.

"Do you know him?" I asked.

"No," Sheila answered, chuckling as we exited the restaurant.

It seemed her parents raised her as a lady, and ladies, as she put it, "should let the man pay for dinner." She lived on a different playing field than I, and soon enough, I would find out just how different it was.

"Would you like another hit?" Darius asked from the adjacent sofa in his living room.

"I can't," I answered through the smoky haze, taking my eyes off his big-screen television.

"Why not?"

"Because I have to work tonight, and my eyes are already so puffy and red. Eye drops aren't even working anymore. I need to quit smoking pot."

Once again, I was frustrated with my life. I'd left Seattle to get away from the stoned me. Life was supposed to be different in another state. I recalled the calendar I'd boldly hung in my kitchen the day I moved into my weekly apartment. Each drug-free and binge-free day, I drew a smiley face and wrote motivational messages. There was no fear of someone reading the calendar, because I didn't know anyone. Life would be different! When I met Darius, I was socially isolated. Before meeting Sheila, he was literally the only friend I had in Vegas. It made sense that I often hung out at his house on my off nights—platonically. Unfortunately for me, my only male friend had a love for pot, and I was mad at myself for giving in to its pull.

"No, what you need to do is get some sleep," he replied.

"I know. Every time I stay the night here, I end up watching music videos all night. Maybe I shouldn't come over here on my days off anymore?" I sat up.

"No, what you need is your own room, and I have two that I never use. You know that I always end up crashing on the couch. My apartment is a lot closer to the Strip, you can catch the free shuttle into work," Darius continued.

"I don't know. I'll have to think about it." I liked having my own apartment. But more than that, I didn't trust myself. Living with Darius would mean getting stoned on a daily basis. I knew myself well enough to foresee that I would be chained to it.

"What's there to think about? You have to think about saving money and time, getting to and from work," Darius said sarcastically.

"Maybe. It is a safer neighborhood." My voice trailed in contemplation.

"I would definitely be saving money, not having to pay for your cab rides over here," Darius joked.

"If you didn't pay for my cab rides, you know I would just stay home!" Cab rides. How many times did I get stranded by jerks who only wanted one thing from me and didn't even have the decency to splurge for a cab ride home? Instead I had to bum a ride from Melinda, ask a total stranger, or walk home. They were either married or never bothered to call the next day. None were big spenders. I'd be lucky if they even bought me a burger! After years of looking for love but finding only a trail of duds, Darius was the only one who treated me with respect.

"Well, I guess I could move in with you, but . . ."

"But there's always a *but*." Darius set his joint in the ashtray.

"You know that I've already moved two times this year, and frankly, I'm tired of it!"

"I'll tell you what to do. Box everything up over the next two weeks, and when you go to Seattle for your birthday, I'll move all your stuff. By the time you get back, you'll have a new home," Darius suggested.

"What about my cat?" My cat was the only rebuttal I had left, and being that Darius wasn't an animal lover, he'd rethink his offer.

"I'll take care of your cat. I'll feed him and make sure he has enough water. I'll even take him for a walk," he assured me.

"Okay, first of all, you don't like cats, and second of all, you don't take a cat for a walk."

"You know, I used to have a dog, and I'm great with animals. I'll have your cat walking on a leash by the time you get back!" Darius grinned.

"Sure you will." I rolled my eyes.

"So quit making excuses. Are you going to move in or not?" He sat up straight and laid an arm along the back of the sofa.

"Okay, okay, I'll pack my stuff!"

Chapter 37

I GOT A BAD FEELIN' ABOUT THIS

By the time I returned from ringing in my twenty-eighth birthday with friends back in Seattle, Darius had, true to his word, moved all my belongings out of my studio and into a waiting bedroom all my own at his place. There were benefits to this new arrangement, aside from Darius now being able to cancel his open account with the cab company. Instead of walking many blocks to work at night, I would simply walk around the corner to the casino and hitch a ride. It was one of the wonderful perks of living in Vegas—free shuttle service. The casinos that were located off the Strip enticed tourists by offering multiple daily runs from the Strip to their hotels in an air-conditioned shuttle free of charge. Not to mention the money I would save on shared rent.

The unfortunate part of my new move, was the unexpected new roommate, Theo, I had acquired while gone. Theo, by the age of eighteen, was supposedly turning over a new leaf. He had gotten into trouble with the law but swore that he was through with the whole "thug life" thing. Even so, I didn't feel comfortable around Theo, nor did I trust him. We got along in terms of watching MTV in a stony haze together, along with Darius, but I wished Theo hadn't moved in. Unfortunately, Darius was desperate for money after his job loss and had rented out both rooms in his apartment to make ends meet, which meant Darius slept on the living room sofa.

I was more than happy to get out of the house on my nights off, and Sheila was coming to my rescue this night in the form of a double date. She had a boyfriend, and unlike me, never had trouble finding one. She likely felt sorry for me. Then again, wasn't that what friends were for, fixing single girlfriends up on blind dates? Sheila suggested to her latest beau, Caesar, a tall handsome cowboy with a charming accent, that he invite one of his eligible male friends along.

I was nervous, but this was a no-strings-attached blind date. If I didn't like him, I wouldn't feel obligated, since we planned to go clubbing and dance the night away. There were always plenty of guys at the bar to flirt with, even if I still felt like the plague when it came to snagging a boyfriend.

Ring, ring . . . I answered the phone, knowing it had to be Sheila, while Theo sat on the couch listening to my conversation.

"Hi. We're downstairs. Are you ready?" Sheila asked.

"Yes, I'll be down in a second." I quickly hung up and snatched a look in the bathroom mirror. I couldn't wait to get out of the house and had the *is-he-going-to-be-cute?* jitters. Faster than my roommates could make out the color of my miniskirt, I headed for the front door.

"Hey, where ya headed off to in such a rush?" Theo asked.

He drove me crazy with his questions. The kid had barely graduated high school, and like my father he was asking me what I was up to. "I'm going out with a friend." I attempted to close the front door behind me.

"Hey, wait up. So it's just the two of ya'll goin' to hit some clubs?" He'd followed me to the stairwell.

"No, she's with her boyfriend and one of his friends."

Theo followed me down the stairs. "Is that who you're going with?" Theo pointed to Sheila and her two male companions standing next to her car.

"Yep, that's them," I said, irritated by his nosiness.

"Hey, hold up!" Theo whispered with urgency as he stood in his bare feet.

Stopping to a dead halt, I turned, writing impatience all over my face. "What is it? They're waiting?"

"Yo, come here. I don't want to be shoutin' and all," Theo whispered, motioning me to come closer.

"Yes, Theo?" I asked with my hands to my ears, in a sarcastic tone.

"Listen. I know you may think I'm young, but I grew up on the streets—"

"I know. I know. The whole thug life," I interrupted, trying to make light of his stern composure.

"I can smell trouble a mile away, and I gotta bad feelin' about ya'll goin' out tonight," he warned.

"Thanks for the tip, and don't worry—you don't have to wait up!" I spun away as I shook my head in disbelief. What was the eighteen-year-old kid talking about? I wasn't about to let him put a damper on my evening.

Go back inside and watch some cartoons, I said to myself as I hopped into Sheila's car and caught a glimpse of him shaking his head in disapproval, as if to say, "I told you so."

Our double date started out normal. After the standard

short introduction, I sat in the backseat with Caesar's tall, semi-good-looking friend. We were headed for our favorite trendy sushi bar. After some wonderful sushi, I noted that not only was my date painfully conceited, he was also a complete cheap-skate, leaving Caesar to foot the bill for all of us. Regardless, I was determined to enjoy being out of the house.

By the end of dinner, I had a great buzz going from the warm saké, which went swimmingly with the desert's comfort-able arid night. Plus, plenty of cute guys would be at the club, and I wasn't about to let an unfortunate blind date ruin my evening. Things were good in my world as I sat in Sheila's back-seat, singing along to the latest jam on the radio.

We passed by the crowded Strip while Caesar made turn after turn onto unfamiliar side streets. We cruised through the industrial part of town, dark and quiet, aside from the occa-sional strip club. The flashy neon lights Vegas was famous for were now only visible through the tinted glass of Sheila's back window.

I didn't understand. Sheila and I had gone clubbing togeth-er many times, but never with her new boyfriend. We usually hit the crowded hotspots on or just off the Strip, but with Theo's words echoing through my head, this night was beginning to feel weird, and I felt vulnerable in the backseat of Sheila's car.

Through the blare of the car stereo, Caesar suggested a club I'd never heard of. From the front seat, Sheila shot a covert expression to her boyfriend, whispering something I couldn't discern. Now uncomfortable, I could barely feel the effect of the saké I'd consumed.

Caesar finally pulled into a nearly empty parking lot.

"This can't be a club. What is this place, Sheila?" I asked.

With a smile plastered across her face, as if I had missed

out on an inside joke, she calmly replied, "It's a swingers' club."

"I have a feeling you're not talking about Rockabilly. Please tell me you're joking?" I shook my head. Was this a bad dream? Who were these people I was with? And for that matter, what had happened to Sheila? Had Caesar slipped something in her drink?

"Don't worry. The guys are just going to see how much the cover charge is," she said, sensing I was not interested in even getting out of the car, let alone walking through the doors of this club.

While Caesar and his cheapskate friend strutted to the club's entrance, I sat in the back seat of Sheila's car, hoping this odd happenstance would soon be over. What could I do? We were in a stark part of town, and I was at the mercy of our driver. It was reminiscent of adolescent peer pressure, except I wasn't thirteen. My only way out was if the club had a pricey cover charge. No way was I going to pay one red cent to get into a swingers' club. I knew my self-absorbed blind date was running on pocket change. Sheila was "a lady," which meant she wouldn't be opening her sleek handbag. So that left Caesar to foot the cover. Surely he wouldn't pay for all of us. That was my only hope. I didn't have the nerve to protest, so I used money as an excuse.

"Sheila, there's no way I'm paying to get into this club," I said.

"Don't worry. We can always go somewhere else if the cover's too high."

"Good!" I breathed an internal sigh of relief. Soon they would slide back into Sheila's car and we would head out to a real club.

"Ladies, we're waiting." Sheila's boyfriend beckoned from

the front entrance of the club.

"Did you pay for everyone?" Sheila asked through the open car window.

"Yes, darlin'," he replied, holding the club door wide open.

It was sickening the way Caesar called Sheila *darling*. Like he was the perfect gentleman showing his girlfriend the time of her life, pulling out all the stops! I was no angel—drinking, smoking pot, and going home with guys that I'd only known for a night—but this was where I drew the line. I'd never been faced with a situation like this, and I didn't know what to do.

From the front entrance of the club, Sheila gestured to me with urgency. "Come on—let's go."

"All right" was all I could respond, and like a follower, I hesitantly closed the car door and caught up with her. I wished I'd put up a fight, but instead I slinked behind Sheila into the club.

The following day I arrived home well after noon, to be greeted by Theo the minute I walked through the door.

"Yo, what happened to ya'll last night? You should have seen Darius! He was sweatin' it when you didn't come home." He laughed.

"Seriously?" I asked, somewhat pleased by Darius's concern.

"For real, dude."

"Theo, I'm not a dude. I'm a chick." I grabbed a bottle of water from the fridge.

"I told him I had a bad feelin' about ya'll going out last night." He shook his head in disapproval.

"Theo, I don't feel like talking." I beelined for my bedroom.

I Got a Bad Feelin' about This

"And then, around five o'clock, when ya'll still weren't home and the sun was comin' up and all, Darius was really sweatin' it." Theo trailed behind me.

"So where is he now?" I stopped at my bedroom door to find the key.

"Darius?"

"Well, yeah, who else would we be talking about?" I unlocked my bedroom door.

"He left a couple hours ago to look for a job," Theo replied.

"Oh, no wonder," I said. "I don't think he was sweatin' it about me last night. I think he's worried about money."

I whirled to close my bedroom door, but Theo stopped it with his long, lanky arm.

"Yo, hold up. You didn't tell me about last night. So was I right?"

"Yeah, you were right about your bad feelin', and no, I don't want to elaborate." I shut the door.

Once inside my room, I lay on my trampoline, trying to shake the previous evening from my mind. It was impossible. The events effortlessly replayed in my head. A large foyer filled with a handful of people, seemingly loners. The tiny wet bar serving nonalcoholic drinks.

Why didn't I have the nerve to tell Sheila no? Then she would have seen that I was serious and told her boyfriend to drive to another club. I stared up at the ceiling. And, for that matter, why didn't I just stay next to the bar? At least then I would have just been bored. But no. Sheila and I had to go snoop around.

"Like, duh! What did I think was going on at a swingers' club?" I exclaimed aloud, hitting myself on the head for added affect.

"You went to a swingers' club last night?" a voice questioned from underneath my trampoline. A familiar voice.

"Darius, you little shit!" I screamed, watching Darius pop his head up in total hysterics.

"You are sick! I can't believe you have been hiding under my bed this whole time!" I jumped to my feet.

"You should have seen the look on your face!" he exclaimed, barely getting the words out.

"Funny! Ha, ha. I'm glad you find it amusing to completely freak me out. And how the heck did you get in my room? The door was locked?" I fumed.

Seeing how upset I was, Darius took another approach and took a seat on my trampoline. "Don't you remember this was my room before it was yours? I know how to unlock the door. So why are you locking it, anyway?"

"Just between you and me, I don't feel comfortable since Theo moved in. I like the way things used to be when it was just the two of us. You know, you're like a brother to me." I sat next to him. Then remembering I was still supposed to be angry, I pinched his tan muscular arm. "One that likes to play cruel tricks on me!"

"I'm sorry. I heard you coming up the stairs, and I thought it would be a funny." His eyes sparkled.

"Lying in wait under my bed? And I didn't even hear a peep from you. That's way too creepy, Darius. You should be in the special forces or something." I managed a smile for the first time that day.

"Tell me what's wrong? You don't seem too happy?" Darius asked sincerely.

"It's not as if you didn't already hear me talking to myself." I glanced away.

I Got a Bad Feelin' about This

"Something about you going to a swingers' club? You don't strike me as the type. I definitely know it wasn't your idea," he said.

"No, it sure wasn't. I just wish I would have had the nerve to tell them I didn't want to go. It's not such a big deal. I mean, we didn't stay long. Thank goodness Sheila and her boyfriend ended up getting into a fight. So we left. It's just . . ."

"It's just what?"

"Sheila and I were bored, so we decided to check out what was behind door number two." I tried to make light of my sad night.

"And?" He leaned over on one elbow.

"Let's just say they weren't playing board games, if you know what I mean," I picked at my chipped nail polish.

"They?"

"They, being the type of people that frequent that type of club. I don't know. I just feel like a jerk. I mean, what did I think was going on? Knitting?"

"Is that all that happened?" he asked.

"Yes, of course!" I flopped to my stomach. "And after we left the room, Sheila and her boyfriend ended up getting in a fight anyway, so we left."

"So you weren't at the place for very long," he stated.

"No, half an hour tops."

"Okay, then don't stress about it. It's over. And now you can mark one club off your list of places you never want to go again." He poked me in the ribs, trying to get a smile out of me.

"For sure!" I agreed. "And by the way, now that you have wheels, I was actually going to hit you up for a ride to the grocery store." I grabbed my purse from the nightstand, knowing

Darius wouldn't say no to me.

"Sure, I'll get my keys." He pushed off the bed and rose to his feet.

"And, Darius?"

"Yeah?" He paused, facing me.

"Thanks for cheering me up."

"Anytime," he replied.

Chapter 38

RIVALS, NOT ROOMMATES

"Hey, what are you doing here?" Linda questioned as I walked into our compact supply room. Linda, having just ended her shift, stood barefoot, counting her earnings for the day. Every time I saw Linda, I couldn't help but notice her absolutely perfect body. It was no fair! She was skinny, not too short and not too tall. She had the prettiest legs, a small but not flat butt, and real breasts. I couldn't comprehend how she'd gotten so lucky, but this night I was more distracted by the surprised look on her face.

I'd worked the Saturday night graveyard shift ever since I'd started with the owner of the cigarette concession. Linda knew that.

"I always work this shift," I stated with trepidation. I also always checked the schedule, but this time had neglected to do so. My weekday schedule tended to fluctuate, but Saturday nights were always the same.

"Well, take a look for yourself. Britney's on the schedule tonight," Linda replied with an attitude.

My heart raced as I walked slowly toward the wall where the schedule hung. At this point it wasn't necessary to confirm Linda's statement. I knew deep down it was true. After reviewing the schedule, I tried to put on my best happy face, the face I had perfected over the years. I never showed my true feelings, but shoved them down. I wasn't like the other self-confident cigarette hostesses I worked with. I didn't blurt out whatever was on my mind to anyone within earshot.

So as usual, I pretended all was well, as if the news didn't bother me. "You're right. Britney *is* on the schedule," I confirmed. "I guess on the bright side, I can go play some nickel slots and have a few drinks."

"I would prefer not to look at the bright side, and as far as I'm concerned, she stole your shift!" Linda stomped her perfectly shaped foot.

"That's the nature of the game around here. Even if she's only been here a couple of weeks, she obviously outsells me." I wanted to stamp my much-larger foot.

"Yeah, but the reason she outsold you is because she's hustling the customers!" Linda planted her butt against the counter.

"What do you mean?"

"I was working a swing shift with her the other night. A customer came up to me and asked how much I was selling yo-yos for, so I told him. Then he said another hostess was selling them for half the price. She's eating her commission just to make a sale. Of course she's outselling you! It's not fair to you or the other hostesses who are selling everything at the set prices!"

"Yeah, you're right," I agreed. "But what can we do about it?"

"I'm going to talk to the owner about this," Linda said. "And I'm really sorry you lost your shift. You deserve to be working tonight."

"Thanks, Linda. Well I guess I should get going. Britney will be here soon." I stepped to the door.

"Have a good night, and don't worry. I'm going to give the boss a call."

"Thanks. Enjoy the rest of your evening." I left and wandered along the crowded Strip, with my tail between my legs. Rather than call the evening a total loss, I opted to cross the street to my favorite casino. At least I could sit at a nickel slot machine and sip free cocktails, alone but surrounded by people. It would pass the time and take my mind off Britney snagging my shift. I wasn't that upset with Britney though, half-price yo-yos or not. Deep down, I was upset at myself.

When I'd moved to Vegas and began working as a cigarette hostess, I'd thought looks were enough to get by on, and I made a lot in tips. But the tips didn't benefit my boss one iota. Our job, as hostesses, was to service a select number of casino players with complimentary cigarettes, and the rest was commission sales. We were responsible for generating revenue for the owner of the concession, period. For the other hostesses, it seemed to be an effortless occupation, four days a week, ten hours a day.

But for me, I had good shifts and bad shifts. When it was really busy, the money came easily. But when it was slow, my sales dipped considerably. I passed the time in the employee lounge, binging on free cafeteria food. Those were the days that I wanted to quit and find another occupation. Much like my four years at the print shop, I was stuck. I was a single young lady supporting myself in another state, far from home. I didn't have the privilege of just quitting my job. Yeah, I'd done it in Seattle plenty of times but this was Vegas, and working in the casinos was the best way to make money for someone like me, with no secondary education.

"Surely it was the casino I worked at," I consoled myself. I slipped another nickel into the slot machine, while Britney was across the street working my shift. "I belonged here at the Palace, why haven't I been transferred yet?" I wondered as I watched a cigarette hostess pass by. Surely if I worked at the Palace, all my problems would be solved. Britney could have my shift. All I wanted was a chance to work at my favorite casino. Well, and maybe a margarita to go with that. I beckoned the cocktail waitress. At least I could drink my troubles away.

Pound, pound, pound. "Yo, dude, have you seen my T-shirt?" Theo yelled from the other side of my locked bedroom door.

"What is he doing?" I asked Darius. "It's three a.m." We were lying under the covers on my trampoline. Yes, somewhere along the way, my relationship with Darius had turned from hang-out buddies who smoked pot, to casual sex, to mutual affection. It had come out of nowhere, at least for me, and transpired over the summer. It was one of those things. I couldn't even say when it started. But one thing I could say, our roommate didn't like this new arrangement.

Bang, bang, bang. "Yo, dude, open the door. I need to find my T-shirt. Is it in there?" Theo yelled even louder.

"I can't believe he's doing this. He's trying to pick a fight. I'm sure of it because you asked him to move out," I whispered to Darius as he threw some clothes on.

Rivals, Not Roommates

My heart raced when Darius opened the door. I'd never trusted Theo and had a feeling he wouldn't vacate the apartment peacefully. In an instant the yelling escalated, and before I knew it, they were on the floor fighting it out like rivals, not roommates.

I grabbed my phone to call 911. I didn't know what else to do. Luckily, that was enough to scare Theo, and he fled the apartment.

The following day I walked on eggshells. I overheard Darius talking to Theo on the phone. Theo apologized profusely and begged Darius to help him move his bed out of our apartment, promising that, in exchange for the favor, Theo would leave on good terms. Darius and I were reluctant but desperately wanted to be rid of him.

That evening Theo showed up at our doorstep with his uncle. They were friendly, making small talk while all three loaded Theo's bed into Darius's truck.

Observing it from an upstairs window, I glanced over to the car Theo's uncle was driving. It had no license plates. Why would he be driving around town without plates? I was beyond worried when Darius ran up the stairs to grab his keys.

"Darius?" I whispered, staring at him intently. "Their car doesn't have any plates."

"I know," he replied solemnly.

"I have a really bad feeling about this. Please just tell them they have to get someone else to move his bed," I pleaded.

"No. I just want to get this over with. Then we won't have to deal with him anymore," Darius insisted.

I followed him downstairs to his truck. "At least call the cops and ask if they can follow you. I don't trust these guys," I whispered through the driver's-side window.

"It'll be okay," He assured me, although by the look in his eyes, I could tell he knew things wouldn't be okay.

I stood there on the sidewalk, staring into Darius's dark-brown eyes, his truck idling in the background. It was a defining moment in our relationship when he looked at me intently and asked, "Would you come with me?"

At that moment my love for Darius was sealed, and even though I was scared to death, no way I would let him go alone. We would face Theo and his uncle together.

After I slid into the passenger seat, Theo quickly said, "Yo, are you ready?" Then giving an affirmative wave, we were off, trailing the unmarked car.

We drove several miles along the freeway and exited to an unrecognizable part of town. Then they weaved like a basket through secluded side streets. It was apparent that our ex-roommate was attempting to throw off any sense of direction we might have had.

Finally, we came to a stop behind their car. We were outside of an apartment complex on a dimly lit road. The whole scene reeked like a low-budget movie. Nonetheless, Darius was determined to be done with Theo, regardless of the cost.

Darius climbed out of the car and whispered, "Lock the doors after I leave. If I'm not back soon, call the police."

Within earshot, Theo and his uncle didn't waste any time engaging Darius in more friendly conversation. Way too friendly.

"Listen, it's late," Theo's uncle said to Darius. "I have to work tomorrow, and I'm sure that you and your girl would like to get home. Let's drop the bed off in my garage."

"Sounds good," Darius agreed.

The three of them picked up the heaviest load and headed

toward the apartment complex. Then they disappeared out of my range. I sat in the safety of Darius's truck, clutching my phone. No one lingered on the street. No cars, no passersby. I was alone. Time stood still. Darius told me to call the police if he wasn't back soon. How long was too long?

I breathed a sigh of relief when the three reappeared. There was only one mattress to go. Again they disappeared. Thinking the worst yet hoping for the best, I could only imagine how Darius must have felt.

Bang!

My heart raced. A gunshot?

Chapter 39

THE SINISTER SIDE OF VEGAS

I heard the sounds of confrontation in the distance. I couldn't make out the conversation but knew it was threatening.

Dialing 911, I caught a glimpse of Darius running toward the truck. In a millisecond I reached over and unlocked the driver's-side door. Darius slid onto the driver's seat, and I could see blood dripping from his face onto his white button-down shirt.

"Was that a gun? Did they shoot you?"

"No," Darius exclaimed, "but I can't see! Can you drive?"

"A stick shift? I don't know how."

"Oh, my eyes are burning!" Darius cried as he turned on the ignition and sped away.

"You're going to have to help me steer. I can't see. They sprayed something in my eyes," he said.

"Okay." I placed a hand on the steering wheel.

"We have to find the main road so I can pull over. My face is burning!"

Back on a main street, Darius wasted no time finding the

nearest house. He pulled into the driveway and jumped from the car, then located an outdoor hose and turned it on.

The sound of the ruckus outside alerted the owner of the home. He came bursting out of his front door to find a young man in a bloodstained shirt, dowsing his face with water.

"What happened? Are you okay?" the man asked.

"A couple of guys jumped me. They sprayed something in my eyes," Darius replied, drenching his face in water.

"Do you need to go to the hospital?" the man asked.

"I think so, but my girlfriend can't drive a manual. Would you give us a ride?" Darius asked.

"Of course," he replied. "I'll get my keys."

At the hospital, the burning subsided, and eventually Darius was able to drive us back to our apartment. His nose also stopped bleeding, which explained the blood on his shirt.

It turned out that Theo and his uncle used some sort of chain as their weapon. Amazingly, Darius had escaped through the garage door shortly after being sprayed in the face. I didn't know what would have happened if I hadn't gone with him that evening.

I tossed and turned all night, tormented by dreams of Theo returning to our apartment with a gun. By the time the sun rose, I was exhausted, yet relieved to see the break of day. There was something so comforting about daylight. Like all fear disappeared when the sun rose. Night lurked just around the corner though. I couldn't comfortably live in Darius's apartment any longer.

Still wrapped in Darius's arms, I pleaded, "We can't stay here. We need a fresh start. I don't feel safe here anymore."

"Everything is going to be fine. I'm here. You don't have to worry about anything." Darius tightened his grip around me.

The Sinister Side of Vegas

I wished such a sweet time of a new romance hadn't been spoiled by the fear of Theo and his uncle showing up at our apartment.

"Seriously, I can't sleep. I keep worrying that Theo is going to show up. And who knows, maybe with a gun this time. This place is filled with bad memories now." I clung to his warm body.

"All right, a fresh start. If it will make you feel more comfortable, that's what we'll do." Darius sealed his promise with a soft kiss.

"I love you," I cooed softly. Finally I could relax and enjoy my new—dare I say?—boyfriend. The thing I had been searching for was right under my nose, and I couldn't wait to move into our own apartment and happily play house together, me tucked in Darius's arms each night.

After six months of living in Vegas, little by little the dark side of what they called Sin City was unveiled to me. If my double-date disaster with Sheila hadn't opened my eyes, my job transfer to my favorite casino sure did. I was elated to finally have my boss's seal of approval. With the transfer came the unspoken statement that I was worthy of wearing the Palace's cigarette girl uniform. It was just the validation I needed, and with it, the embarrassment of Britney snagging my shift melted away. But on the other side of the casino chip, the sinister side of Vegas was now in full view.

It was 1:00 a.m., and I had situated myself directly across from my favorite nightclub. Resting my cigarette tray on a receptacle, it made the perfect pedestal. Not only did the dimly lit location serve as a showcase to display the flashing jewelry I was selling, it also provided needed rest for my arms.

The spot I'd chosen was strategic. I could listen to my favorite songs from the club's entrance just yards away and also sell my goods to everyone who passed by.

There I was, nodding my head to the beat of the music with lighted yo-yo in hand, when a man approached me. *Hopefully, he'll purchase a pricey cigar.*

He stopped in front of my tray. "Hello," the man said with a friendly smile.

"Hello," I replied.

"It looks like you have the best spot in the casino," he remarked.

"I think so. No cover charge, no drinks being spilled on me."

"If the music is this loud out here, I can't imagine what it's like on the dance floor," the man said, still smiling innocently.

"I know it's loud, but I love it! Would you like a cigar?" I asked, motioning my hand toward my cigarette tray.

"No thanks. I don't smoke," he replied.

Terrific, he's not purchasing anything. I loathed men who just wanted to talk. There were paying customers out there, patrons in search of cigarettes or cigars and even lighted yo-yos they would take back to little Johnny or Sally. This guy was not only wasting my time, he was also obstructing my view.

"Do you like to dance?" he asked coyly.

"Of course. Who doesn't?" I replied naively, wondering when this cheapskate chatterbox would leave.

"Would you like to come up to my suite and dance for me?" he asked, not blinking an eye.

"No thanks!"

"Money is no object . . ."

"I said no thanks," I replied, even more adamantly.

"All right," he said hesitantly, as if waiting for me to change my mind "It's a shame though. I'm willing to pay you much more than you will make standing here . . . waiting for someone to purchase a cigar."

Oh, if I were only one of those girls who had the nerve to tell a guy like that exactly where he could go!

Maybe this was what Hayle was trying to rescue me from, I wondered as I watched the man who'd propositioned me disappear in the distance. Maybe that was why Hayle had wanted me to go to college. He must have visualized a path for me that I couldn't see or that I didn't believe I was even capable of achieving.

A few weeks later, I stood, resting my tray, by a small cocktail lounge chatting with a server in the wee hours of the morning. I'd never met her before. She was a kindhearted girl. The casino was pretty quiet at 4:00 a.m., and I welcomed any conversation that would pass the time.

"So how old are you, Shana?" the waitress asked.

"I just turned twenty-eight," I said.

"Oh, you look great! I thought you were in your early twenties," she marveled.

"Thanks. It's my chubby cheeks, which I loathed as a teenager. My mother always told me I would appreciate them when I grew older!" I laughed.

"You must have a boyfriend, hmm?" she asked.

"I do. He has dark-brown eyes, thick lashes, and an amazing olive complexion. Of course, it's always the guys that get the great lashes. It's no fair!" I said, discreetly slipping off my heels to give my aching feet a break.

"I agree. I have to curl mine for a half hour." She laughed.

"And apply three coats of mascara!" I added.

"Any plans to marry?"

"I don't know," I said hesitantly. "I mean, how do I know if he's the one?" *But if he isn't, why am I playing house?*

"Has he asked you to marry him?" she asked.

"Many times. In fact, he's the only guy who's ever asked me to marry him. Most of them seem content just living together," I said.

"He wants to marry, but you're a little scared?" she asked sincerely.

"I guess. He's a hard worker. He's nice to me and cute. I'm just not sure if I'd be happy with him, you know, forever," I confided.

"In my country, some women do not get to choose who they marry. The family arranges the marriage." She leaned against a barstool.

"How awful!"

"I know we just met, Shana, and you seem like a very kind lady. I hope I don't offend you, but you said something curious . . ."

"What is it?"

"You said that you didn't know if he would make you happy forever. But happiness comes from within. The most wonderful man in the world can't make a girl happy unless she's happy with herself," she said with all sincerity, noticing a customer waiting for a drink. "It was nice talking with you, Shana. Good luck to you."

"Contentment comes from within?" It was as if a lightbulb had gone on in my head. Watching the cocktail waitress in the distance, I contemplated my life. I wasn't happy with myself, and no man could ever change that fact. I was looking for someone to sweep me off my feet and make everything all better, but no man could perform such a feat. Only I could change me. Which meant that no matter what guy it was, eventually, after all the butterflies flew away and I settled into the relationship, I would still be left with the reality of all my hang-ups and insecurities. No man, no matter how seemingly wonderful, could ever fix me. Unfortunately, this epiphany was truly depressing.

Chapter 40

SLIDING BACKWARD

"Hmm, what a novel concept," I pondered, days after my encounter with the cocktail waitress. Being happy on the inside . . . but my happiness came from an external source: a sunny day, lounging at a casino pool in my newly purchased bikini. That made me happy. Well, kind of. If I added three or four slushy margaritas with salt around the rim. Or how about shopping at my favorite designer outlet store, finding a great pair of jeans that fit like a glove? This made me happy. Especially if I'd just consumed lunch, the largest blended coffee known to man with extra whipping cream and caramel on top. These were my favorite things, along with sunset drives in a rented convertible through the barren desert at dusk with a joint in hand; working out at the gym for three hours just so I could step on the scale and see the number 125; going to hip new places with my boyfriend, drinking microbrew out of a pint glass; and eating jumbo shrimp dipped in cocktail sauce. All these things that I did to fill my time in Vegas made me temporarily happy on the inside. But what this cocktail waitress spoke of was different, an inner joy I hadn't experienced since adolescence. How could I obtain such a thing? If everything were stripped away, all of my favorite things, and I was left with just me . . . how would I cope?

Several weeks after my conversation with the cocktail waitress, I decided to hang up my plastic heels for good. The casino I had so desperately wanted to work at and thought my happiness—a.k.a. self-worth—was dependent on—even this casino soon lost its luster. Sure the tips were great, but my ability to sell overpriced cigarettes, cigars, and lighted trinkets was lacking in the shadow of the other cigarette hostesses. Instead of taking it in stride, I handled my inferiority complex by hitting the food court after my shift ended each morning. The scenario was always the same: buy a bunch of delicious food, stuff myself silly, and then search for a secluded bathroom to throw up in. That was always the hardest part, finding a place to purge in secret. It had become the story of my life, and oh, how I hated it . . . how I hated myself.

For the other hostesses, it was such an effortless means of making an income. I knew it because I overheard their conversations each evening as I stood barefoot on the supply room floor getting ready to start another long shift. While I arranged my tiny backless dress so that my bra wouldn't show, I listened in on all the gossip.

"Did you work during the big boxing match last week? I heard that one of the boxers was playing cards all night!" said a beautiful dark-haired hostess named Taylor.

"I was slammed all night. I made a killing, but as for the boxer, he doesn't even smoke. Wouldn't you know," a pretty blond hostess named Sasha said.

Sasha was even more intimidating than the rest of the hostesses because not only was she selling like crazy on the casino floor she was also attending UNLV to become a teacher.

"I had the worst customer, I swear, of all time yesterday . . ." Taylor continued on as she counted her earnings and chain-smoked simultaneously.

"Tell me about it! The same thing happened to me. It's probably the same man. Was he at the roulette table with this skinny little redhead?" Sasha interrupted.

"Yes!" Taylor stubbed out her cigarette. "He was such a jerk, acting like he was a billionaire or something. It's always the ones that don't have any money that try to act like they do!"

"I hear ya, sister!" Sasha agreed, shaking her head in disbelief while she changed into her street clothes.

"It's too bad we couldn't all be like Shana." Taylor turned to acknowledge me. "Nothing ever bothers you. I never hear you complain!"

The other hostess agreed as the two of them continued their conversation while primping in front of the mirror. I didn't say a word. These two hostesses had no clue how I dealt with stress. If they only knew that while they were enjoying their lives, going to the university and building up their savings accounts, I was spending my life throwing up. It was such a wasted life! I blamed my binging on my occupation, and since being a cigarette hostess was causing me to throw up every day, I knew it was time to say goodbye.

When I finally did give notice and hung up my plastic shoes for good, I did it in the worst way possible. Usually responsible, I ignored the endless ringing of the phone as I lay in bed glued to Darius's side. By not showing up for my final graveyard shift, I ultimately left another hostess to work a double shift. It was cruel and unthinkable, not to mention out of character on my part.

But much had changed since Darius and I had moved. He'd started a new job, which meant that he could support us while I searched for something better. But that wasn't the reason I didn't show up for my final shift. I was afraid of what my new man would be doing while I worked the graveyard shift. Blame it on his bachelor friends. Blame it on the city, with its unlimited amount of nightclubs. Or maybe it was Joel's little one-night stand that left me scared. Whatever the case, all of a sudden, I was paralyzed with fear. So afraid that I couldn't bear to leave him alone.

Once Darius and I established ourselves as a couple, I began what would quickly become a joke between the two of us, a not so funny one: my long list of fly-by-night jobs. Some lasted four or five days, some lasted three weeks, and others three months. But they all ended a similar way. I quit, and my perpetual job search continued. My live-in relationship with Darius was so different. With Joel everything was split down the middle, kept separate, and we each paid our own way. I would have never dreamed of not working while living with Joel. But Darius had the attitude that what was his, was mine.

"Don't you have to work tonight?" Darius asked while I cleared the small dining table in our weekly apartment.

"Actually no."

"They didn't schedule you?" He scratched his brow.

"Well, they did. Please don't get mad, but I quit," I replied.

"Why? What was wrong with this job?"

It was a question he was quite used to asking. This would then lead to my arm's length of excuses.

"I wasn't getting enough hours. The pay was too low," or, with regard to my five-day stint at a famous coffee chain, "They made me mop the floors."

In my defense, I truly was a hard worker. I just had a few problems that plagued me. One was Darius's income. For the first time since I'd left the family nest, I had someone supporting me.

The second was that I had access to pot on a daily basis and couldn't function on the job when stoned.

Third, I was ashamed to be working for minimum wage. The sincere pit boss named Tom who had been so concerned when he found out I was walking into work each night? Well, he ran into me one day while ordering his morning coffee. Only instead of me being in line next to him, I was wiping down the counter and emptying the trash. He had the most shocked look on his face, wondering what on earth I was doing. It was as if I were sliding backward instead of climbing the ladder of success. I felt about an inch tall. All my life I had dreamed of being a "super-duper model," or at least having a career that I loved, and in my eyes, my life had fallen way short of my expectations.

So I continued on a roller-coaster ride of jobs, joints, and food binges, while Darius worked overtime.

"We should open up a printer repair business," Darius suggested one evening while we relaxed on the patio of our latest rental. It was located far from the Vegas Strip but was dirt cheap, the tiniest place I'd ever lived.

"And?"

"And run our own business. We've saved more than enough capital to invest in a business and I have plenty of experience in sales and repair," he explained.

"What am I supposed to do?" I asked.

"You will handle all the bookkeeping, answer the phones,

schedule appointments. There's so much for you to do, and I promise you will never be bored," he insisted.

"It sounds like you have everything planned, but I want to move back to Seattle. You know I'm tired of Vegas. The excitement has worn off. Trust me, you would love living in Seattle. We can use the money to establish our lives there," I urged.

"Wouldn't it be better to stay here two more years and double or even triple the money we've saved?" he asked.

"You've saved. You're the one who's been working," I added.

"My point exactly! You'll never have to apply for a job again," he said with a mischievous grin.

"Don't think I don't see that smile on your face. I know you're thinking about my revolving job status." I pointed my finger at him.

"Well, now that you mentioned it . . ." He tried to hold back a smile. "Are there any jobs left in Vegas?"

"Very funny." I swatted him on the arm.

"You can work nine to five, Monday through Friday, with the weekends off," he said.

"I just don't think opening up our own business is the answer. I want out. I don't fit in here. I'm not a Vegas girl. I'm a Seattle girl. I love listening to jazz music on a drizzly winter day bundled up in multiple layers of clothing. I miss the smell of saltwater in the air and eating clam chowder on the ferry," I said, reminiscing.

"No, you miss the coffee stands on every corner!" Darius nodded knowingly.

"That too," I agreed, "but mostly I miss home."

"We're not staying here forever, just two more years. That way I'll feel more comfortable moving to Seattle with plenty of money to reestablish ourselves," he reasoned.

"We don't need a ton of cash, and I have family in Seattle. We'll be fine," I replied.

"You need to see things from my perspective too."

"Which is?"

"I know you miss your family and your hometown, but what about us getting married?"

"What does that have to do with moving to Seattle?" I asked defensively.

"You want me to leave Vegas, but you're not willing to get married. We've been engaged for six months."

It was true. I had no rebuttal. I'd accepted his proposal but was hesitant to set a date. I didn't want to lose him but also didn't want to commit to what I viewed marriage as: forever. So instead of walking down the aisle, I agreed to go into business with Darius. My decision was swayed by one thing—money, the quest to get rich. And it taught me a lesson I'd never forget.

Chapter 41

EXIT DOOR

$\mathcal{E}$xcitement was in the air as Darius and I embarked on our new business venture. In the first few weeks, we moved about town in search of office space, business license, and supplies.

Our storefront was on a busy strip of town near two casinos. It took no time for our business to prosper. At first I enjoyed my new career. What other job would pay me to grab my morning coffee and run errands each day? Sometimes the errands were business related, and other times they were mundane tasks, like doing laundry. A few puffs of weed helped break up the monotony though.

One fine spring day, which equates to upper 80s in Vegas, I tried a new laundromat, as my load of clothes was huge. That day I saw two faces I thought I had left behind—Hayle and his wife.

"Shana? Is that you?" Hayle asked from several yards away.

Seeing Hayle's face, while grabbing my last load out of the dryer, was unexpected—and also unwanted. I was stoned. It had been a long time since I'd seen him, since my first few months living in Vegas. A lot had changed, especially my lifestyle, which consisted of gourmet coffee and pot.

"Wow, it is you! I hardly recognized you. Your hair is long, and it looks like you lost some weight!" Hayle said with his dazzling white smile.

"Wow, it has been a long time!" Though taken completely off guard, I tried to appear enthusiastic. I was sure that Hayle and his wife knew I was stoned, eye drops or not. It was reminiscent of my mother seeing me stoned in junior high. I felt paranoid and scared. This was something I didn't do—I never hung out with non-stoned people while stoned. I hid my addiction to pot. I didn't wear it proudly, like a badge of honor. I retreated to places where either no one knew me, or the other people were stoned too.

"What happened to you? I asked about you at the casino, and they said you were working at another casino. I tried your phone, but it was disconnected," Hayle said, beaming from ear to ear.

"Yes, I did get transferred, but after a while I got tired of selling cigarettes. You know, it's a hard lifestyle." I chose my words carefully. I had a goal. I wanted Hayle to think I was happy, healthy, and excited to run into him. An utter lie. I couldn't wait to escape his presence. It wasn't just that I was stoned out of my mind—it was the fact that Hayle lived a clean life.

Technically I'd accepted Jesus Christ as my "Savior" at twenty-four. But my lifestyle surely didn't reflect it. I knew I wasn't pleasing God by the way I was living, and truthfully, I was trying to hide from God. Like the Creator of the universe had no clue where I was, duh. But nonetheless, I tried. If I couldn't hide from God, I could at least put on the best show possible for Hayle.

I stood there across from Hayle and his wife with a fixated smile, figuring out how I could verbally sugarcoat my life and be on my way.

"You aren't selling cigarettes anymore?" Hayle asked with enthusiasm.

"No. I got so tired of that. You were right, and I want to thank you for all you did," I replied.

"Don't mention it. I'm just so happy to see you!" he said, shaking my hand.

"Yes. So I got engaged to a really great guy, and we opened up a business together."

"Wow! A lot has happened in—what has it been?—a couple of years?" Hayle said, clearly amazed.

"Has it been that long? Wow, time does fly," I said, as if I were also amazed. But it was more like dazed.

With a somber expression, Hayle asked, "Are you happy? Is your fiancé good to you?"

"Yes, he is very nice, and he ran his own business before, so he knows the ins and outs. Everything is going great!" I said enthusiastically.

"Praise the Lord, sister! I want to meet him!" Hayle said.

"Definitely. We should get together for dinner. Why don't you give me your number?" I said, adding, "Unfortunately, I misplaced it."

"Of course. That is what I thought. Otherwise, I know you would have called," Hayle said as he wrote down his number on a scrap of paper from his shirt pocket.

"I'll give you a call soon!" I promised, grabbing my large laundry bag, "It was so nice running into you. I hate to rush, but I better be getting back to the office. I'm the one who answers the phones. We'll get together soon."

"Yes, we will get together soon. God bless you, sister. It's so good to see you again!" He replied.

By the time Hayle finished saying goodbye, I was halfway through the door. To Hayle I might have seemed like a diligent new business owner eager to get back to the office, but I was really attempting to shake the event from my guilty conscience.

While the weeks continued to pass, I lived a lonely existence of running errands and staying stoned. Even though I had Darius, he was busy tending to the needs of our growing cliental. When he wasn't working, one of his many friends popped in to hang out. I retreated to the comfort of my car, which was willing to take me anywhere in Vegas at a moment's notice.

Each day I made up an excuse to leave the ringing phones and walk-in customers behind, to make my escape. I was a lonely young woman secluded by my addiction to pot, ceasing contact with family and friends. All I had was Darius and his friends. I tried to stay numb so I wouldn't have to face the fact that I hated my life, but had no courage to change it. I spent much of my time at the athletic club, my ultimate place of escape. I savored my time at the gym each day, and I never wanted it to end. For a few hours a day I could forget about my messed-up life.

In the evening, after I returned from the gym and closed up shop, Darius would take me out for dinner and drinks at one of Vegas's many restaurants. Whether it was filet mignon and wine or jumbo shrimp and microbrew, he tried to offset my waning emotional state. While Darius worked hard, I kept myself anesthetized, and devised a plan to get out of Vegas for good.

"Excuse me. I don't mean to interrupt, but I noticed the title of your book. It looks interesting," a woman said from the treadmill next to me, one evening at the gym.

"I was visiting my family in Seattle and stumbled across it in a thrift store," I said.

"Who is the author?" the woman asked.

"That's the amazing part! It's written by the pastor of my old church."

"What a great find," she agreed. "By the way, my name is Kate."

"Nice to meet you, Kate. My name is Shana," I said, shaking her hand as we both continued to walk.

"You're from Seattle originally? How long have you lived in Las Vegas?" she asked.

"Too long," I replied with a chuckle.

"Oh, really?"

"No, not really. I just miss my hometown. I've only lived here a couple of years, but it seems like a lifetime," I confided.

"Do you have a church in town that you go to?" she asked.

"No. The only church that I've ever loved is in Seattle." I traced the pastor's picture on the back of the book.

"Wow, it sounds like you really miss home. So what keeps you here? A job transfer?"

"No, I met someone a few months after I moved here, and he wants to stay," I said.

"You two must be pretty serious," she assessed.

"We're engaged."

"Have you asked your fiancé if he would be willing to relocate?" she asked, wiping her face with a hand towel.

"A zillion times!" I sighed. "He actually really likes Seattle, but . . ."

"But?"

"We have a business together, and now I feel like I'm stuck here," I said.

"That must be hard."

"Such is life, right?" I sighed.

"I'm sorry I can't be of more help, but I would love to invite you and your fiancé to my church in Spring Valley," she said.

"Thanks. I'd love to try it," I replied.

"Great. I'll give you the address and service times," she said enthusiastically.

Kate jotted down the information and handed me the slip of paper.

"It was so nice meeting you. I have to get going now, but I really hope to see you there," she said with a sincere smile.

"It was nice meeting you too. And thanks for the invite!" I waved goodbye.

The following weekend I was determined to attend the Saturday evening service at Kate's church. To ensure that I would go, I didn't smoke any pot for the entire day, which actually wasn't that hard. I was tired of getting stoned and wanted to be free from its snare once again. Whether my new resolution would last for only a day or several months, I wasn't sure. Every time I gave it up, my hope was that I would quit smoking pot forever.

I had the same intention each time I vowed to stop throwing up too. But inevitably, life's circumstances overwhelmed me, and I would succumb to my old coping mechanisms. Yet each time I vowed to quit an old habit, I did it wholeheartedly. I really believed that this time would be different.

I carefully selected something to wear. It had been months since I had attended a church service, and I was hopeful that maybe this time I could turn my life around for good.

"Are you going somewhere?" Darius inquired from the doorway of our office bathroom.

"Yes. A lady invited me to her church in Spring Valley. Do you need the car?"

"I can drop you off and stop by Richard's while you're at church. How long will you be there?"

"Two hours, at the most." I said as I zipped my skirt.

"All right. Are you almost ready?"

"I just have to put my shoes on." I slid my feet into some flats.

"Sounds good. I'll be waiting in the car."

After Darius dropped me off, I faced my fear and walked inside Kate's church. I found a seat and surveyed the room but didn't see Kate. Many people introduced themselves, but I still felt awkward and alone. I wished that Darius was with me. He was the only person I had in Vegas. While he hung out with one of his many friends, I sat in the semi-crowded church by myself.

After the service ended, I exited the church's large glass doors and stepped out to view another gorgeous Vegas sunset, sprinkled with palm trees. I felt good. I hadn't made any new friends, nor had I run into Kate, but I was in my right mind. I was even a little hopeful. It wasn't that the hour and a half I'd spent at church had miraculously transformed me. What it had given me was a reason not to smoke pot, even if it was only for one day. I saw undeniable joy on so many people's faces. People were living normal lives and seemed genuinely happy! They weren't letting life pass them by in a stony haze, hanging out with a bunch of other people doing the same thing, like it was normal. If I had learned one thing about addiction, it was that just because a bunch of people were in the same room doing the same thing, that didn't make it normal! It just meant I gravitated toward people with the same messed-up way of dealing with life as me, and frankly, I was tired of it. I wanted out, and my short stay at Kate's church left me with the burning desire to be free.

I didn't make it back to Kate's church the following week-end. Unfortunately, I returned to my old familiar friend mari-juana and began packing my bags in secrecy. I planned to leave Darius and the business behind. To simply walk away as if I were playing a board game and had soon grown tired of it. But in my mind it wasn't an impulsive move. I had wanted to leave Vegas months ago. My roots, like the evergreen trees the Pacific North-west was famous for, grew deep, and I wanted to go home.

So I laid in wait for the opportune time to sneak away. My bags were secretly tucked away in our office warehouse. I knew that eventually Darius would go out one evening with a friend, and by the time he returned, I would be crossing the state line. I would flee under the cover of darkness, with all of Vegas's neon lights far behind me.

Scenes

Molly goes away for a week to see her family in Seattle.
She is currently rethinking and planning her life
Often which she has considered instead of actually doing.
Reflecting upon past indiscretions
Molly feels raped of her precious youth.
Her boyfriend—beautiful, prickly, sweet, energetic, aggressive
Who's ripe to eat.
He haunts her soul. It feels like Halloween every day;
Ghosts enter from every which way.
She clings to him like a baby.

Chapter 42

REST STOP

I drove all night through California, finally pulling into a rest stop in the wee hours of the morning to catch a couple hours of sleep. After waking, I continued on through Oregon and into Washington. I was finally home! I wasn't ready to face family members though, not until the tiny amount of weed I had left was gone.

It was then, at a waterfront hotel in downtown Seattle, that the reality of what I'd done set in. It was 3:00 a.m. when I finally called Darius.

"Hello?" Darius answered.

"It's me," I said solemnly.

"Where are you?" Darius asked in an exasperated tone.

"Seattle," I replied, just as solemnly.

"What is going on with you? I came back to the office, and all your things were gone. You just disappeared." Darius sighed. "I don't get it."

"I couldn't take it anymore. I couldn't take another day there."

"Another day here? I don't understand what was so hard for you. You had plenty of free time to do the things you wanted to do. You went shopping and bought new clothes—"

"I know, and I went and got coffee every day, and worked out at the gym, and the list goes on. But I wasn't happy, and I was stoned all the time. I'm tired of being stoned," I explained.

"You weren't happy because you had too much time on your hands. You see me. I keep myself busy. There's no time for me to sit and wonder whether I'm bored or not. You could have gotten a job if the business didn't keep you busy enough."

"What you're saying is all true. I did have too much time on my hands. I could have gotten a job, and yes, it probably would have kept me busy, but I would still have been in Vegas. That was my fatal mistake. I wanted us to move to Seattle, but I had dollar signs in my head and I chased after money. I thought it would make me happy, and we had plenty of it, but it didn't make me happy."

"Shana, I don't know if there's anything or anyone on this planet that can make you happy. It comes from within."

"You know, there was a cocktail waitress who told me the exact same thing," I said, recalling her words.

"It's true. No career or location can change how you look at life."

"Well, at least I'm not stoned now. I can't stay stoned and miserable the rest of my life."

"What are you going to do? Do you think moving back to Seattle is going to make you happy?" he asked.

"I don't know if it's going to make me happy, but I can think clearly now. My mind won't be in a haze anymore," I said.

"Where are you going to stay?"

Rest Stop

"With my mom and dad. They'll be flying south for the winter soon. I can stay at their house and keep an eye on things while they're gone. After that, I don't know. What about you?"

"I'm going to keep doing what I've been doing, working, keeping myself busy. The business is doing well, and I need to make a living. I'm staying put. I'm not the one that left," he replied.

"I know. I'm the one that left, and now I have to figure out what I'm going to do, whether I get a job and where . . ." My voice trailed off.

"See, wouldn't it have been easier to stay in Vegas until the lease was up, like we planned?"

"We had another year and a half on the lease. I couldn't take another week, let alone a year and a half!"

"Then why did you sign the lease in the first place? Do you think life is a game?" he questioned in frustration.

"No, I don't think life is a game," I said. "I told you, I made a mistake. I thought a big bank account was going to make me happy, make Vegas bearable. And it didn't, and I really don't want to talk about this anymore. I'm going to catch a ferry over to my parents' place. It will be morning soon."

"All right, give me a call when you can."

"I will. I'll call you in a few days. Take care," I said softly.

"You too," he replied.

After hanging up, I drove to the ferry terminal and waited to board. The hour-long ride would give me time to catch some much-needed sleep. Not only had I lost a lot of weight due to my excessive pot habit, my eyes were also a hazy shade of red, telling the story of my life. The last thing I wanted to do was face my parents in this condition. Sleep was the only thing that would help.

The ferry docked on the still, sleepy peninsula. I was in my parents' neck of the woods, the place where they had graduated high school before relocating to the city to find employment and raise a family. I remember taking the long trek out to what I viewed as, the middle of nowhere, when I was a teenager, to see the piece of property they bought in Belfair. They sold our family home, the one I'd spent seventeen years growing up in, during the time I lived in Ballard and worked at the print shop.

While I was "single in Seattle," my parents were bicycling across the United States enjoying their early retirement years. That is when my father injured himself in the middle of the Arizona desert and spent time recovering in the town of Yuma, and where they purchased a tiny piece of land for their RV. Finally they had found their slice of paradise after working and raising kids for so many years in the rainy Pacific Northwest—a sunny place to escape the drizzly gray winters.

While I was living in Las Vegas, they decided to build on their property in Belfair. I'd only visited their new home once, with Darius. It seemed they had come full circle, returning to the place of their roots. Now if I could only remember how the heck to get to this place! But first I had to grab a latte. Regardless of whether I was in the middle of nowhere or not, there was always an espresso stand just a stone's throw away.

I located a familiar landmark with one hand on the wheel and the other holding my latte.

"Yes, this is the hill I turn up!" I exclaimed, relieved.

After ascending, I still had another ten-minute drive up and down a winding road in the middle of the forest. I'd labeled it "God's country." There were no streetlights, probably more wild animals than people, and a view of the Olympic Mountains that looked like a huge painting in the sky.

Rest Stop

The farther I drove, the smaller the road became, which meant my parents' home was nearby.

As I curved through a canopy of mossy trees, I recalled Darius and me driving through this same stretch of road on vacation. He had loved the oxygen-rich air, towering evergreens, and relaxing around the firepit at night. It was a bittersweet moment. I took a final left turn onto the lakeside road that led to my parents' home and up their narrow gravel driveway. The girl from the Pacific Northwest had returned home with a piece of Las Vegas still in her heart.

My parents welcomed me home with open arms. It had been several years since we had spent any significant time together and the three of us easily slipped into a normal daily routine. We woke in the morning and had breakfast. Usually mine consisted of a glass of orange juice and two vanilla cupcakes, still slightly frozen, which gave me more time to savor the sinful frosting. It was my sugar fix. Then we would all meander to the car. My dad always packed an insulated bag full of snacks, being a diabetic since I was a child. It made sense, considering that any excursion, living on the peninsula, spanned several hours, all major towns being a forty-minute drive from my parent's house. It took a bit of getting used to. I was a city girl and had never lived in a rural community. All this extra driving filled my days though, and there was the added benefit of barely any traffic lights or traffic for that matter! It was just pure road.

Our daily treks were a mix of business and pleasure. The pleasure part was shopping every day and the business was listing the items online, getting paid to enjoy a hobby, considering that any lucrative employment, for me, was miles away in the city. My mother knew every thrift store on the peninsula. The two of us were on a constant search for vintage collectibles. If it was old, looked cool, and the price was right, we scooped up the find and tucked it safely in our shopping cart. Both of us had our own unique style. I leaned toward toys and clothing; my mom loved knickknacks. And my dad, munching on his snacks, was our designated driver.

In the evening I capped the night with a couple glasses of white Zinfandel and dinner with my parents in front of the TV. It was easy for me to stay off pot when I was in the company of those who didn't smoke it and not isolated, living on my own. I simply exchanged pot for wine. One vice for another. It was the same thing with bulimia. I was in a constant state of companionship with my parents. They were holding me accountable and didn't even know it.

After several weeks of our routine, the weather cooled, which meant my parents would head south soon. The following week we said our goodbyes, and they climbed into their fully stocked motor home.

I waved and watched them descend down the gravel driveway. I breathed a secret sigh of relief. It wasn't that I didn't love my parents, but I was twenty-nine years old and longed to be on my own once again, but . . . would I be able to stay clean? Pot wasn't the root of my trepidation. I knew no one on the peninsula aside from causal conversation in the checkout line. But food, that was different. Food, a legalized drug for me, was an accessible cupboard or a car drive away.

Inside my parents' now silent home, I decided that I must keep busy. I was alone, but I didn't want to be lonely and fall into bad habits. I purposed every day to get out of the house, grab a late-morning latte, and drive to a thrift store to earn spending money but also keep my mind occupied. An idle mind was my enemy.

In the afternoon I returned to answer email, list more items online, and box up packages to take to the post office.

In the evening I hauled in wood before dark, fired up the woodstove, and locked myself in for the night. This was the scariest part for me, when darkness fell on the forest that surrounded my parents' home. I was a big chicken and savored those glasses of wine each night to help me fall asleep.

After six weeks my parents returned in time for Christmas and the upcoming new millennium. For me, cabin fever had set in. I needed freedom. No matter how great my folks were, I was back to sleeping on my parents' living room sofa. I devised a plan to fly to Vegas to ring in the new year.

Once in Vegas, I rented a car and settled into my weekly. I had time, transportation, and a credit card—there was no stopping me. Darius stayed with me each night, but during the day was busy at work. Before I knew it, I was boarding a flight home. It was time to return to my parents' house far from civilization.

Back at my parents' again, I felt stuck. Maybe I should move someplace tropical, like Miami? Or get a job in Seattle and spend four hours each day commuting to and from work?

Maybe I should drive down to Yuma and stay in my parents' vacant RV? What a brainstorm! I couldn't wait to tell Darius the news!

"Hello?" he answered from his office phone.

"Hi, guess what!" I exclaimed, practically jumping up and down with excitement.

"You won the lottery."

"No, but I came up with a brilliant idea . . ." I paused for emphasis.

"So what is it?"

"I'm going to Yuma!"

"For?" he asked. "Are you out of acne medication already?"

"No, but that's a good idea. I will stock up while I'm there," I replied.

"Then why are you going?" he asked.

"To sell stuff!" I said, as if it were the most brilliant idea on earth.

"Sell stuff?"

"You know all the things I've been selling online? Well, I can go down there and sell it. I hear that yard sales are a big hit."

"Is this along the same lines as moving to LA to be a coat-check girl?" he questioned.

"Okay, now you're making fun of me."

"I'm not trying to, but what do you expect me to say? You're driving hundreds of miles so you can have a garage sale?" he asked.

"The way you put it, it does sound ridiculous. But it's not, I swear!"

"Okay, I'm listening," he said patiently.

"My parents left their RV in Yuma. I can stay for free. I will sell the rest of the stuff I've been collecting for the past three months and stock up on acne medication at the same time. Plus, I hear the weather is great, and it's freezing here!" I affirmed.

"I think you just want an excuse to get out of your parents' house." he assessed.

"That too, but their RV is empty," I said, trying to convince him that I was onto something.

"Why don't you just come to Vegas?" he asked.

Rest Stop

"I will, on the way back."

"So when are you leaving?" he asked.

"As soon as I can pack everything into my car," I replied.

"Make sure you call me."

"I will, but right now I have to go get a piping-hot white chocolate mocha with whip!"

"Of course you're getting coffee. I should have known."

"I'll call you soon!" I hung up and bounced over to the corner espresso bar. I would be leaving. I had a plan, and more importantly, a purpose. I was lost without a purpose.

Chapter 43

DID SOMEONE SLIP ME A MICKEY?

The following week I hopped into my fully packed sedan, beeped my horn, and drove down the gravel driveway. Through my rearview mirror, I watched my parents wave good-bye. It was a bittersweet moment, leaving my parents again. To the onlooker, my actions probably made no sense at all. I had missed my hometown and my loved ones so much while I lived in Vegas, yet here I was leaving again. It reminded me of when I was in my early twenties.

I loved the family gatherings with all my relatives during the holidays. We played games and went to the movies with full bellies after too much turkey and pumpkin pie. But no matter how much fun I was having, sometimes I had to leave because of my bulimia. I hated missing out on the fun and companionship. But a stronger force drove me. I had to go throw up, even when it meant leaving all my loved ones, only to be isolated and alone.

That was how I felt when I saw my parents wave goodbye from my car mirror—something inside of me needed to run.

It took all of forty-eight hours to realize my stay in Yuma would be short. Those big plans to have my own little flea market fizzled. I didn't want to be an entrepreneur on my own, with no one by my side. And who did I call for comfort when I felt all alone? Darius, of course. He'd been my security blanket ever since we collided on the Vegas Strip, my source of comfort as the new girl in town. Now, while I nervously munched on a bag of chips and watched TV in my parents' RV, I reached for the phone to find comfort in Darius.

Not wanting to feel like a complete fool, traveling from Seattle to Yuma with my car full of merchandise and not enough courage to go it alone, I decided to chalk my journey up to a trip to Mexico to buy my meds. As I didn't have health insurance, I could purchase over-the-counter acne pills for the condition that had plagued me since I was a teenager. I could also buy Valium, a pill I enjoyed once in a while since my years at the print shop, when a friend introduced me to it. I usually consumed it until the bottle was empty, and when it was gone, I was done. I wasn't dependent on it but enjoyed the occasional bottle while it lasted. This bottle would be more like a treat, a reward for not purging or getting stoned. I was proud of my accomplishment!

With that in mind, I awoke early and prepared for a fun day across the border.

I set out in my car and drove the short distance to the border. I parked on the side of the road where vendors sold fresh mangos swimming in lime juice and chili powder.

From there I joined the crowd of Americans making their way into Mexico. Once there I got the business part over and purchased my medication and bottle of Valium.

Now famished, I was free to go grab a bite to eat. Of course any authentic Mexican meal wouldn't be complete without a blended margarita with salt around the rim. The tangy adult slushy went along so well with a basketful of warm chips and spicy salsa.

What a wonderful escape, I thought while I soaked up the outdoor atmosphere of a true Mexican cantina.

After lunch I took in a little shopping and purchased a pair of hoop earrings. But it wasn't enough. *Life sure isn't fun without someone to share it with.*

At this point I had already popped a Valium with one margarita under my belt, and it was only noon. I couldn't leave Mexico so soon. What was there to do back at my parents' RV? Did I really want to spend the rest of my day watching TV? No. I opted to stay in Mexico for a little while longer, but I had already eaten and shopped. Considering my options, the only thing left to do was sit at an outdoor bar and drink.

Talk about a lapse in judgment! I sat at the bar alone, sipping on margarita number two, when a local sitting next to me struck up a conversation. Between the Tequila and Valium, I felt quite brazen.

"Do you know where I can get some pot?" I asked the man.

"*Sí, en mi casa.* It's only a five-minute walk from here. Let's go." He stood to his feet.

"No thanks. I'm not going to your casa."

"I understand, senorita. We just met. I will go to my house and come back with it," he said.

"All right," I agreed.

"I will be right back. Don't go anywhere."

"I won't. I'll wait right here."

After the man scurried away to retrieve some weed from his home, I sipped my margarita, taking note of two men working behind the bar. I began to sweat. Paranoia consumed me as I observed the two engaged in a hushed conversation just a couple yards away.

Was I the subject of their conversation? Did they know the man I was talking to? I wondered as I watched them snickering, with an occasional glance in my direction. Or, goodness forbid, had they put something in my drink? I stared down at my empty margarita glass.

No, they couldn't have. A female had served me when I first sat down at the bar, I assured myself.

"Would you like another margarita, Senorita?" the bartender asked.

"No, thank you. I'll take the check please." I rose.

After paying, I quickly exited the bar, making my way back onto the tiny dusty streets. Weaving through the crowds and past the merchants who beckoned for my attention, I made my way toward border patrol.

Fear had completely set in now. What was I thinking, attempting to purchase pot across the Mexican border from a man I'd never met? And why in the world was I even inquiring when I had successfully stayed off pot for so long? All I wanted to do was cross the border and return to my car parked on US soil.

By the time I reached my car, I had only one goal: to return to my parents' RV. I was still shaken up about what could have happened to me if I'd waited for the man to return. I was glad to be in the safety of my car and felt okay about driving, until I merged onto the freeway and was seeing double.

It was the longest twelve miles of my life. I drove with one eye shut. I focused on the white line and followed it as it curved from right to left through the barren landscape. With one hand on the wheel and the other covering my eye so that I had single vision, I finally reached my parents' RV.

I crawled inside and sought refuge the only way I knew how—by binging on food.

By the end of that evening, after purging every last morsel consumed, I knew it was time to leave Yuma. I had already overstayed my welcome.

The following day I repacked my car that I'd just unpacked. I was glad to be leaving Yuma and my short, fuzzy memories behind me. With a large bottle of Valium in hand, I popped another pill.

I drove in a state of numbness and . . . approached a fork in the road. I was faced with two choices.

Should I take the left turn that would lead me back to Vegas, or should I continue down this road, destination unknown? I was truly that confused. My existence and future was as indecisive as flipping a coin.

I pulled over on the side of the dusty road to consider my options: either turn left back into Darius's arms, or continue down the path of the unknown.

If Vegas, Darius and I would be married. That much I knew. I had a secret. It happened during my millennium vacation in Vegas. Darius and I had applied for a marriage license, but I was afraid to follow through with the nuptials. So instead I'd flown back to Seattle, still unwed.

But God had shown me something during that vacation. Even though I was on the run from God, He still had His way of getting my attention.

My initial outbreak of herpes had put the fear of God in me. When I had gone to church with my sister and heard the pastor say that sex outside of marriage was considered sin in God's eyes, I knew it was true. I felt a heavy sense of guilt. So much so that when I returned to our apartment that Sunday afternoon, I told my then-boyfriend, Joel, we were sinning by sleeping together, but he just looked at me as if I were nuts. Joel and I had never had a conversation about God, nor had I, up until then, ever attended church during our relationship, which was probably why he thought I'd gone cuckoo. I'd felt guilty for a day. I soon disregarded the pastor's warning.

God had even gave me a chance when Joel and I had broken up that fateful weekend, the weekend I had purposed in my heart to walk away from him for good. To change the path I was on. It was as if God had given me a moment away from Joel to stop and reflect. Was I where I wanted to be in life? If not, would continuing down the same path get me a positive outcome? Although the answer was a resounding N-O, I again ignored God's call. Well, of course, that ignored call was how I had ended up with herpes and pregnant.

Fast forward several years to my millennial trip to Vegas. After applying for the marriage license, Darius was anxious to wed. It was only a two-week vacation, and each night he asked if we could go to the chapel. We even purchased a cheap wedding ring, intending to buy a nice one after we were married. But I was hesitant. Night after night I came up with an excuse why I couldn't get married. Yet at the same time, I was having sex with him.

During this vacation I encountered my second herpes outbreak. The virus had lived dormant for years. It was as if God was telling me, "You're not going to play house anymore." Unable to have sexual relations with Darius during my outbreak in the latter part of my stay in Vegas, I flew back to Seattle. I wasn't ready to commit, yet at the same time, I wanted Darius to take care of me. Our relationship and future were in neutral.

Did Someone Slip Me a Mickey?

And so was I—in neutral while I sat in my idling car on the side of the road, unsure as ever.

It didn't help that it was my favorite time of day, twilight, a time when the sky turned into a majestic tapestry of color. I could be in any sunny location at dusk, and it would reek of ambiance to me. Like tropical-scented candles and tiki torches all ablaze in the yard, on a warm summer night. It was just one of those things, twilight, that I wished could last for hours. But I didn't have hours to sit on the side of that desert road. I had to make a decision before nightfall.

On one hand, that Thelma and Louise spirit cried out to me to run and just keep running as I continued driving down this unknown road.

On the other hand, I was scared. I would need to earn an income soon. Did it make sense to continue on a remote road through unknown terrain? Eventually my bottle of Valium would run dry and I would be forced to face my decision sober. Would I rather face that decision in Vegas back in Darius's arms, or alone, chasing after that Thelma and Louise dream?

The driving part was easy. I had driven to Vegas with my cat in search of a new life. I had driven up the California coast by night trying to escape from Vegas. And I had driven away from my parents' home to seek freedom in Yuma. If there was one thing I was good at, it was grabbing a little weed and hopping into a car for a long one-way journey. Yet now it seemed, in all my impulsiveness, I was faced with the biggest decision of my life. In which direction would I steer my car this time? And how would that decision impact my future?

Pulling back onto the road, I switched on my high beams, turned on my left blinker, and prepared for the long drive to Vegas.

The time was 10:47 a.m. I had been officially married for eleven hours. The momentous occasion took place just before midnight at a drive-thru wedding chapel.

Darius had a half-eaten burger on his lap when we said our "I dos." It doesn't get any simpler than that. A fifteen-minute wedding, and we didn't even have to get out of the car. What wasn't simple, though, was the day after our nuptials. That was when I realized marriage wasn't going to solve my problems.

At 10:47 a.m., as my new hubby proceeded to go about his usual daily task of earning an income, it was just another day at the office for him. But for me, it was a different story.

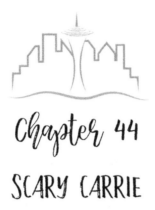

Chapter 44

SCARY CARRIE

I didn't know what to do with myself. My first inclination was to loathe my new husband and seek an annulment. I decided to earn an income instead. I spent my days tootling around thrift stores in search of vintage items to sell. This would at least keep me busy during the day while my husband worked. At night, I opted for a few glasses of white Zinfandel, since I was still off pot. The wine made life bearable, and I looked forward to glass number two each night.

All the while, I knew that the answer to my problems couldn't be found in a large cardboard box full of vino. After a couple months of marriage, I began my search for outside intervention. I started attending Overeaters Anonymous meetings.

Just shy of my thirtieth birthday, I was in a desperate state. The pattern was always the same for me. I would manage to drill up enough willpower to abstain from whatever substance was controlling me. I would supposedly strike oil and enjoy a moment of freedom. But those moments never lasted. Eventually my well of willpower would dry up. Circumstances would change for the worse and I would respond the only way I knew how. While Darius and I were business partners, I never threw up. Not even once. While I stayed with my parents, I never purged either. There was a little struggle while I stayed alone at my parents, but I thought I had it under control. I thought I was free. My trip to Yuma, circumstances changing for the worse, threw me violently back into the eating disorder. In a desert of barrenness without even an ounce of willpower in reserves, I was helpless and hopeless.

"Hi, my name is Shana, and I'm a bulimic," I introduced myself to a group of twelve strangers. I didn't say much. I mostly listened to others confess their innermost struggles. It didn't matter though—I found comfort just being around a group of people who could empathize with my ongoing battle with food. Something that was intended to nourish my body had become my nemesis, and to be with others who shared the same struggle! It was a safe place to seek solace, a place where I could let my guard down and didn't have to pretend that life was just peachy, like I had everything under control.

To think of all the years I had so feverishly hid my "disorder with a name." From my coworkers when I snuck off to the bathroom after lunch with the girls. From my friends when they pounded on my apartment door and I slid along the floor like a slug to avoid them catching a glimpse of me through an open curtain. Or all the times I took that evening shower so my live-in boyfriends wouldn't know I was throwing up. It was an exhausting task to live a life of secrecy motivated by addiction and shame. To be with others, admitting I had a problem, was such a relief.

As silence hovered over the room, I told the group that first day, "I've struggled with food for many years now, and I just need a place to come that's safe, a place that I can confess this struggle with people who won't judge me but actually understand. I need a place to go where I don't have to hide anymore."

Even though the words I spoke were minimal, it was a milestone that kept me coming back for more. Yet as all good things come to an end, so did my attendance at Overeaters Anonymous shortly after I landed a full-time job.

Or was it my encounter with Carrie that scared me away?

It was a meeting I'd wished I never attended, a standing-room only meeting on the west side of town. It was such a contrast to the small intimate group that met just up the street from my apartment. When I first walked into the large building, I immediately recognized some familiar faces and felt at home. It wasn't until after the meeting that a young woman I had met at a meeting introduced me to a few of her friends.

As we chatted in a mini circle, from across the room I noticed a dark-haired, middle-aged woman with a muscular build looking our way.

She must know one of the women I'm talking to, I thought as I watched her make a beeline in my direction. In an instant this woman who'd been staring intently at me, as if trying to pry into my soul, was standing just inches away.

"Hello. I don't think we've met before. My name is Carrie. Is this your first meeting?" she asked.

I felt uneasy but tried to play it cool and shook her hand. "Hi, no, we haven't met. My name is Shana. This is the first time I've been to this meeting. I've been attending one up the street from my apartment for about a month."

"So you just recently started attending meetings? Did you finally realize you couldn't do it on your own?" she asked.

"Yes. I've struggled with bulimia for years."

"I used to throw up too," she replied, eager to continue her interrogation.

"I haven't binged for several weeks now, but I know I still need support to stay on track. I'm happy to be here, and I really like all the people I've met." I didn't like Carrie, and was trying to say all the right things, hoping she would go bye-bye.

"Yes, accountability is imperative to recovery," she replied in the same aggressive way.

It was as if she wanted to skip the formalities and cut to the chase.

Boldly she asked, "Do you drink?"

"A little," I replied, on the defense. By the tone of her voice, I knew Carrie had an agenda attached to her inquiry.

"I've been sober for two years now. So how much do you drink?" she asked.

How do I escape this nosy woman's presence? Who did she think she was anyway?

I was calm as I answered her question. "I have a couple glasses of wine in the evening every now and then."

"Is it every night?" she asked, like a hungry lion ready to pounce on my answer.

"No. I don't think I drink every night," I replied carefully.

"Do you think you can make it through one night? Can you get through one night without having a drink?" she asked with an intense passion.

It was apparent that Carrie had struggled getting through just one night without drinking and felt that I needed her in-your-face support.

"I can get through a night without drinking," I affirmed, feeling attacked but playing it cool.

"How about tonight? Can you go home tonight and make it through the evening without having a drink?" She put me on the spot again.

"Yes, of course I can," I said.

"Okay, I'm going to give you my number. You can call me at any time. I don't care if it's 3:00 a.m.," she replied.

"I'm fast asleep by three," I joked, my forced laugh an attempt to get her off my back. *Excuse me. Maybe you have issues with alcohol, but I don't, thank you very much.*

"I mean it now! If you're struggling tonight, you give me a call. I am also writing down the time of an AA meeting I go to. It's on Tuesdays at ten a.m. Please come if you can," she said.

"All right. Well, it was nice meeting you, Carrie."

"I'll be seeing you, Shana," she replied.

Thankfully, that concluded my conversation with Carrie. By the time I reached my apartment, all I wanted to do was pour myself a glass of wine and shake off the encounter. Floating down the river Denial, I walked straight to the refrigerator and poured myself a glass.

I landed a cool job shortly after my encounter with Carrie, which was excuse enough to stop going to meetings. I would be too busy with work. Besides, I hadn't thrown up for weeks. If anything, a new job would keep me even busier because there would be no time to binge.

In my new position of "entertainment waitress," I would serve burgers out of baskets and hop on top of the bar with my fellow employees to perform choreographed skits to songs like "Grease Lighting" in an outdoor restaurant, smack dab in the middle of the Vegas Strip, among a slew of onlookers recording it all.

You would think that part of the job would have had me

sweating bullets, but no. Dancing on the bar to reminiscent tunes, and laughing when I forgot part of the skit was the highlight of my day. It was those damn burgers in baskets that sent my heartbeat rising!

The first days at the restaurant were nerve racking, at best. The friendly part wasn't a problem for me. It was the flustered part. I was a friendly, flustered waitress with a serious learning disability when it came to memorizing table numbers. I discovered what the restaurant term "in the weeds" meant only a week into my new job. That was the afternoon that this friendly, flustered waitress almost lost it. If I could have walked out that day, I would have. But I knew there were too many customers counting on me.

My section was completely full. Every table and seat was occupied. Orders needed to be taken. Baskets lined up in the kitchen, waiting to be served. And under the hot Vegas sun, everyone's sodas desperately needed a refill. If that wasn't enough, there were requests for extra napkins, condiments, and plenty of "Excuse me, miss. This isn't what I ordered."

By the end of the day, when I climbed into Darius's idling car, I counted my tips and had a pity party.

"How was your day?" he asked, greeting me with a smile.

"Horrible." I pouted, staring down at the stack of one dollar bills in my hand.

"Well, it couldn't have been that bad. It looks like you made some tips," he said.

"Forty-eight bucks. I can't believe it! All that hard work for nothing." I waved a hand in disgust.

"Was it pretty busy?" he asked.

"My section was busy. I couldn't keep up with all the customers. They just kept coming!" I relived the day in my mind.

Scary Carrie

"That's what a restaurant is, a place full of customers waiting to be served," he remarked.

"I know, but I'm just not good at juggling all those tables and orders." I shook my head in disappointment.

"Did you ask the other servers to help you out?" he asked.

"Sort of," I replied sheepishly.

"Well, there's your problem. You should have asked one of the servers to cover an extra table. Then ask another server to pick up a couple of your orders from the kitchen and deliver them. That's what table numbers are for," he advised.

"That's my problem," I replied. "I can't remember the table numbers for the life of me. They're all just one big blur. There I am asking another server if she could deliver an order to the guy way over there wearing the red baseball cap. It's a mess. I'm just not cut out to be a waitress."

"Cheer up. It's not going to be that busy every day," he assured me.

As the weeks passed, it turned out that Darius was right, and I didn't find myself in the weeds often. But it was always in the recesses of my mind.

Some days I managed okay, with just enough customers. The night shift was even better, especially after the kitchen closed and the house band played with a backdrop of shining neon lights beneath the open sky. I loved serving cocktails to crowded tables while "Thong Song" echoed from the sound system.

But I soon found out I wasn't cut out to wait tables. Shamefully, I had lied during the interview with the manager. I'd told him I had prior experience as a food server, which I did, if you counted the one day during my high school culinary class when I attempted to wait on three tables and broke under the pressure.

For the remainder of the year, my instructor allowed me to man the helm of the ice cream station, taking one order at a time.

Yet I still found myself feeling inadequate, like a Christmas tree in the middle of the desert. I was tired of trying to compete with everyone and falling short, then beating myself up internally for not performing the way everyone else did, seemingly so effortlessly. For once in my life, I wanted to be great at something.

When the opportune time came to ask my manager for the week of my thirtieth birthday off, I devised a plan. Instead of flying home to see my family, I would hunt for a new job in secret. If I told Darius my plan, he would scratch his head in disbelief. I already knew what his response would be: "You just started this job. You're making great money. Why would you leave?" And I knew it would have truth to it. But still, he didn't understand me. Darius was a great server; he'd worked in many restaurants. In fact, anything that required self-assurance, he excelled at. He was fearless, and as far as I was concerned, couldn't relate to my plight in life. Was there anything that I could be great at, and more importantly, was there anyone who could understand my inner struggle and feelings of inadequacy?

"Darius, can you drop me off at the gym?" I asked on the eve before I was to return to work.

We walked out to our car on another warm Vegas evening, I had an unusual skip in my step.

"You're in a good mood," he said.

"Oh, I didn't tell you?" I slid into the passenger seat.

"Tell me what?"

"About my job interview?" I knew full well why I hadn't told him about my job-hunting quest. "Yeah, I had an interview today with this really great lady."

"Okay?"

"She's really rich and owns a production company, and she is looking for a personal assistant. That means I'll get paid to go shopping and run her errands. Does that not have my name written all over it?"

"Yeah, it sounds good, but you already have a job, and you're making pretty decent money," he said.

"I know, but frankly, I'm just not cut out for waiting tables. I get the job done, but barely at that. It's not my forte."

"Forte? You get paid a lot of money to serve drinks and burgers in baskets."

"That's on a good day though," I interjected.

"Okay, but even on your worst day, you still make great money, not to mention that you get paid to listen to a reggae band under those sprinklers."

"The outdoor mist cooling system? It's a hundred degrees outside! The waitresses would be fainting without it!" I exclaimed.

"You're not going to get any sympathy from me. I've been to your work. You might as well be serving cocktails on the beach in Jamaica and getting a tan! Everyone's on vacation and in a good mood."

"I know. You make my job sound so good. But it's just not me."

"And this job is?" he asked.

"A personal assistant? Are you kidding? That's my dream job!"

"I thought working as a coat-check girl was your dream job."

He would never let me live that one down.

"Maybe I was a bit off on the coat-check career, but this job is going to be wonderful." I slapped my hand on the dashboard, for emphasis.

"What do they produce? Movies?"

"I'm not exactly sure. But their office is incredible. It's elegantly hip." I beamed proudly.

"How much are they going to pay you?" he asked, clearly irritated by my response.

"I don't know. I didn't ask. But the owner, who I'd be assisting, I think she really liked me!" I beamed again.

"Oh no." Darius sighed.

"Oh no, what?" I sat up straight, indignant.

"Here we go again. You've had more jobs than I can count, and you've only been at your new job for a couple of months."

"It seems like years."

"You get free meals, health insurance, paid vacations." He sighed again.

"I know, honey," I replied in a reassuring tone.

"So when should I pick you up?" he asked, changing the subject while we sat idling in front of the gym.

"At nine. Oh, I forgot to mention my whole point. If a guy named Raul calls on your cell, that means I got the job. He works for Eileen. He's her . . ." I paused. "Actually, I have no idea what Raul's job title is."

"Did you ask any questions on this job interview?" Darius asked sarcastically.

"No, and I don't care. I just want the job." I scooted out of the car. "I'll see you at nine."

After a calculated workout, faithfully burning off a thousand calories on the cardio machines, I made my way out to the parking lot to wait for Darius. Just a few short minutes later he arrived, greeting me with the good news. My new boss wanted me to report to her office at 8:00 a.m. I was thrilled! Sure it was a little early, but it was worth it. I'd obtained my dream job and had already envisioned how wonderful it would be.

Chapter 45

HE STILL HAS MY NUMBER

Vegas' June sun blazed down on me as I strolled down to our apartment's laundry room, with a spring in my step and a honey cigar dangling from my lips. Having just finished out my first workweek as Eileen's personal assistant, I was content, despite the many loads of laundry I had that Saturday afternoon.

I entered the tiny laundry room through a slightly opened door and was immediately greeted by two smiling faces. By the warmth of their smiles, an onlooker would surely presume that these two young ladies—foreign exchange students?—had known me for years.

"Hello," they greeted in unison.

Taken off guard by their kindness, I scrambled for a place to rest my cigar.

"Hello. I'm glad to see I'm not the only one who does laundry during the hottest part of the day," I joked.

"Yes, it is, but my sister and I are quite used to the heat. We're from Ethiopia. My name is Fanna, and this is my sister,

Lebna," the young lady said.

"It's nice to meet you. My name is Shana." I set my laundry basket on top of a dryer.

"Do you live in this complex?" Fanna asked.

"Yes. My husband and I have been living here about four months now. And you?" I asked as I flipped open a washer lid.

"We live in the next complex over. We moved to Las Vegas to attend the university," Fanna replied.

"How nice," I said, knowing that at the age of thirty, I would never attend a university. It wasn't that I was resentful, but more like regretful as I smiled back at the two beautiful Ethiopian girls while they folded their laundry.

I could sense that they took their education seriously and lived a clean life. They probably worked, too, in combination with their studies. *How admirable*, I thought as I glanced down at my ashen cigar. It seemed I'd chosen such a different road in life.

"Tell me what your secret is," I said, breaking the silence.

"Secret?" Fanna questioned, looking up from her pile of clothes.

"Yes. It seems every Ethiopian woman I meet has the same natural beauty. Is it in the soil?" I poured some detergent into the washer and turned the water on.

"Thank you. You're so kind," Fanna replied, laughing. "Are you acquainted with many women from our country?"

"Not really," I replied, remembering Hayle and his beautiful wife, who had extended such kindness to me. Unfortunately, my addictions controlled me, not the other way around, and I had run from them. "But I did have a friend in Seattle who loved Ethiopian food. She took me to her favorite restaurant, and that was the first time I ever tasted the veggie combo. I am indebted to her for life!"

"Wow, I am impressed. I don't meet many Americans that love Ethiopian food!" Fanna said as her sister nodded in agreement.

"I am sorry that we have to leave now, may I give you our telephone number?" Fanna asked, placing the last piece of folded laundry in her basket.

"Sure," I said, startled by her request.

"Lebna and I meet with some other students from the university on Friday nights at our apartment. We study the Bible together. Everyone brings a refreshment. We would love for you to attend," she said, handing me their number.

"Thank you." I took the slip of paper.

"It was nice meeting you," Fanna and Lebna said in unison as they grabbed their laundry baskets.

"You too," I replied as they turned toward the door.

"Please don't forget to call," Fanna said, holding the door for her sister.

"I won't," I promised.

After they left, I continued on with the arduous task of doing laundry. I reflected on what had just happened. It seemed peculiar to me. Like more than just a coincidence that in a ten-minute span of time, two women I didn't even know had invited me to a Bible study at their apartment.

I stood there frozen, looking down at the slip of paper Fanna had handed me. Focusing on their names and telephone number, it made me think of God and that He still had my number. Regardless of how many times I'd moved and how many times I'd run, He knew where I lived and that I would be doing laundry with a cigar dangling from my lips that Saturday afternoon. It seemed that God was still calling me after all these years. Despite all of my rebellion and I'll-do-it-my-way attitude, even when my way never worked, God still knew how to reach me. The question was whether or not I would answer His call, and if so, when?

Chapter 46

ALREADY HAD ME PEGGED

Click, click, click went the sound of my wooden sandals as I raced to my car. It was 7:30 a.m. and already warm. It looked like another desert scorcher underneath a cloudless blue sky, and my favorite thing of all time, with palm trees sprinkled throughout the city.

I loved early summer mornings in Vegas; they were the rare occasions to roll down the car window without having to use the air conditioner.

Another reason I loved summer mornings in Vegas were the breakfasts, which had become my favorite meal of the day.

"Good morning. What can I get you started with today?" a cheerful voice beckoned over the intercom.

"I'll take a twenty-ounce blended coffee with lots of whipping cream and caramel on top." Then with the latest jam blasting on my car stereo, I sat in the drive thru awaiting my fix. Although I was born and raised in Seattle, I didn't get "hooked" on blended frappes until moving to Vegas. That was when I'd landed a job at a well-known coffeehouse for all of five days.

During my short-lived career, I spent much time blending up icy-cold concoctions for eager waiting customers.

After I'd decided I wasn't cut out to be a barista, I'd left the company to play the part of frequent customer instead.

Idling at the drive-up window, my mouth already salivating to get my fix, I handed the cashier a crisp twenty-dollar bill.

You can't put a price tag on this kind of happiness! I thought while I snatched up my favorite purchase of the day.

Pulling back onto the wide Vegas streets, I began my usual tricky maneuver of navigating a manual transmission while inhaling a mound of whipping cream dripping with caramel, sans lid. It was my five-minute euphoria of the day, which was about the same amount of time it took me to reach the posh office of my new employer.

After pulling into the parking lot, with empty cup in hand, I exited my car feeling like a million bucks. I had a new designer haircut, complete with highlights, and a sleek wardrobe, thanks to the clearance rack. No more uniforms, no more nylons in one-hundred-degree weather, and no more plastic heels! For the first time in my life, I was free to be myself and enjoy a career that fit my personality.

I felt like my life was just beginning. All those years of working in dungeon-like warehouse settings, getting stoned to pass the day, or worse, binging on thousands of calories to endure the day, were over. The commission-based casino jobs had left me feeling inadequate in comparison to the other girls who could sell an overpriced item so effortlessly without blinking an eye. Those days were a thing of the past, along with propositioning businessmen who had promised me a quick buck if I would only accompany them up to their hotel rooms for an innocent massage. Only in Sin City. Indeed, the road of life hadn't been perfect, but I was optimistic. It was finally my time to shine.

"Top of the morning to you, Chelsea!" I said, shutting the darkly tinted glass door behind me.

"Girl, I don't know where you get that kind of energy at eight in the morning," Chelsea replied with a muffled voice.

Resting my empty coffee cup on the office's sleek reception desk, I patiently waited for the other half of Chelsea's body to appear from behind the counter.

"You know, I feel a little awkward having a conversation with your butt," I remarked, trying not to stare at the only visible part of Chelsea's body. "But since we're on the subject, how did you get so toned, and not to mention, flexible?"

"I'm sorry. Could you repeat what you just said?" Chelsea replied, bending her body back to an upright position, her blond hair flying through the air.

"I was just saying that you are the first executive secretary I have ever seen touch her toes while organizing files. I work out for three hours a day, and my body nowhere near resembles yours." I shook my head in disbelief.

"Oh please, you're a twig!" Chelsea retorted.

"Are you kidding? Chelsea must have put on ten pounds since we moved to Vegas," chimed in Brad, the tall baby-faced sales executive from the background. "Why do you think she's not bending her knees?" He laughed. "She's afraid she'll bust a seam."

"Very funny," Chelsea replied, glaring at Brad from behind a pair of studious-looking glasses.

Brad, Eileen's one-man sales team, was a young thirtysomething, like the rest of Eileen's employees, and he always wore a suit. He spent most of his time on the phone and was one employee that I could have done without. Even though Brad was friendly, it was his outspokenness that intimidated me, and more importantly, his ability to size me up in a short amount of time.

The jig was up. Only two weeks into my new job and Brad already had me pegged as the girl with an eating disorder.

"Well, I think Chelsea looks great," I said, halfway glancing at Brad, who was now standing at the front desk too. "And I'm sure you haven't put on ten pounds since you moved to Vegas." I directed my attention her way.

"Well, actually Brad is telling the truth. I have put on weight, but that's because I'm not dancing anymore," Chelsea replied.

"Dancing?"

"I'm a professional dancer by trade. When Eileen decided to open a west coast office, we unanimously agreed to relocate and help out with whatever she needed. But, Brad . . . I'm still trying to figure out what his job title is!" Chelsea joked, giving Brad a playful wink.

"I'm Eileen's right-hand man," Brad said confidently.

"You've never been her right-hand man. Get over it!" Chelsea laughed, giving Brad another wink.

"And me, I hung up my leotards to handle all the office work. But it's not forever. It's just until this new location is up and running. We're all making sacrifices. Would you like me to throw that away?" Chelsea asked, noticing the empty coffee cup still in my hand.

"Oh sure," I replied, not realizing I still had a firm grip on the colossal-sized beverage.

"Now I know where you get your energy from at eight in the morning," she said, tossing my cup in the garbage.

"Knowing her, that was probably breakfast," Brad remarked, still standing at the front reception desk.

"Don't you have work to do?" Chelsea glared at Brad in my defense.

"Speaking of which, I should probably get to work too," I said, happy to escape Brad's discerning eye.

"What are you going to do?" Chelsea asked, watching me head toward the stairs.

"I'm going to vacuum the conference room upstairs," I replied.

"Oh, speaking of which, Eileen called. She wants you to clean the windows in the conference room. She has a VIP flying in today on his private jet. They'll be stopping by the office at one p.m.," Chelsea informed me.

"Did she mention if I would be picking up her client?" Brad inquired.

"You wish!" Chelsea said. "I know you just want an excuse to take Eileen's car out for a spin!"

"That's okay. Actually, today's a pretty busy day for me," Brad replied nonchalantly.

"Yes, and I have windows to clean!" I turned on my wooden sandals to make my way upstairs.

"Oh, and Shana?" Chelsea beckoned.

"Yes?"

"Eileen is going on a business trip this weekend. If you're available, could you stop by her house?"

"Let me guess, cats and plants. Oh, how I loathe cleaning litter boxes!" I said from the top of the stairs.

"Normally, Raul would take care of it. But he's accompanying Eileen on this trip."

"I'm just kidding. Of course I'll stop by her house," I said as we continued our conversation from a distance.

"You know, you could make a day of it. You and your husband could barbeque poolside!" Chelsea suggested.

"Oh, good idea!" Our conversation ended as I walked through the conference room, staring at the sea of glass before me. I consoled myself by remembering the many generous perks included in the title of "personal assistant" that made cleaning windows all the more bearable.

Palm trees and a warm breeze, cocktails under a sun-drenched blue sky, an aqua-tiled pool set among a lush, tropical garden, waterfalls, the sound of ambient music echoing in the background, swinging in a hammock, sand between my toes, a barefoot walk on the beach under the moonlight. *These are a few of my favorite things . . .*

<hr>

"Ah, this is the life!" I reached for my mai tai that seemed to be evaporating under the intense Vegas sun.

"Absolutely!" Darius concurred from an opposite chaise lounge.

"You know, I think I could really enjoy living in Vegas if I had Eileen's house and car and clothes." I laughed.

"I wouldn't mind having her outdoor grill. Should I fire it up? Did you marinate the steaks?"

"I did, and yes, you should. I'll get the steaks." I stood. With mai tai in hand, I passed through Eileen's posh sitting room. It was one of my favorite rooms to relax in at the end of my workday. The furniture looked like a showroom display at one of those pricey import stores. There was an eclectic mix of oversized pillows one could get lost in and tons of magazines to pass the time with. *What a wonderful place to unwind,*

Already Had Me Pegged

I thought, wondering if Eileen ever had a chance to do so. It seemed that each week I was unpacking her suitcases while she simultaneously prepared for another business trip.

Interrupting my train of thought, Darius called from the patio, "Are the steaks ready?"

"Actually I was waiting for the butler to come and do that," I joked.

"Well, it looks like the butler must have the weekend off, so could you please grab the steaks? I'm starving!" Darius poked his head through the open-air terrace.

It was apparent that Darius was trying to reel me back to the reality of his growling stomach. If I had learned one thing over the years, it was not to come between a man and his empty stomach.

I opened the state-of-the-art refrigerator. "Here you go," I said, handing him the steaks.

"Thanks. Are you going to make a salad while I grill the steaks? Or are you waiting for the butler to do that too?"

"I will make it." I sighed. "While I pretend that I'm Cinderella and this is my castle . . . and you are my prince, of course." I added.

"Good save, but don't you get enough of this castle five days a week?" he asked, manning the grill through a plume of smoke.

"Work with me." Lifted my hand in the air dramatically, as if life was so bittersweet. "Alas, after today my beautiful gown will turn . . . to but tattered rags."

"Oh please. You're wearing a bikini with a beach towel wrapped around your waist!" He rolled his eyes for added effect.

"Excuse me, but you're kinda ruining my whole dream I've

got goin' on here."

"Oh, forgive me. Please continue while my stomach growls."

"Thank you. This will take but a minute." I lifted my hand in a dramatic display of distress. Then clearing my throat, "Alas, after today . . . at the stroke of midnight, my beautiful gown will turn back to tattered rags and I will go back to mopping Eileen's floors for minimum wage."

"Don't remind me that you quit your job at the restaurant to mop floors, which, if I recall correctly, your new boss slipped and almost broke her ankle on those floors that you mopped!" Darius noted while he turned the steaks.

"I used a product that Eileen had underneath her sink, and how was I supposed to know that the floors would be that slick? Plus, she wears stilettos!" Darius always had a way of not letting me live down my blunders. I was just grateful my boss hadn't actually broken something on those waxed floors.

"All right, so the steaks are almost done. Is the salad still waiting to be chopped?" Darius asked.

"You can call that salad practically chopped!" I said triumphantly.

In an instant I was back to the reality of preparing lunch, with or without a butler. Taking one last look at the palm trees that surrounded the pool, I made a mental note. Whether or not Eileen actually ever got the chance to sit back and smell the roses of all her hard work, there was one thing for sure—I would! For one day I would live the dream, which included Darius yelling "Salad!" in the background.

It was midafternoon; I was in Eileen's kitchen that overlooked the pool. It should have been the perfect setting, getting paid to be surrounded by luxury. But instead, I found myself engrossed in a large bowl of cereal as I heard the sound of a key in the front door.

Fear instantly gripped me. I stood there motionless. At the rate my heart was pumping, a person would think a robber was at the front door. But as the lock turned, I knew that robbers didn't carry keys. Within seconds I heard Eileen's voice in the entryway.

"Brad, I have a meeting in half an hour. Please carry my bags upstairs," Eileen instructed.

My heart sank as I attempted to gain my composure. I had been caught off guard in the middle of a binge, and all I could do was hope that they wouldn't suspect the guilt written all over my face.

"Wow, I think that was your shortest business trip ever!" I exclaimed, greeting Eileen from her immaculate kitchen.

"Yes. I caught an early flight out of New York," she replied, grabbing a bottle of water from the refrigerator.

"I hope you don't mind that I helped myself to a bowl of cereal?" I said, hearing Brad's approaching steps behind me. Eileen I could surely fool, but Brad already had me pegged. There would be no fooling him.

"That's fine. You can help yourself to anything, but what I'm looking for are the leftover steaks. I don't see them in the refrigerator," Eileen said, standing with the door ajar.

"I'm sorry. I cleaned your refrigerator and threw out what I thought was old," I replied. I had consumed much of the steaks during what was quickly becoming a regular occurrence.

"Those steaks were perfectly fine. Please don't throw out the leftovers," she said sternly.

"I'm really sorry. I won't," I promised. I didn't lie, technically. I had thrown out the remaining steaks in an attempt to cover my trail. How could I account for half the missing steaks? No, it was safer to destroy the evidence completely and never leave a trail.

That was the thing about being bulimic. It was an exhausting life, like living in the witness protection program or on the run from authorities. A dark cloud continually hovered above me, and I lived in constant fear that somebody would find me out.

This day, it was Brad I feared as I turned to acknowledge his presence while Eileen ran upstairs to change into fresh designer clothes.

It took all my might to turn slowly in Brad's direction with a plastered-on smile, hoping beyond hope that he wouldn't mention the oversized cereal bowl still sitting on Eileen's kitchen countertop. Luckily, he didn't say anything that day, as Eileen returned right away, in a hurry as usual.

But it was what Brad didn't say that bothered me. It was the presuming looks and subtle Carpenter tunes he'd recently begun to sing in my presence that got under my skin. Insinuating that I was anorexic without actually coming out and saying it—which wasn't even the part that really bothered me. I saw more strength in someone who could control what they put in their mouth. I viewed myself as weak, someone who couldn't control what they put in their mouth. What monster would shove massive amounts of food, like a wild animal, into her mouth, not stopping to breathe? If that wasn't horrific enough, then vomiting it all up. The stench still lingering on my breath and telltale teeth marks on my knuckles. It was a heinous act. I would have rather died than to be found out and labeled *bulimic*.

Already Had Me Pegged

Why would I think that an eating disorder I battled with for a decade would seemingly disappear just because I landed a job as a personal assistant? I had fooled myself again, thinking I was free from this detestable bulimia. Then again, I reasoned, maybe if my new job had turned out to be a real personal assistant and not just a glorified maid with an occasional trip to the mall thrown in, maybe then I wouldn't be throwing up. It was the only way I knew how to cope in times of dissatisfaction. I didn't voice my opinion—I just shoved my opinion down my throat!

By the time I returned to our apartment that evening, I was depressed and if there was one thing I knew, change was necessary. Whenever I resorted to the binge-purge cycle again, I knew I needed to make a change.

"Hi, hon," I said glumly to Darius. The smell of rubbing alcohol permeated our small apartment while he joyfully cleaned printers in what should have been our dining room but was converted into a makeshift warehouse.

"Hi. What's wrong? Did you have an exhausting day spending your boss's money?" he joked, yet was the only one laughing.

"You know, that was so funny I forgot to laugh," I replied, minus any smile.

"You're in a bad mood. What happened? Has your job lost its luster?" He paused the motion of his cleaning rag.

"It lost its luster when I started cleaning the men's bathroom at the office." I conjured up a smile.

"Did your boss actually ask you to clean the men's bathroom?"

"No, but I wanted to keep busy," I said.

"Well, that's your problem. You're working too hard." His hand pushed the rag across the printer again.

"I don't know. At first I didn't mind all the cleaning—"

"Oh no, here we go again." He rolled his eyes.

"Don't give me that look! I know exactly what you're thinking, and you're wrong!" I retorted.

"Wrong about the bad day you had or wrong about the number of days left until you give boss number . . . twenty-seven? . . . notice? I know you've established too good a rapport to just not show up for work." He threw his rag to the floor.

Even though the truth hurt, Darius's assessment was accurate. "Ouch, that hurts," I said as I lurched to the sofa.

"So when are you going to start looking for a new job?" he asked.

"Actually . . ." I hesitated.

"Do I need to pour myself a drink for this one?"

"No, seriously?"

"Oh, I'm serious about pouring myself a drink all right, because by the sound of it, you're about to drop a major bomb on me." He headed toward the fridge.

"What? All I said was 'seriously.'"

"I know, Shana, what you're 'no, seriously?' translates to. Many cardboard boxes!"

"What about the house in LA?" I questioned.

"I knew it! You want to move," he said.

"You should be happy, living inches away from your entire family, eating breakfast, lunch, and dinner together!" I pointed out.

"And that's precisely what I don't understand. You don't like living like that." He sat beside me on the sofa.

"I know, but I'll get a job, which will keep me busy. And you'll be spending your days remodeling your family's newly purchased house that, I might add, no one is living in."

"It is pretty tempting, not having to pay rent," he added.

"Exactly! It's perfect," I said.

"But what I don't understand is that when I mentioned the house a couple months ago, you didn't want to have anything to do with it," he replied.

"Well, times have changed," I muttered.

"I don't think I will ever figure you out," he said, shaking his head in amazement.

"Not in a gazillion years, so you might as well just give up trying."

"Well, there is one thing I do know. You must really want to get out of Vegas."

"I do," I said as the wheels turned inside my head. I knew, too, that my husband loved Vegas, and the only way I would ever get him out of Vegas would be through California. He would be near his family, and I would be one step closer to my California dream.

There I went again, but this time, not on my own, to the land of opportunity. In my eyes it was my last chance at fame and fortune, to finally make something of my life and fulfill my destiny. I mean, why else would I have walked down the street as a grade school kid, having a mock conversation with myself, pretending to be interviewed by a late-night talk show host? What ten-year-old child did that? Unless . . . unless my gut instinct was finally about to come true!

I had spent my adolescence secretly posing in front of the bathroom mirror, envisioning myself as a super-duper model with my picture plastered on the cover of every fashion magazine. Why else had I grown up with such a burning desire to become famous and significant? Because that was where true happiness resided, right? If I was somebody and everyone thought I was beautiful, then I would be happy. Finally I would be happy! If I had the pricey SUV and a house in Malibu with all the latest designer clothes that fit my skinny frame like a glove, then I would find happiness, right? At the end of this rainbow that had eluded me for years, I knew with all my heart, or at least dreamed with all my heart, that was my destiny. All this stuff, the achievements and accolades, would finally bring me to the pinnacle of genuine happiness and peace with myself. Not the kind of joy found in a bottle or food or a joint, but true lasting joy. I was sure that this life was waiting for me in LA, a bright new future!

Chapter 47

RESTLESS

Our first day in LA was spent unloading a large truck filled to capacity with everything we owned. Actually, most of my time was spent watching as my husband and mother-in-law lifted huge boxes from the rental truck. Darius looked gorgeous with his T-shirt haphazardly wrapped around his head, catching all the drops of sweat from the California heat.

After settling into my sister-in-law's home, Darius quickly began the arduous task of remodeling the dollhouse we would soon call our own. Then as the days turned to weeks and I realized the enormity of my Hollywood dream, I became disillusioned. In all my teenage fantasies of moving to California, I'd never envisioned being a valley girl. My dreams had always been wrapped up in Hollywood and its homes nestled in the hills. I loved winding roads with names like Mulholland Drive and Laurel Canyon. I could just picture old-time movie stars speeding through in their convertibles after dark. What about all the nightclubs on Sunset Strip and the warm sand of Malibu Beach between my toes? What girl wouldn't dream of living in

LA surrounded by palm trees, beaches, and sunny weather?

But I soon discovered that my dream was going to be just that, a dream. Sure, I tried to knock on doors, but the operative word was *tried*. Was I aggressive, giving it every inch of my being? Sadly, the answer was no. I gave up and threw in the towel, which seemed to be the story of my life.

Plan B was reverting back to my old familiar way of staying stoned to make my mundane life interesting. But one thing I could testify to—I wasn't throwing up. Eating breakfast, lunch, and dinner with my husband's family had been good to me in that respect. It kept me accountable. So now I was an accountable girl with an eating disorder in remission, spending much time with my husband's family and wondering if my life would ever amount to anything.

The highlight of LA was a one-week trip to Hawaii with my family. It was the honeymoon Darius and I never had.

Each day we set out on a new adventure around the island in a rented convertible. It was truly paradise. I walked barefoot on the beach at midnight, holding Darius's hand. He had purchased a lei from a vendor on the beach, and the smell was intoxicating. We strolled along the shore, letting the warm waves splash against our feet, taking in all the tropical island had to offer. It was a feast for the senses. The smell of saltwater and fine cuisine, aromatic flowers, the texture of the sand between our toes, and statuesque palm trees under a moonlit sky.

It was my new definition of paradise and love at first sight. By the time we boarded the plane bound for LA, I had already made up my mind. Now I just had to convince Darius that our destiny was in Hawaii, waiting for us like a sweet-smelling lei. In my mind I had it all figured out. We would return to LA and sell everything. Then we would purchase two one-way tickets to Hawaii. Once we arrived we would sleep on the beach. We'd have to make a living, and of course I dreamed up the perfect plan. Darius and I would take our spot on the sidewalk among all the other glorified entrepreneurs, vying for happy tourists' dollars.

But instead of a guitar, Darius would play the drum and I would be his Caucasian belly-dancing wife. All I needed was a long dark wig and authentic attire. I was sure we could earn enough money to get us off the beach and into an apartment. By the month's end, we would be established and living in paradise.

Yet my perfect plan was interrupted indefinitely once we were back in LA. It seemed my bottle of microbrew didn't taste good. This was terrible because my New Year's resolution had been to give up smoking pot, for the millionth time!

How am I going to cope now, I wondered, *and why am I throwing away a nearly full bottle of beer?* It was unheard of.

"I think I'm pregnant," I said as I sat in our freshly painted bedroom.

"How do you know?" Darius asked, staring at me with full attention.

"Well, I missed my period, I feel gross all the time, and the thought of consuming an alcoholic beverage makes me nauseous," I replied.

"So go to the doctor and find out for sure," he said, with urgency.

"Don't worry. In another eight months we'll know for sure if I'm pregnant!" I smiled.

"We're not going to wait until you're in labor to find out if you're pregnant or not!"

"Actually, I think we'll know a little sooner than labor, hon.

When I can't bend down to tie my tennis shoes, it will be a dead giveaway." I laughed.

"Seriously, go to the doctor," he insisted.

"I'll ask your sister to take me," I said.

After a trip to the doctor's office, I discovered that (A) I definitely was pregnant, and (B) it looked like it was going to be a very long gestation! Suddenly I experienced cabin fever. Just as I had at my parents' place after they returned home from their winter break in Arizona. Except this time, instead of living with my parents, I was living with my husband's family.

Darius had been correct in his assessment. Whether it was his family or my family, it didn't matter. I needed space. I had been on my own for too many years.

In the middle of a rainy winter in LA that left me house-bound, my mother and father happened to be passing by on their way to Arizona. I knew their stay would be short. They just needed a hearty dose of vitamin D to get them through the gray winter blahs of the Pacific Northwest.

With this in mind, and the wheels spinning in my head again, I broached the subject on my parents' last night in LA.

"How long will you and Dad be gone?"

"Two weeks. Why?" my mother asked.

"Well, I was thinking that maybe you could pass back through LA on your way home and I could drive back with you," I said.

"Oh, for a visit?" she asked.

"No, permanently," I replied.

"Why? Has something happened?" she asked, concerned.

"Well, for starters, I'm two months pregnant."

"My lands! We've been here for two days and you haven't said a word!" She hugged me.

"I guess I was waiting for the right time. I'm sorry to spring this on you all at once, but I want to move back home," I confided.

"Well, what does Darius have to say about this? He is moving with you, isn't he?" she asked.

"Of course, but not at first. I thought if I ride up to Seattle with you, I can stay with my big sis for a few months. Her house is close to downtown, so I can easily get a job and ride the bus into work. My expenses would be low enough that within a few months I can afford an apartment. Then Darius will drive up with the car and all our things."

"Well, that's a lot to absorb at once, but yes, of course you can ride back home with us," she said.

"Thanks, Mom." I breathed a sigh of relief. I was going home, and this time I sensed it would be for good.

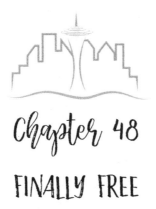

Chapter 48

FINALLY FREE

*W*hen I moved back to Seattle, I signed up with a temp agency, and they found me a long-term job downtown. After a few months I saved enough money to rent a cute one bedroom near the water on the peninsula. Then came a commuter car for my long ride into Seattle via ferry, and eventually Darius with all our belongings.

Even though I'd actually stuck with a plan for once, the most important change was what was taking place on the inside, in my soul. During my stay with my sister, I started attending church with her—the same church I had visited when I had lived with Joel. The one in which the pastor had addressed the whole congregation with the nugget of truth, that sex outside of marriage was sin. The pastor had been speaking to everyone, but I'd felt as if the statement were for me alone. That was what real truth did when it presented itself—it resonated in one's soul. I'd felt convicted, a.k.a. guilty as charged, but not committed to change my life. Then had come the STD and unwanted pregnancy.

The night all those years ago I had accepted Jesus as my Savior at that church, I had heard truth. My heart had agreed that, yes, I was a sinner and would never be good enough to get to heaven on my own. I couldn't volunteer enough hours or donate enough money to my favorite charity to earn my way in. But the fantastic news I learned was that Jesus paid my admission fee! It was a bloody price Jesus paid with His life. All I had to do was agree with this truth and accept Him as my Savior. I did that night. I walked to the front of the church and invited Jesus into my heart!

But had my life changed? Not instantly, no, because I still didn't understand the part about Jesus being Lord. Of course, my choice to stop attending church and reading my Bible didn't fare well. I still wanted freedom, what I perceived as freedom. But had I really been free? I'd still thrown up, gotten stoned and drunk, and had risky relationships with the opposite sex.

When I moved in with my sister and started attending that same church on a weekly basis, I was finally ready to accept God's offer. I was married, so there was no temptation to chase after guys. I was pregnant, so there were no late nights at the bar or getting stoned. It was time for my life to change and to actually, finally, *begin*.

The process was gradual—not overnight. It actually started months earlier when I had given up pot for the last time and gotten pregnant a few weeks later. Even though I wasn't honoring God with my life yet, I felt that He honored my decision to quit pot with the gift of a baby. I'm not proud to admit this, but once I had moved back home and started attending church, I was still binging and purging while pregnant, though not as often.

God was working on me, a little at a time. When I was six

months pregnant, Darius said his goodbyes to his family in LA, and the guy that only knew sunny days became a permanent northwesterner. I continued to attend church, even taking discipleship classes with my sister before Sunday morning services. I read my Bible daily, and scratching my head, wondered why the first four books of the New Testament kept repeating the same stories. Things started to move at lightning speed when I was baptized, my public declaration to follow Christ, but it was a solo venture—my husband's decision wouldn't come until much later.

When I gave birth to my son, God took away the bulimia that I had struggled with for an entire decade. I refer to it as a supernatural deliverance, a miracle that I cannot take credit for. After years of fighting a losing battle, poof—it was gone! My tendency toward emotional eating wasn't taken away in an instant, but God mercifully deleted the chapter from my past of binging on massive amounts of food and throwing it up. And He replaced it with this thing called godly fear. It's like the time I tried to dabble in alternative religions. God drew a clear line in the sand for me that I was not to cross. I have that sense now, deep down in my soul, for smoking pot and purging. I feel that God has been so gracious to me by taking away the desire for those things I once had no resolve over, that if I were to ever go back it would be like a slap in the face, and I love Him too much to ever do that.

About a year into my journey with God and being a new stay-at-home mom, I started typing up my story. I think it was honestly out of boredom, but was it? It only took a couple of chapters in to realize that God wanted me to write a book. It took me years to accomplish the task while I simultaneously raised kids and my husband worked hard to support our family. I, of course, told everyone and their brother that I was writing a book. I was excited and couldn't wait for the book to be published!

But something happened along the way. I was scared, really scared, emotionally paralyzed. How could I publish a book with the dirty laundry of my life strewn out for all to read? And what about my three kids? They were older now, they understood stuff! Now I had to admit to my kids who their Bible-thumping mom truly used to be?

If it weren't for God, I would have given up. I would have continued to hide my messy story, too ashamed to share it with others. But God wouldn't let me give up. Everybody and their brother whom I had blabbed I was writing a book to wouldn't let me give up either.

I had a dream during this time of internal turmoil, which summed it up well. A monster-sized black bear was chasing me—it's a secret fear of mine, living in the Northwest and the notion of running into a bear. This bear crawled in after me through an open car window. I escaped to a public bus, and that darn bear followed me onto the bus! When the bus came to a stop, I finally got my big break. I could exit the bus and be free from the scary bear. The only problem was that two passengers had just walked onto the bus through the same exit door that was still waiting, open, for me to escape through. I could escape with my life, but what would happen to the others still trapped on the bus?

That dream set my mind in motion. What about the young teenager who just threw up for the first time and feels completely alone? What about all the people still getting stoned to numb the pain of life's hurts, or those desperately seeking companionship in all the wrong places to feel loved. And the list went on and on. Was I going to bury this book, my story, that God had entrusted me with, because I was too afraid of what people might say or think of me?

Finally, there was Jesus. The Bible says that He stands patiently knocking at the door of our hearts, waiting for us to open the door and let Him come in. It also says that He wants to be our Shepherd and care for us, that Jesus longs to give us rest for our weary souls! I don't know about you, but I definitely need to be cared for, loved, and accepted. So how could I keep these precious promises to myself? I have been given a God-sized chance to tell my story. I had to swallow my pride and my fear. I had to make up my mind that I would trust God and walk through whatever door He chose to open for me.

How about you? Will you trust Him? Will you surrender your soul to Jesus who died for you and waits patiently for you to accept His offer?

I want to end this book with one last song, "More Beautiful You," by Jonny Diaz. This song has been the anthem in my mind and inspiration in my heart to press on, to finish what I started. Publishing this book is not for me. I'm more of a don't-draw-attention-to-yourself type of person. I could have continued on with my simple life of being a wife and mom, gardening for a few months out of the year, but this song will not let me! It's as if it was written just for me. It sings to me that this book is way more than just an adventure through my crazy messed-up past.

Remember the little girl named Kristi who sat on the porch with her deep summer tan, golden highlights, nose sprinkled with freckles, and face beaming with happiness? That was the same day I met Sunita. It was a sweet time. For those thirty days, I felt like that little girl with freckles chasing after the ice cream man. The blissful innocence of childhood before life got all tangled up with drugs, drinking, and eating disorders. When life consisted of a portable radio, my favorite can of orange pop, and peddle power.

My favorite line in "More Beautiful You" encourages the listener that there is hope to view life through new lenses and a clean slate, like that of a child. But how? After the huge mess I made of my life and all the haunting memories, could I possibly see the world through the innocence of a little girl? The answer is God. When I asked Jesus into my heart, He made His home inside of me. I'm no longer alone. I am reminded of this truth each time I grab my Bible and head off for a quiet place to spend time with God. Whether I am journaling my heart out, venting frustration over a bad day, or thanking God for a wonderful day, I'm no longer alone. I'm spending time with my heavenly Father, and like a little girl crawling up on her daddy's lap, I can tell Him everything. God speaks to me too. When I read the Bible, He tells me who I am, a daughter of the King! He also tells me that I'm forgiven and washed clean of my ugly past. My new life is in Jesus. It is sweet moments like these that reveal how God truly sees me, as His princess, and how I can embrace Him through little-girl eyes! I'm not just occasionally happy anymore—I have God to thank for that!

DEAR READER

When writing this book, my goal was to make it an entertaining read yet at the same time address serious struggles. I know from experience that addictions of any kind are anything but fun and often leave the person feeling enslaved and hopeless. For any of you who feel this way, I would like to encourage you by sharing a more in-depth look into the spiritual aspect of my journey.

The first thing I did, as a new Christian, was find a church home. A safe environment surrounded by like-minded people, where I could grow spiritually closer to Jesus. The Bible talks about the importance of regular church attendance, and I now understand why. I need people in my life who can lift me up when I'm discouraged and pray for me when I desperately need guidance from God.

Attending a weekly women's Bible study was foundational for me. The first smiling face I saw was a retired widow named Evelyn. I learned so much from the group of ladies she led through each week's study. There was food, fellowship, laughter, and tears. These were precious moments in an environment where I was learning the Bible and also able to tap into the deep reservoirs of knowledge from the ladies who surrounded me. I spent so many years isolated in addiction, lonely years— at Bible study I was no longer alone! It was also a great way to meet people so that when I attended weekly services there were familiar faces in the crowd smiling back at me.

My first Bible that actually got used had to be retired recently. The pages had been flipped through so many times that they were literally taped together. Bibles can be expensive. My latest Bible was purchased at a thrift store. I have already underlined multiple verses and scribbled notes in the margin. Though I never attended college, I study the Bible as if it were a textbook for life!

Prayer, if I'm honest, is more of a struggle for me. Sometimes I feel like I'm just talking out loud to myself. I discovered something I do enjoy though, and that's praying Scripture. As I read through the Bible, I write down verses that really speak to me, either in a journal or in the back of my Bible. Then I find a quiet place and turn those Scriptures into specific prayers to God or praises. For instance, as a mom, sometimes I mess up. When I should be listening to my kids, I lecture instead. That's when a verse about taking the time to listen and not being in a rush to speak comes in handy. I will pray the verse, asking God to please help me to listen to my kids instead of automatically getting angry with them. Another verse might reveal how mighty God is and how He really isn't limited. I will often set a verse like that to praise by thanking God for what He has already done in my life and what He is yet to accomplish—like publishing this book!

Worshiping God through music is something I love too. In this book I mention several songs. I wanted to present a soundtrack to my life. Many of those songs, although mentioned in the book, I no longer listen to. I feel that it is important to fill my mind with music that will encourage me and bring God glory for all He has done for me. Christian music has a ton of different genres. It really does change the atmosphere around me when I play godly songs that speak goodness and life. I dance around my garden all the time listening to Christian music, and embarrass my kids in the process!

Renewing my mind was and is huge. It's nonnegotiable. I had so much crud, and to this day the buildup still needs a thorough spring cleaning. When I feel down in the dumps, it is probably related to what I am meditating on. I can be in the kitchen munching away, not realizing what I'm doing, and then stop myself. Why am I eating? It may be that something from my past surfaced and I was feeling ashamed about it. That is when a verse that speaks about God's forgiveness and acceptance of me in Jesus is like gold. I speak God's promises aloud, those verses that I underlined in my Bible and wrote in my journal. This world, and especially my past, is so messy. I must purposely renew my mind, not what I think about myself but what God says is true in the pages of the Bible. I love Joyce Meyer because she addresses this topic of renewing the mind.

Lastly, practically speaking, it's not a good idea for me to be alone with a sheet cake. I'm trying to be a little lighthearted here but in all seriousness—know your weaknesses. Try to be aware of what may trigger you to make a wrong choice. I love sugar, but I consider it a nemesis because I have a natural bent to not be able to stop once I start eating it. The same goes for chocolate. Maybe some people can eat just one square and walk away. Instead of beating myself up for not having the same willpower, it's wise for me to abstain. That way I don't have to deal with the guilt that follows.

I hope that this is able to help you on your journey to a new life in Jesus and that you leave the past behind and walk forward with God.

Shana

AUTHOR BIO

Shana Donyaei looks forward to her favorite holiday each year—summer. A time when she enjoys watching the ferry float by from her deck, gardening, and sunset walks along the beach with her husband, three kids, and German shepherd. On any given day, you can find her in the check-out line at the grocery store and in her kitchen, where she loves to whip up yummy ethnic cuisine. She resides on the beautiful Kitsap Peninsula, near the town of Manchester, in Washington state.

Made in the USA
Monee, IL
03 December 2020